flex appeal

flex appeal by Rachel ™

RACHEL McLISH
with BILL REYNOLDS

WARNER BOOKS

A Warner Communications Company

Copyright © 1984 by Flex Appeal, Inc.
All rights reserved.
Warner Books, Inc., 666 Fifth Avenue, New York, NY 10103

 A Warner Communications Company

Printed in the United States of America
First Printing: August 1984
10 9 8 7

Library of Congress Cataloging in Publication Data

McLish, Rachel.
  Flex appeal by Rachel.

  1. Bodybuilding for women. I. Reynolds, Bill.
II. Title.
GV546.6.W64M43   1984   646.7'5   84-3684
ISBN 0-446-38105-5 (pbk.) (U.S.A)
    0-446-38106-3 (pbk.) (Canada)

Front cover photo by Michael Neveux.
Back cover photo © Harry Langdon.
Exercise photos by Michael Neveux.
Special thanks to Joe Weider for contributing photos.

Designed by Giorgetta Bell McRee

To the only perfect person I know—
my dear friend Jesus Christ

Special thanks to:

World Gym of Santa Monica, California, the Santa Monica Bodybuilding Center, and the Warner Center Club of Woodland Hills for allowing me to be photographed in their superb training facilities.

Bill Reynolds for typing and retyping the manuscript and for explaining my exercises in a comprehensible manner. Bill, you are a true expert.

Michael Neveux for your patience and artistic abilities that make your photographs among the best in the sport.

Joe Weider, all the bodybuilders, fitness enthusiasts, and fans who make bodybuilding what it is today. Without you there would be no bodybuilding, no *Muscle and Fitness* magazine, no championship titles, and, no book.

Contents

Introduction

Would you believe me if I told you that you want muscles? That you can totally reshape your body during the next few months? Fulfill your physical potential? Dramatically improve your health and physical fitness? Normalize your body weight? Increase your strength level by more than 50 percent? Develop valuable personal qualities that carry over into everyday life? You probably wouldn't believe me.

Only five years ago I would have been locked away for making such promises, but today the bodybuilding training that can give you these results is widely sought after. A muscular, fully toned body has become the new American ethic. The reason you picked up this book is because you want MUSCLES! You may agree with me; you may disagree with me; you may even be a little upset about the accusation I just leveled at you. Whatever your response, the fact remains . . . I repeat: *You want muscles!*

Every man and woman living in the twentieth century has had a deep desire for a developed musculature, especially men and women today. The only difference between the 1980's and the 1940's or fifties or sixties is that now people in general are more assertive and aggressive when it comes to picking and choosing what is best for Number One. We are not as easily swayed by sociologically induced concepts and fads that have in the past directed the way we looked, felt, and even acted. Perhaps we are more oriented toward survival in these days of uncertain world tranquillity. Perhaps it's because we are striving to save the family unit, and all else seems insignificant in terms of fashionable gimmicks. We have to come to grips with ourselves in discerning what is best for us; each of us must ask "What is in it for *me?*" and "How can *I* benefit from it?" Truly we live in a period in which we suspiciously regard the miragelike propaganda we are bombarded with day after day as just more ways that someone is trying to make a fast buck. We've learned and relearned that the hard way: Time and again the ever fleeting dollar slips through our fingers as we reach for another shining promise of ecstasy and hope. And it is the element of persistence in our humanness that keeps us coming back for more.

Where bodybuilding is concerned, the positive addiction that one may come to experience will transform one's efforts into rewards too wonderful to describe, like love. Love is wonderful. Love is perfect. Love is great. Love is … You see? You lose the essence and the meaning when you try to define and analyze the nature of it. Fitness is wonderful. Fitness is great. Fitness, like love, cannot be bought. . . . I can only show you the many ways you can acquire this wonderful (pardon the understatement) thing, to feel and be in shape. Oh, what a feeling!

But there's a catch: Perfect love is unconditional; fitness *isn't*. I feel it's a really encouraging revelation that there are certain absolute steps to take in order to achieve this end result. These absolute, factual steps are exactly what the following pages are about.

flex appeal

Photo by Emmanuel Tanjala

CHAPTER 1

the magic of bodybuilding

Thanks to Jane Fonda, aerobic exercise has become a way of life for millions of previously sedentary women. It is a good form of exercise because many women who ordinarily wouldn't are now exercising regularly. But weight workouts will do the job better and much more quickly. I'd like to see every woman in America lifting weights either in a spa or at home in her own little gym. It would be the physical salvation of American women.

My ultimate goal in life is to make every woman on this planet realize it is a scientifically documented fact that everyone needs exercise, so they may as well pick some form that will also have a direct beneficial effect on their physical appearance. I want the women of the world to know that bodybuilding—not necessarily competitive bodybuilding, but weight training—is the only way to have the most beautiful body imaginable.

I'm sick and tired of hearing women say, "Yech, I don't want to get muscular." They can't. They'll merely develop a beautiful body by lifting weights. As proof of this contention, I've been training extremely hard with weights since 1976, and I don't think that many men or women would consider my body to be unaesthetic or unfeminine. If I am too muscular for your taste, that's okay. But remember, I am a world-class *bodybuilding* champion. I'm merely sharing secrets that I have collected over the past seven years to give you complete and total control over your physical being.

I've taken aerobic exercise classes for years, and I've taught similar classes while involved in the gym and spa business. Most women don't realize that a class is not necessarily good for the body just because the workout is difficult or painful. Many classes are actually detrimental to a woman's body, because they put a great deal of strain on the joints; or they yield little in terms of body shaping, because few of the muscles are exercised through their full range of motion. The quick partial reps students are encouraged to do with zero weight resistance have little positive effect on the body.

I also feel that a large number of aerobics instructors fail to work every part of the body sufficiently during their classes. Instead they concentrate on a few muscle groups and push for a lot of short reps to achieve a burn in those muscles. Then they emphasize to the class the "benefits" of this burn, even though it has little to do with how much benefit a women gets from a class. And the freehand exercises done in group aerobics classes are far inferior to systematic weight-training workouts, both in terms of sculpting a woman's body and improving overall health and physical fitness. I feel that nothing can beat regular weight training, gentle stretching, and aerobic activities like running and cycling to build a beautiful body and optimize a woman's health, physical fitness, and sense of well-being.

Physical fitness has become a *very* big industry, with Americans spending billions of dollars each year on sports equipment, clothing, spa dues, and special foods. But many people are being ripped off. Besides receiving subpar instruction in aerobics classes, people often waste their time on resistance training because the instructors simply aren't qualified to teach it. It's not that the instructors lack the desire to help; it's usually that the personalized instruction lacks enthusiasm and the ability to motivate, qualities that will help someone get into shape.

I feel that gym owners and instructors have a responsibility to their members. I don't feel that the average American has to have a degree in exercise physiology just because he or she wants to get into shape. You should be educated by the gym instructors, who have been letting women down for years. That's one major reason why I wrote this book—to give you the type and quality of instruction that you probably won't get in a gym. Whether you actually work out in a spa or at home, this knowledge can mean the difference between success and failure of bodybuilding training.

To me the most exciting aspect of weight training is that *you* can use it to change *your* body and *yourself* in a positive manner. Bodybuilding is a means of self-determination because you alone are responsible for your success or failure in reaching your physical goals. Whether you simply wish to improve your appearance, health, fitness, and sense of well-being, or desire to compete successfully in bodybuilding shows, you are totally responsible for what you get from your training.

I've been training extremely hard with weights since 1976, and I don't think that many men or women would consider my body to be unaesthetic or unfeminine. © *Harry Langdon 1982*

YOUR ALTERNATIVES

There are essentially two paths that you can take with your weight training. For most women, bodybuilding training and the maintenance of a healthy diet are used to change personal appearance. As I said, this can be done in a totally feminine context. The muscles that you develop eventually take the shape of the new feminine contours of your body.

A minority of highly motivated women decide to enter bodybuilding competition. If you have the desire to succeed competitively, and if you possess certain genetically determined advantageous physical qualities, competitive bodybuilding can be tremendously rewarding. At the very least you can learn a new degree of self-discipline and an appreciation for the rewards of hard work. If you have the talent, you might even win a national or international title. I have been able to earn a good, satisfying living as a professional bodybuilder.

The lessons that you learn in bodybuilding training and competition will have valuable applications in other areas of your life. For example, if a woman can consistently discipline herself to diet strictly for competition, she will experience no difficulty in, say, sitting down every night at a set hour to do school homework. In later life she will have no difficulty maintaining a lean figure, because normal dieting for the sake of a lean feminine appearance is very relaxed in comparison to dieting for an upcoming competition.

Virtually all successful bodybuilders are extremely goal-oriented individuals, and it's difficult to accomplish any challenging task without the ability to set long-range goals, break them down in-

With his expert eye, Joe Weider (right) directs a Harry Langdon photo session. That's me sitting on the bars. Photo by Bill Dobbins

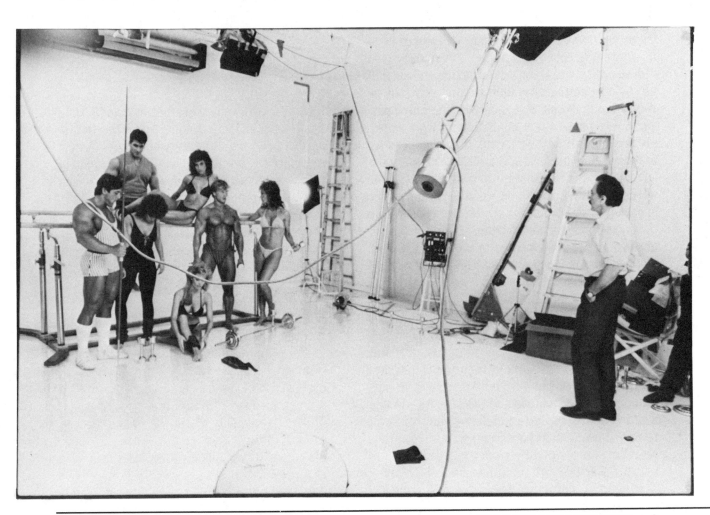

to short-range goals, and pursue each goal with single-minded determination and maximum energy. I feel that a woman's self-image will drastically improve as a result of bodybuilding training and maintaining a balanced, health-promoting diet.

Competitive bodybuilding for women has exploded in popularity in much the same manner as weight training and other forms of exercise that are intended to improve physical appearance, health, fitness, and well-being. In 1979, the first year of organized bodybuilding competition in America, there were just two contests, which drew a total of only forty women. During 1983 there were two hundred shows, which drew 3,500 entrants. Three 1983 competitions were large professional events with a total of more than $100,000 in prize money offered.

HOW I GOT STARTED

I was very active as I was growing up. I looked up to my brother because he was the only man around besides my father. I thought it was tremendous that he could be strong, play football, and generally be very athletic. When he actually let me play some game with him, I'd feel so unbelievably privileged. My brother, Ralph, gave me my first real incentive to increase my physical and athletic potential.

I also wanted to be like my two older sisters, who were and are very beautiful women. Perhaps some considered me a tomboy, but beauty comes from the inside, and you are a woman regardless of your physical activities. I wanted to be like my sisters, but I also wanted to play football and other sports. I was determined to do what I wanted, even though some of the activities I engaged in were labeled masculine sports in those days. Times change!

When I was a sophomore at Pan American University in 1976, I found myself getting out of shape, and I *hated* it. I had been in tremendous physical condition as a young girl and while I was in high school. My sister Yolanda and I used to fool around a little with my father's weight set, but I'd never been to a health club. However, I went to one while searching for a way to get back into shape, and I totally fell in love with the atmosphere of the place. They had chrome-plated machines, which I

thought were terrific toys, and there were mirrors everywhere. From dabbling with my father's weights, I knew that the best way to tone up my body was resistance training. I lived in an area (southeastern Texas) where all of the women wore shorts and halter tops as a means to stay cool in the subtropical climate of the Gulf of Mexico, so I *had* to improve the way I looked.

I joined a gym and started working out solely for the sake of vanity. I wanted to look better, and within a few weeks of bodybuilding training and following a good diet I completely improved my appearance. I went from being someone with skinny limbs and too much body fat to having a firm, well-toned feminine body. It worked for me, and I knew it would work for other women. Soon I was instructing others in the techniques of bodybuilding, and every woman (there are literally thousands) with whom I have personally worked has received equally gratifying results from her workouts. I'm confident that you will experience similar results.

WHAT TO EXPECT

What results can you expect from regular and systematic bodybuilding training and a health-promoting diet? Of course, every woman reacts at a different pace to exercise and dietary stimuli, but in general I feel that six to eight weeks of training and diet can give you these results:

- The loss of three to five pounds of fatty tissue and the gain of one or two pounds of muscle, which will noticeably reshape your physique
- An increase of 20 to 30 percent in your beginning strength levels in most exercises
- A noticeable improvement in cardiorespiratory fitness
- Distinct improvement of sports participation results
- Improved self-confidence
- A greater sense of well-being
- An improved ability to fall asleep and to sleep more soundly
- Plus many more "hidden" benefits.

These may sound like impossible expectations,

Regular weight training will distinctly improve your performance in other sports.

Photo by Luke Wynn

but you *can* achieve each of these goals after only a brief period of regular bodybuilding training and only a moderate change in your dietary habits. Virtually any woman can expect similar results from bodybuilding training and diet.

HOW IT WORKS

The human body's system of skeletal muscles is remarkably adaptable. A muscle of a sedentary woman maintains only the amount of mass and strength necessary to complete daily physical chores successfully. But if that muscle is subjected to an overload of weight, it adapts to that load by growing a bit larger, better toned, and stronger so that the increased load can be lifted with ease. And if you systematically increase the overload you place on a muscle, that muscle will continue to grow slowly in mass and strength.

Weight training used to be referred to as progressive resistance training, paying credit to the gradually greater overload you place on a muscle. The range of loads that you can put on a muscle is wide in weight training, from as little as 2½ pounds in each hand to more than 500 pounds in some exercises. So, unlike calisthenic exercise—for which you must have a certain strength level to do some exercises, and in which you can never use resistance greater than your body weight—weight workouts can be made adaptable to the beginning and ultimate strength levels of the strongest and weakest individuals. That's one major reason why bodybuilding training is so superior to freehand exercise.

SOME BODYBUILDING MYTHS

Because it is still such a new activity, there are a lot of ridiculous myths associated with bodybuilding training. You have probably heard a few of them: "It's going to make you look like a man." "You'll ruin your back." "Lifting weights will make you muscle-bound." Let's take note of the five most common bodybuilding myths and explore the truth behind each of these false beliefs.

(1) Bodybuilding will make you appear masculine. Well, do I look masculine to you? I hope not! In reality the natural hormonal balances in a woman's body preclude the development of large, well-defined muscles *unless* she makes the mistake of resorting to the use of anabolic steroids. A woman will always have smaller muscles and lower strength levels than a man, because her body secretes primarily the female sex hormone, estrogen. A big, strong man gets much of his muscular development because his body secretes primarily the male sex hormone, testosterone. Therefore you will find that any gains that you make in muscle mass will be seen on your body as new feminine curves (actually, you will *uncover* those curves that are hidden by fat). And if you enter bodybuilding competition, the slow rate at which you add muscle mass to your physique will sometimes be discouraging unless you go into the sport with the realization that your hormonal makeup will make it difficult to achieve fast gains in muscle mass and strength. I have been training for seven and a half years; champions are certainly not made overnight!

(2) Bodybuilding will slow you down. Since athletes in virtually all sports train with weights specifically to increase speed and strength, it is difficult to believe this myth, but it still has many disciples. In reality, scientific studies done as long ago as the early 1950's established that strength training increases the speed of muscle contraction. Reaction time (the speed at which you can initiate a muscular contraction once your eye perceives a stimulus to contract) is unchanged by weight training or any other physical activity, but the speed with which you contract a muscle once the contraction is initiated is significantly improved.

(3) Bodybuilding will make you muscle-bound. In truth, men and women with larger-than-average muscles that were gained from heavy weight training are significantly more flexible than the average person. This is because proper weight training emphasizes making complete movements of all muscles—from full extension to complete contraction and back again to full extension—in every rep of each exercise, a practice that fosters an improvement in joint and muscle flexibility.

(4) You're sure to injure yourself by training with weights. If you follow the safety procedures recommended in this book, maintain proper biomechanical positioning during each exercise (also defined in this book), and warm up correctly prior to training, you will never injure yourself while working out with weights. Most of the weight-related injuries that I've seen have occurred when a novice comes into a gym to "try out" a few exercises without prior instruction, without using correct exercise form, and without properly warming up.

(5) Muscle turns to fat as soon as you stop working out with weights. It's surprising how many people still cling to this old-fashioned belief. It is physiologically impossible for muscle tissue to be turned into body fat. However, you must cut back a bit on the number of calories you consume each day if you decide to stop regular weight training, running, or any other type of exercise. If you don't, you will grow fatter over time, but you already know that!

One of the ridiculous myths associated with bodybuilding is that it will make you appear masculine. Do I look masculine to you? © Harry Langdon

DISADVANTAGES OF BODYBUILDING

There are a couple of minor disadvantages to bodybuilding, but both of them can be overcome if you take the correct practical or psychological steps. First of all, the inherently repetitious nature of bodybuilding training can make the activity boring if you stay on the same training program for too long. That's why I will recommend later in this book that you change workouts every four to six weeks. By changing training programs from time to time, you won't have any problems with becoming bored with your workouts.

A second minor disadvantage of bodybuilding is that it will cost you a bit of money to do the activity properly. You will need to spend money on gym dues and special food supplements, to say nothing of new workout attire. However, you can minimize the emotional and financial impact of bodybuilding by realizing that you won't be ill as often when you are in regular training as you would be if you didn't work out. In most cases your savings in health bills even balance out the money you spend on dues, clothing, and food supplements.

ADVANTAGES OF BODYBUILDING

There are seven distinct advantages to bodybuilding training, many of which I touched upon earlier in this chapter. Let's discuss these advantages:

(1) Bodybuilding allows you to fulfill your physical potential. As mentioned earlier, the heavier stress of bodybuilding training causes your body to make physical changes very rapidly and to a much greater extent than any other type of exercise. Only through systematic bodybuilding can you exact the changes in appearance and strength that allow you to fulfill your physical potential completely.

(2) Bodybuilding greatly improves your health and physical fitness. Any type of exercise will improve health and physical fitness, but bodybuilding does it more quickly and to a greater extent than other forms of exercise. Normal weight training has been criticized for not increasing aerobic fitness to the same degree as running, swimming, cycling, and other aerobic activities. But by using a special form of weight workout called *circuit training*, you can dramatically improve your aerobic conditioning as you increase strength and improve your physical appearance.

(3) Bodybuilding helps to normalize body weight and greatly improves physical appearance. If you are either over- or underweight, you can combine bodybuilding training with a specific type of diet (outlined in detail in Chapter 8) either to lose enough fat or to gain enough pounds to reach a normal body weight. And in normalizing your body weight, you will drastically change the appearance of your body.

(4) Bodybuilding gives you valuable reserve strength to meet life's emergencies. If nothing else, weight training will make you much stronger than you have ever been, which will allow you to meet traumatic, even life-threatening, situations with an increased chance of survival. In other words, not only will you be better able to carry a heavy bag of groceries from the car to your kitchen; increased strength levels will also make it more possible for you to survive an auto accident, fend off a mugger, or emerge injury-free from a sports situation that would ordinarily result in an injury to a joint or muscle.

(5) Bodybuilding allows the use of an unlimited range of weight resistance. I fully explained this when I told you that you can use as little as $2\frac{1}{2}$ pounds in each hand or as much as 500 pounds in some exercises. This factor makes bodybuilding training markedly superior to calisthenics, which force you to use at least a substantial portion of your body weight in every movement, and limit you to using only body weight in those exercises in which you have become exceptionally strong.

(6) Bodybuilding allows you to stress specific muscles in relative isolation from the rest of your body. There are weight-training exercises that stress individual muscles, and at times only a part of a muscle, in nearly total isolation from the rest of the body, something that can't be achieved with most other forms of exercise that work the body as a unit (e.g., swimming and dancing). This factor is

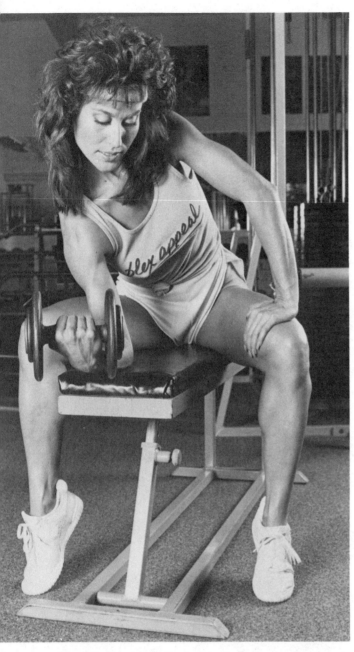

Dumbbell wrist curls stress the forearm flexor muscles.

extremely important in competitive bodybuilding when a weak muscle group must be brought up to par with the rest of the body by training it as hard as possible in isolation from the rest of the physique. It is also important in injury rehabilitation when a single weakened muscle must be exercised with great intensity to bring its strength back in line with the remainder of the body's muscle groups.

(7) Bodybuilding develops valuable personal qualities that carry over well into everyday life. I also touched on this aspect of bodybuilding when I discussed how the self-discipline, goal-orientation, and the ability to work hard in pursuit of a goal work well in other situations of life, such as when disciplining yourself to sit down at a certain time each evening to do schoolwork.

LOOKING AHEAD

The next six chapters of this book are paired: Each pair consists of a chapter of training advice and a chapter of exercises and workout programs for each of three ability levels. Chapter 2 focuses on beginning training advice, and Chapter 3 presents beginning-level exercises and routines; Chapter 4 is devoted to intermediate training advice, and Chapter 5 reveals intermediate-level exercises and routines; Chapter 6 presents advanced training advice, and Chapter 7 focuses on advanced-level exercises and training programs.

The final four chapters are devoted to advanced aspects of the bodybuilding life-style. Chapter 8 is devoted to discussion of bodybuilding nutrition; Chapter 9 discusses competition-level training; Chapter 10 focuses on home workouts (including stretching, calisthenics, and aerobic training); and Chapter 11 is devoted to a discussion of the psychology of bodybuilding.

You'll probably find some of the unfamiliar information in *Flex Appeal* somewhat difficult to master the first time you read through the book. Therefore, I suggest that you extract the information from specific chapters as you advance through your bodybuilding training. This will make an invaluable reference book, as the information I present has been around for a while now, and will never *ever* go out of style.

Photo by Emmanuel Tanjala

CHAPTER 2

beginning training information

*I*t's essential when you begin training with weights that you are set on the most direct path toward success in bodybuilding. You're after results—*visible* bodyshaping results—so why not go for them in the fastest way? It's surprising how many women jump right into a gym, spa, or weight room with no knowledge of what they are doing when they start tossing around barbells and dumbbells, even after they've been "taught" how to work out by their local gym instructor. As a result, they don't get the body results they're after, they grow bored and discouraged, and they may even injure themselves by following unsafe training practices.

In this chapter I'll give you all of the information you'll need to begin receiving great results from your weight workouts immediately and safely. Some of the important general information I'll cover includes basic bodybuilding and weight-training terminology, an equipment orientation, the importance of physical exams prior to starting resistance training, correct exercise form and cadence, training tempo, correct breathing patterns, workout frequency, where to work out, when to train, what to wear, how to determine

appropriate starting poundages, the correct repetition ranges to achieve your goals in bodybuilding, the recuperation process (sleep and rest), basic nutrition practices, fundamental mental aspects of bodybuilding, breaking into training and how to cope with muscle soreness, how to warm up, the safety rules that you need to know, the self-evaluation process in bodybuilding, and how to combine weight workouts with aerobics and stretching to achieve optimal physical fitness. In short, I'll tell you everything you've always wanted to know about bodybuilding, but didn't know who to ask about it or, for that matter, what to ask about!

POSSIBLE BODYBUILDING GOALS

There are five distinct directions in which you can go with weight training. *Strength training* is the most basic form of weight training. In strength training you work out with weights to improve the power of the skeletal muscle groups of your body. Strength is a valuable quality to have, particularly if you are an athlete. Of all the qualities that combine to form a champion athlete, such as a particular body type, skill, fast reaction time, endurance, strength, and flexibility, strength is the one that can be developed most quickly. And increases in strength can result in dramatic improvements in athletic performance.

A closely related form of weight training is the use of resistance workouts for *rehabilitation of joint and muscle injuries*. Physical therapists have long understood that resistance training of an injured part of the body results in more rapid rehabilitation of the injury. Through heavy bodybuilding, an athletic injury can quickly be cured and the injured athlete returned to competition, often with the injured body part stronger than it was prior to the injury.

A third common function of weight training is *health and physical fitness promotion*. This type of training will not only increase strength but also improve aerobic conditioning, which leads to better health. And because weight training allows you to stress intensely nearly every skeletal muscle in your body, it is superior to "leg-only" sports, like running. Weight training is by far the most intense form of training available to the average person.

The fourth function of weight training, and by far the most popular, is *body sculpture*, in which you use weight workouts in conjunction with sound dietary practices to reshape your body. In effect, this is a mild form of bodybuilding. You may, for example, wish to reduce the size of your thighs, firm up the flesh on the backs of your upper arms, or add feminine contours to your tush. This body sculpture function of weight training involves toning and building up your muscles, but let's face facts: Everybody wants muscles, whether or not they realize it. Most women desire a firm, shapely, tight body, and the only way they can attain this physical presence is by toning, sculpting, and building muscles. I certainly want more muscle, and I'm sure you do, too, so read on!

The final branch of weight training is actual *competitive bodybuilding*, a sport in which women athletes attempt to develop their bodies to the maximum. I have competed as a bodybuilder for several years, winning a number of world championships and Miss Olympia titles, and have found professional bodybuilding to be a most rewarding, enjoyable, and satisfying career, a personal fulfillment that goes far beyond competition and even everyday training.

There is incredible diversity of goals among body-builders. Can you imagine how I felt when a seventy-eight-year-old woman I'd coached hugged me and expressed heartfelt thanks that she could now walk for blocks without the walker physicians had said she'd need for life? Or the thrill of seeing newfound confidence in a formerly shy and inhibited housewife who hadn't previously considered that exercising with weights was for her too? Or the improved health of Rafael, who, with adult-onset diabetes, had been in grave need of muscle stimulation and improved blood circulation? Compared to these success stories, a superenthusiastic Lori who spends nearly all day in a gym, pursuing a professional bodybuilding career, pales by comparison.

What I'm trying to say is that the goal you choose to set in weight training and bodybuilding is highly personal, and I will respect whichever path you choose to follow in the activity. Toward that end I will attempt to give you all of the information you will need to know to optimize your chance of reaching your goal in bodybuilding and weight training. I want more than anything else for you to make bodybuilding your lifetime life-style, so *let's go for it!*

BASIC DEFINITIONS

There are several terms commonly used in weight-training and bodybuilding circles. You should be thoroughly familiar with them before entering the weight room. A general understanding of these terms will also help you to follow what I describe in the rest of this book. More esoteric bodybuilding terms will be defined in the glossary at the end of the book.

An *exercise* is the actual movement that you're doing. Indeed, an exercise is often referred to as a *movement* in bodybuilding circles. In a calisthenics program a push-up or a sit-up would be an exercise, while in weight training a bench press is a good example of an exercise.

A *repetition* (which is frequently abbreviated as *rep*) is each full and individual cycle of an exercise. For example, when doing push-ups, a repetition consists of the complete downward movement from a position with arms straight until the chest touches the floor, as well as the return back up to the starting position.

A *set* is a group of repetitions (normally in the

Here I am at the 1982 Women's World Championships with Joe Weider on my right and Ben Weider on my left, two of the most important figures in the world of bodybuilding.

range of 8 to 12 for most exercises) done without a pause between reps. Several sets of each movement are ordinarily done with a *rest interval* (a pause of about 60 seconds to allow your muscles to recuperate a little) before the next set is begun.

A *routine* (also referred to as a *program* or *training schedule*) is the entire accumulation of exercises, sets, and reps that you do in one *workout* (or *training session*). Often the term *routine* refers to the actual written record of these exercises, sets, and reps.

Contraction is the shortening and tightening of a muscle during a repetition of an exercise. There are two types of musclar contractions: *isotonic contraction,* in which force is exerted against a moving object, such as a barbell or exercise machine; and *isometric contraction,* in which force is exerted against an immovable object, as when statically flexing the muscles while posing.

Resistance (also referred to as *weight* or *poundage*) is the amount of opposing force provided by a machine or free weights (a barbell and dumbbells) as a muscle contracts in an exercise. The amount of resistance that you use must be increased over a period of time in bodybuilding training.

Overload is another term for resistance. It is the amount of stress placed on a muscle that is over and above the amount the muscle is ordinarily accustomed to bearing. In bodybuilding and weight training this overload is provided by lifting heavier and heavier weights.

Intensity is the quality of effort that you put forth during the performance of an exercise or an entire workout. Intensity is similar to resistance in that it is often a function of the weight applied to a muscle group.

There are two types of exercise. You have probably heard of *aerobic exercise,* which is low-intensity, long-lasting exercise, such as cycling, jogging, and swimming, that builds endurance and burns body fat. For an aerobic effect you must maintain your pulse rate at 80 percent of your maximum target pulse rate for at least 20 minutes. (You can calculate your maximum target pulse rate by subtracting your age in years from 220, so a twenty-five-year-old woman would have a maximum target pulse rate of 195 beats per minute.) Aerobic exercise uses abundant supplies of oxygen to burn energy extracted from fat cells, so it's an excellent form of movement for burning stored body fat. I highly recommend a combina-tion of aerobics and bodybuilding training to build and reveal detailed musculature.

The second type of exercise is *anaerobic exercise,* which is of much shorter duration and much higher intensity, burns more oxygen than the body can supply, and results in an oxygen debt. This type of exercise burns primarily glycogen (cell carbohydrate) stored in the muscles and liver for energy. Since bodybuilding training is primarily anaerobic work, you should also perform regular aerobic workouts with it in order to burn off excess body fat more effectively.

One of the most important concepts in bodybuilding training is *isolation,* which involves limiting stress from an exercise to a specific muscle, and often to only a part of that muscle. By carefully choosing movements to isolate a particular part of a muscle or muscle group, you can actually alter the shape of that muscle or group.

Nutrition is the various practices of taking food into the human body. Bodybuilders have made a science of nutrition by applying it either to add muscle mass or to strip fat from their bodies totally to achieve optimal muscular definition.

The final object of bodybuilding is to induce *hypertrophy,* or an increase in muscle mass and strength that results from heavy exercise. Hypertrophy is often referred to as *muscle growth*.

EQUIPMENT ORIENTATION

There are so many pieces of resistance training equipment in spas and gyms that it would boggle your mind to attempt training without knowing the name and understanding the functions of each piece of equipment beforehand. Generally speaking, weight-training equipment can be divided into two categories—free weights (barbells, dumbbells, benches, and other equipment) and exercise machines (e.g., those manufactured by Nautilus Sports/Medical Industries, Universal Gym, Questar, and a wide variety of other manufacturers).

Free Weights

By far, free weights are more commonly used by serious bodybuilders than machines are, although the gap between the two modes of training is rapidly closing. Free weights are also much less expensive for home gym use. A complete set of barbells, dumbbells, and a bench will cost you under $300—a one-time investment—which is approximately the cost of a year's membership at a Nautilus or fitness-training facility. The cost of equipping a home gym with exercise machines can run into many thousands of dollars.

Under ideal circumstances a serious woman bodybuilder should train in a gym that provides both free weights and a variety of exercise machines, for only then can she be assured of optimal workouts. There are many gyms across America, Canada, and the rest of the world that have both types of equipment, such as the world-famous World Gym in Santa Monica and Gold's Gym in Venice, California, both great gyms in which I've often trained.

The most fundamental type of free weight is a *barbell,* which consists of a metal rod four to seven feet long to which metal discs called *plates* are fastened by means of cylindrical clamps called *collars.* Many bars are equipped with a rotating *sleeve,* a metal tube fitted over the bar that allows the barbell to rotate more freely in a bodybuilder's hands during an exercise. Most sleeves have grooves, called *knurlings,* cut into them to assist a bodybuilder's grip when her hands are sweaty.

Most barbells used in home gyms are adjustable: You can change the weight on the bar by loosening the outside collars and either adding or removing plates. If you have an adjustable barbell set, you must add in the weight of the bar itself when calculating the poundage you're using. It's best to merely weigh the bar, or you can estimate its weight by multiplying the length of it in feet by five pounds (e.g., a five-foot bar will weigh about 25 pounds).

In large commercial gyms, most of the barbells are "fixed," with the plates either bolted or welded permanently in place. In this case the poundage of each barbell is either painted or etched on the inner and/or outer plates of the barbell. Normally, fixed barbells

Squats with the Olympic barbells. (Note the squat rack in the background.)

are provided in 5- or 10-pound increments ranging from about 20 pounds to over 100 pounds.

There is also a specialized form of barbell called an *Olympic barbell,* which is used in weight-lifting competitions. It is also used by bodybuilders for heavy leg and back exercises such as squats and bent rows. An Olympic bar weighs 45 pounds (or 20 kilograms—about 44 pounds) unloaded, and the collars that secure plates to the bar weigh 5 pounds (or 2½ kilograms—about 5½ pounds) each.

Barbell plates are normally made of cast metal, although some are made of vinyl that is filled with concrete. Unfortunately the vinyl plates are so bulky that it's difficult to get a lot of weight to fit on a bar. Still, the vinyl plates are much easier on wooden floors if you happen to work out in your bedroom. Barbell plates most commonly come in the following poundages: 1¼, 2½, 5, 7½, 10, 15, 20, 25, 50, 75, and 100 pounds.

Dumbbells are merely short-handled barbells 10 to 15 inches in length that are intended for use one in each hand. All of the other characteristics and terminology of a barbell are the same in a dumbbell. In general, barbells are used for heavy back, chest, and leg movements, while dumbbells are used for lighter arm and shoulder exercises, although these functions do overlap to a significant degree.

The two remaining common pieces of free-weight apparatus are an *exercise bench* and a *squat rack.* Many upper-body exercises are performed on a flat exercise bench with a support rack attached to one end to hold the barbell between sets. There are also incline benches so that you can do chest, shoulder, and arm exercises while reclining backward at an angle on the bench surface. And there are decline benches, which allow you to lie on your back with your torso angled so that your head is at the bottom end of the bench for certain arm and chest movements.

The squat exercise for the powerful thigh, hip, buttock, and lower back muscles is one in which you can soon use such heavy weights that you won't be able to lift the barbell unassisted to a position across your shoulders. In this case you can rest the loaded barbell on a squat rack consisting of two upright posts with cups at the top ends to cradle the bar. With a squat rack you can merely step under the bar, position it across your shoulders, lift the weight from the rack, step back, and do your squats.

The following are many other types of free-weight apparatus whose functions you will understand as you read the exercise descriptions in later chapters: hack machine, leg extension machine, leg curl machine, standing calf machine, seated calf machine, high pulleys, low pulleys, seated pulley rowing machine, lat pull-down machine, T-bar rowing machine, curling machine, Smith machine, preacher bench, dipping bars, chinning bar, leg press machine, abdominal board, Roman chair, wrist roller, neck strap, and pec deck.

Exercise Machines

Nautilus manufactures the most popular and strongly promoted exercise machines; I have seen Nautilus machines in use all over the world. I have also used them in my own training. The machines are constructed with rotating cams (pulleys) that have varying radii, a feature that places direct resistance on the working muscles in such a way that the resistance varies in intensity according to how strong a working muscle is in each position as it contracts. This is called variable, rotory resistance, and it is a feature that makes Nautilus machines stress the working muscles much harder than normal free-weight movements *if* you use each machine properly and with total mental concentration (more on how to do this will be revealed a bit later).

I use Nautilus machines freely in my bodybuilding workouts, but only in conjunction with free weights and other machines. Some bodybuilders feel that they can get optimal workouts using only Nautilus machines, but I disagree. I simply can't do enough exercises for each muscle group on Nautilus—or on any other single brand of machine, for that matter—to

Dumbbell Flyes on a decline bench.

keep from becoming bored on machines. In bodybuilding, variety is indeed the spice of results, and it can't be achieved by training exclusively on machines, or even just on free weights, for any extended period of time.

The Universal Gym Company produces a number of units on which several bodybuilders can train at one time, a feature that makes them ideal for use in schools and other high-use institutions. Each machine incorporates exercise stations at which you can perform movements for all major muscle groups. Still, Universal machines offer very few exercises for each specific body part.

Many other manufacturers sell exercise machines of varying quality and price, and many of them are available for use in larger gyms. A few of the brand names that you may notice are Polaris, Flex, Hydra Gym, and Cam II. Keep in mind that all of these machines are good, but they give much better results to a serious bodybuilder when used in combination with free weights than when used alone.

PHYSICAL EXAMS

If you have been physically inactive for a year or more prior to adopting a bodybuilding life-style, you definitely should have your family physician give you a thorough physical examination before you begin working out. A physical exam can reveal whether you have any hidden health problems that may be aggravated by intense weight training. If you do have such problems, your physician can perhaps recommend a slower-than-normal rate of progression.

If you are over forty years of age, I recommend that you also have a stress-test electrocardiogram (EKG) in conjunction with your physical exam. This is particularly important for men, who have a much greater risk of heart and vascular disease than women (although women *are* catching up!). The EKG will give your physician a clear picture of the health of your heart and circulatory system.

In the event that your physician's recommendations regarding speed and intensity of progression in your training differ from my own, you should definitely follow his or her advice. Your physician knows your health better than I do.

AGE FACTORS

While one will probably make the best progress as a bodybuilder between the ages of about fifteen and forty-five, women of all ages can enjoy and benefit from a program of regular bodybuilding training. No matter what your age is, you will be able to reshape your body significantly by training consistently and monitoring your diet. However, up to the age of about fifteen, the body is not mature enough to make optimal bodybuilding gains. After the age of forty or forty-five, your body will begin to slow down and you won't be able to make gains as quickly as you did in your twenties and thirties. But it's *never* too late to benefit from bodybuilding workouts.

HEREDITY

Much has been written and said about the role of genetic potential in bodybuilding. As a result, it is widely contended that only genetically gifted women can become champion bodybuilders. In my experience in the sport, I have found that this is not necessarily true.

Your genetic potential *can* limit the degree to which you can develop your physique. However, it is only to a small degree that your potential can dictate the speed at which you make bodybuilding gains. About 5 percent of all women who enter bodybuilding have optimal physical potential for the sport, and these women will become champions most quickly. Another 5 percent of women bodybuilders have such poor potential that they probably won't become champions regardless of how hard they train or how carefully they watch their diets. The remaining 90 percent of all women in bodybuilding have the genetic potential to become winners *if* they are prepared to pay the price—in other words, if they're prepared to work hard and consistently *and* follow a healthy bodybuilding diet.

I prefer to look at my genetic potential as an *enabling* factor rather than a *limiting* factor in bodybuilding. I have been genetically blessed in some respects, as have most titleholding women bodybuilders. Therefore some bodybuilding qualities have been easier for me to attain than others for which I have been less genetically gifted. But the beauty of bodybuilding lies in striving as hard as you can to improve your weak points.

In the final analysis only *you* are responsible for unleashing your total physical potential. I have put in the type of dedicated work that it takes to become a champion. If you want to be a champion, you must commit yourself to do just that!

RESISTANCE PROGRESSION

Periodically increasing the resistance in each exercise is the way we systematically overload a skeletal muscle to make it stronger, improve its tone, and increase its mass.

There are three basic methods by which you can increase resistance in an exercise:

(1) Increase the amount of weight being used in a particular movement.

(2) Increase the number of repetitions that you perform with a given weight in any exercise.

(3) Do the same number of reps and use the same weight in a movement, but gradually reduce the length of time you rest between sets of the exercise.

Experienced bodybuilders use the third of these methods (which is called *quality training*) prior to a competition. But most people use a combination of the first two methods of increasing resistance. This combination involves increasing reps through an established repetition range, then increasing the weight and decreasing the repetitions once you reach the top of the suggested range, only to begin working up in reps again.

For example, let's say that you are required to do 8 to 12 repetitions of an exercise (*8* and *12* are the *guide numbers* of repetitions that you perform for the movement). In your first workout you might do 8 reps (the lower guide number) with a certain weight. Then, in each succeeding workout, you add 1 or 2 repetitions to the movement until you have reached the upper guide number of reps (in this case 12). At that point you add 5 to 10 pounds to your barbell and drop back to the lower guide number of reps, then gradually work up again to the upper guide number.

In all upper body exercises, you'll generally be able to add 5 pounds to your bar each time you drop back down to the lower guide number. For leg and back movements you can probably add 10 pounds fairly easily, and a few stronger women may be able to add more.

In Table 2-1 on page 20 you will find a four-week sample progression chart showing how you can gradually increase the weight and number of reps in the barbell bent rowing movement. Note that 35×8 is a type of bodybuilding shorthand that means to do 8 reps with 35 pounds.

Table 2-1 should give you a clear idea of how progression of resistance works when you're doing a single set of an exercise. However, you will ordinarily do multiple sets (usually three or four sets) of each exercise in a bodybuilding program. If that is the case, you must reach the upper guide number for *each* of the sets before you increase the resistance. In Table 2-2 you will find an example of how you might progress doing three sets of 8 to 12 reps in the barbell incline press over a four-week period.

You should normally be able to add one or more reps to each exercise every workout. But keep in mind that your body will experience natural up and down energy cycles. When you're experiencing a down day, you will find it difficult to add a rep. Don't worry about this, however, because you'll easily be able to add as many as two or three reps on an up day, and you may even be able to go up in weight for some movements.

Don't rely entirely on this method to measure your progress, however. It has two drawbacks: (1) It can become mechanical and boring; and (2) it's unrealistic to add new reps over an extended period of time. I believe that it's best to change exercises from time to time in order to get more varied stimulation of a body part. Sometimes only one new exercise changes the sequence of exercises for a muscle group so dramatically that it's as if you changed every movement. But of course you should gradually increase resistance in all of your exercises if you wish to induce muscle hypertrophy.

Table 2-1: Progression When Performing a Single Set of a Movement over a Four-Week Period

	Workout 1	Workout 2	Workout 3
Week 1	45 × 8	45 × 9	45 × 10
Week 2	45 × 11	45 × 12	50 × 8
Week 3	50 × 9	50 × 10	50 × 11
Week 4	50 × 12	55 × 8	55 × 9, etc.

Table 2-2: Progression When Performing Three Sets of a Movement over a Four-Week Period

	Workout 1	Workout 2	Workout 3
Week 1	45 × 8	45 × 10	45 × 11
	45 × 8	45 × 9	45 × 10
	45 × 8	45 × 8	45 × 9
Week 2	45 × 12	45 × 12	45 × 12
	45 × 11	45 × 12	45 × 12
	45 × 9	45 × 10	45 × 11
Week 3	45 × 12	50 × 9	50 × 10
	45 × 12	50 × 8	50 × 9
	45 × 12	50 × 8	50 × 8
Week 4	50 × 10	50 × 11	50 × 12
	50 × 10	50 × 10	50 × 11
	50 × 9	50 × 9	50 × 10, etc.

CORRECT EXERCISE FORM

While experienced bodybuilders use ''cheating'' movements very effectively in their workouts, it's essential for less experienced trainees to maintain strict form in all of their exercises. Try to move only those parts of your body specified in the exercise descriptions in this book. Until you learn how to cheat to make a set harder rather than easier (this takes time and experience), don't allow any other part of your body to assist in a movement. Swinging or jerking a weight up is self-defeating, since cheating removes stress from the muscles you're trying so hard to work in a particular exercise.

It's also essential that you move the weight relatively slowly over the full range of motion possible in each exercise. You must move each working muscle from its full degree of extension to its full degree of contraction and back again to full extension with every repetition. Moving a weight slowly keeps bar momentum from robbing your muscles of some of the muscle-building stress they should receive. Moving the weight slowly and over a complete range of motion in each exercise guarantees that the muscles being worked will receive maximum stimulation.

The speed of each repetition is quite important. At first you should take three to four seconds to raise the weight up for each repetition and four to five seconds to lower it back down to the starting point. It's always a good idea to lower the weight a bit more slowly than you raise it because you get a considerable muscle-building effect from the downward (negative) cycle of a movement, and you cheat yourself out of much of the benefit of a rep when you fail to resist powerfully the pull of gravity as you lower a weight. Lowering a weight slowly also tends to prevent muscle, tendon, and joint injuries.

As you gain experience as a bodybuilder you can experiment with raising the weight faster or slower than I've just recommended. Changing the tempo of an exercise in this way can produce different effects on your muscles. So can changing your foot stance, grip width, or body position a little from set to set or from workout to workout.

I believe that this type of variety in your workout helps you to become more aware and in tune with your muscles and the way they work. Develop a good relationship with your muscles, be kind to them, teach them, punish them (in a constructive way, of course), stroke them, show them new tricks, treat them to fabulously nutritious meals, and they'll never let you down.

Develop a relationship with your muscles and the rest of your body. Such a relationship doesn't just happen; it evolves and grows. And when you do your part, your muscles will naturally respond to your workouts. The expression of this type of love relationship between you and your beautiful physical presence can feel exhilarating. Narcissistic? Not really, because it comes from the heart and is something to deeply enjoy.

Rest Between Sets

I recommend rest intervals of about sixty seconds between sets for the average woman. Many experienced bodybuilders rest only twenty to thirty seconds between sets just prior to a competition, while competitive weight lifters often rest as long as four to five minutes between sets. But as a good, safe rest interval, I suggest that you stick to sixty seconds. This length of time will keep your body warm, thus preventing injuries while allowing your muscles to recuperate sufficiently for you to do justice to your next set.

How to Breathe

This is the question that I'm most often asked by beginning bodybuilders at the training seminars I conduct across America, in Canada, and throughout the world. It's best to breathe out during the exertion phase of a movement and breathe in during the relaxation phase. After a few workouts this pattern will become so automatic that you probably won't even think about it.

Never hold your breath while you are lifting a very heavy weight, since this can cause you to black out. If you faint while doing a bench press on a flat bench, the weight crashing down on your face and neck might cause you some problems. In other exercises you might fall and hit your head, so be sure that you never hold your breath in the middle of a heavy set.

The Urge to Go Heavy

I'm sure that sooner or later you'll want to do one or more "maxed-out" sets in your workouts. Human nature dictates this desire in every one of us, and I just want you to be prepared to handle this urge safely when it hits. So what's it feel like to do a very heavy set? For an answer to this question, consider the following scenario.

You slap more plates than ever before on your barbell, or you move the weight selector pin farther down the weight stack than you world normally dare. You stare for long seconds at the weight, perhaps hating it for its ability to thwart your efforts to lift it. You become keyed up, and your pulse rate zooms. Perhaps you even feel a tendril of fear.

Suddenly your mental focus flips into a do-or-die mode. You're juiced to the limit and feel the triumph of power surging through your body. You laugh at the weight, perhaps even suppress an urge to curse the weight and all of the corruption in the world. You think of millions of people suffering far more than you will suffer when lifting the weight. Your eyes have fire in them and your breathing quickens. Mentally and physiologically you're now ready for a total effort.

You position yourself on the bench, grasp the bar, and become one with the equipment to the point that you feel neither the barbell nor your surroundings, only your muscles exploding with energy. With your mind focused totally on explosive muscle contraction,

*A rest interval of about sixty seconds between
sets will keep your body warm and prevent injuries.*

Photo by Emmanuel Tanjala

you begin to blast out reps: one ... two. *My God,* you think, *I've never done this before! Am I really doing it? Yes! Another? Yes!*

Oh, what a feeling! It's muscle motion. No, it's even better, its *Flexdance!* Every fiber of your being goes into a final slow, almost painful rep, then it's over. For a moment it feels anticlimactic to put down the bar, but suddenly you begin to feel the blood coursing through those muscles you've just forced to the limit. It feels sensational, and in the gym mirror you can see your muscles throbbing larger than ever with the pump they've achieved. Could this muscle pump be what the legendary—and oh, so carnal—Arnold Schwarzenegger calls the ultimate physical sensation?

Certainly a good pump does feel great, both physically and mentally, after you max out like this. It becomes a positive addiction to the point where you'll shoot for a good pump again and again in future workouts.

WORKOUT FREQUENCY

In the hours following a heavy weight workout, the muscles in your body undergo profound changes. Fatigue by-products are slowly removed by the bloodstream and new supplies of muscle fuel (glycogen)

The final, almost painful rep of a "maxed-out" set.

and oxygen are brought into the muscles. The trained muscle cells grow in mass and strength as soon as the muscles have recuperated from a workout *if* the body is given proper nutrients and is allowed to rest sufficiently.

In order for the muscles to receive this crucial rest, it's best for you to train each muscle only every other day. This training frequency allows for full recuperation and therefore full benefit from a workout. If you train your muscles every day, your body won't receive enough rest to recuperate fully, and your muscles will fail to increase in mass and strength. In some cases they might even shrink in size and grow weaker.

As a beginning bodybuilder you should train three nonconsecutive days per week. Novice bodybuilders usually train on Mondays, Wednesdays, and Fridays, and rest on Tuesdays, Thursdays, Saturdays, and Sundays, since this leaves the weekends free. Of course, any other convenient combination of three nonconsecutive days can be used.

After two or three months of steady training, you may shift to a split routine in which you train half of your body on Mondays and Thursdays and the other half on Tuesdays and Fridays. Split routines allow you to do shorter workouts, which in turn allows you to expend more energy on each muscle group. Since a muscle group can rest while another is trained, you will still give your muscles plenty of recuperation time between workouts.

Sleep and Rest

I just explained that your muscles need at least forty-eight hours of rest between workouts for full recuperation and muscle growth to occur. To allow for complete recuperation between workouts, you must maintain regular sleep habits. The amount of sleep necessary is an individual matter, however. (If you feel sleepy and can't concentrate well during the day, you definitely need more sleep.) The key to getting enough sleep is to avoid too many late nights partying, studying, or working.

You should also attempt to keep yourself in a restful state of mind during the day, rather than running around like a chicken with its head cut off. It's very difficult to make optimal gains when you're expending large quantities of nervous energy during the day. Avoid stress and you'll get better results from your bodybuilding endeavors.

WHEN TO WORK OUT

There's really no set time to train with weights. You should simply fit your workouts into your daily schedule whenever possible or, like most of us fanatics, organize the rest of your life around your training schedule. Most bodybuilders seem to prefer to work out in the morning, late afternoon, or evening, but you can find dedicated bodybuilders pumping iron any time in between as well.

WHERE TO TRAIN

The best place to work out is at a health spa, a large commercial bodybuilding gym, a school, or a YMCA/YWCA with a well-equipped weight room. In these establishments you'll find a wide variety of equipment, including many types of exercise machines, which you can use to make faster progress as a bodybuilder.

If you don't have access to a good gym, however, don't despair. Many men and women who have become prominent bodybuilders started working out at home with an inexpensive adjustable barbell and dumbbell set. That was the case with me, almost. I first began training along with my sister Yolanda, at the tender age of four, with my father's weight set back home in Harlingen, Texas. My father would train with weights, and Yolanda and I would sometimes mimic his workouts. What a great dad I knew I had. As far as I was concerned, no one could possibly be stronger or have better muscles than my father!

At the beginner's level of training, you may actually be better off working out in your own home gym. But as you become more advanced, you may find that you prefer a greater variety of exercise equipment in order to maintain a high level of interest in training through greater workout variety. At that point you'll be better off training in a large gym or spa. You will also find that having other good bodybuilders training in the same gym with you develops a valuable sense of camaraderie and inspiration that spurs you to greater bodybuilding results.

WHAT TO WEAR

Any type of athletic clothing can be worn when your're working out with weights. The key to choosing what to wear lies in finding clothing that won't bind your joints as you exercise. As I mentioned earlier in this chapter, in the section on correct exercise form, bodybuilding training requires moving the limbs over their full range of motion. Tight-fitting clothing restricts such freedom of movement.

Most women bodybuilders wear shorts and either a T-shirt or tank top. Other women, myself included, often wear leotards and/or tights as well. Needless to say, hard bodybuilding training and other forms of exercise will inevitably cause you to perspire. It happens to everyone. I prefer for the sake of hygiene not to train with bare legs or a bare back in high-use gyms. It's unpleasant to say the least, when you sit or lie back on a piece of equipment plastered with the sweat of some inconsiderate oaf with zero knowledge of gym etiquette. Yuck! So if you fail to cover your legs and back, be sure to carry a towel around during your workouts. It'll come in handy.

Whether or not to wear a bra should be determined by individual needs for support, comfort, etc. In cold weather you may choose to wear a full warm-up suit while you train. Otherwise, choose clothing in any fashion you wish in order to enhance the appearance of your hard-earned body. I find that I am much more positively motivated to train hard when I know I'm looking good in the gym.

I strongly recommend that you wear shoes when you're working out. Whenever you're using heavy weights in an exercise, the archs of your feet will be momentarily compressed. Therefore you should wear shoes with built-in arch supports (most good running shoes have these built-in supports) to protect your feet from injury. The tread pattern on the soles of the running shoes will also help to keep your toes from slipping off the calf block when you're performing heavy calf movements.

I and many other serious women bodybuilders prefer to wear a wide leather weight-lifting belt when doing heavy exercises such as squats, deadlifts, barbell bent rows, and overhead presses. These belts help to support and protect your abdomen and lower back from injury when you're pumping really heavy iron. They're available in many sporting-goods stores or through advertisements in *Muscle & Fitness* and most other bodybuilding magazines. They cost between $20 for the most Spartan belt and more than $50 for a custom-made weight-lifting belt.

APPROPRIATE STARTING WEIGHTS

The starting poundages for each exercise in the beginner's program in the next chapter have been selected according to what my experience indicates is what an average woman can comfortably handle. Of course, you may be either stronger or less fit than the average woman, so it may be necessary to adjust the weights after your first workout.

How do you know if the poundages you're using are appropriate for you? A set done with the correct poundage can be completed for the required number of repetitions without undue strain. If you can easily do more than the required number of repetitions, you should increase the weight a little for your next workout. And if you have to struggle to complete the required number of reps—or you can't complete them at all—you should reduce the weight for your next training session. As a general rule, when you can complete 15 full, strict repetitions of a movement with a particular weight, it's too light and should be increased by 5 to 10 pounds.

I won't presume to provide you with suggested training poundage once you advance beyond the beginning level of training. You will very quickly develop an uncanny feel for your body's strength capabilities and will be able to judge accurately the training weights that you should use in more advanced programs.

HOW MANY REPS?

The number of repetitions of an exercise that you perform will have a degree of effect on what that movement does for you body. Generally speaking, low reps (5 to 8) tend to develop muscle mass and physical strength quickly; medium reps (8 to 12) give you a good combination of muscle quality and mass; and high reps (more than 15) tend to develop local muscular endurance and higher muscle quality (i.e., definition, or the muscle quality apparent when your fat percentage is down to a minimum level) than muscle mass. By choosing your rep ranges carefully in the early stages of training, you can achieve your bodybuilding goals more quickly. Later, as a more advanced bodybuilder, you will learn specifically how to train your muscles with maximum intensity.

With a bit of bodybuilding experience under your belt, you will discover that you must use varying numbers of reps for each muscle group. Upper-body muscles tend to respond best to reps in the range of 8 to 12, while the thighs respond best to a rep range of 10 to 15. Calves can be trained with 15 to 20 repetitions, and abdominals with reps in the range of 25 to more than 100.

BASIC NUTRITION TIPS

Bodybuilding nutrition is discussed in detail in Chapter 8, but to point you in the proper direction nutritionally, I'm including a few suggestions on diet in this beginning-level chapter. They'll help you get the most out of your initial training efforts.

In essence you must follow health-promoting eating habits if you wish to make optimal bodybuilding gains. This involves eating fresh, low-fat meats (such as fish and poultry), low-fat (or, better yet, nonfat) milk products, fresh fruits and vegetables, seeds, nuts, whole grains, and eggs.

You should also take a multipack or two of vitamins, minerals, and trace elements each day as insurance against progress-halting nutritional deficiencies. These cellophane packets of capsules and tablets are available in health food stores. You should take each multipack with a meal, since the vitamins, minerals, and trace elements are absorbed better when they're consumed with food.

To give you a general idea of what a bodybuilding diet looks like, here's a typical one-day menu:

- **Breakfast**—one or two poached eggs, one slice of whole-grain toast, half a grapefruit, herbal tea, one vitamin-mineral multipack
- **Lunch**—broiled fish, rice, salad, iced tea with lemon

- **Dinner**—one broiled chicken breast, one baked potato, one or two steamed vegetables, one glass of nonfat milk, one vitamin-mineral multipack
- **Snacks**—trail mix, "health food" cookies or bread, raw vegetables, fresh fruits, tea, coffee.

As you gradually learn more about nutrition for bodybuilding by reading nutrition books and nutrition articles in bodybuilding magazines, you can refine this basic diet to suit your personal needs.

BASIC MENTAL ASPECTS OF BODYBUILDING

A detailed discussion of the mind in bodybuilding is given in Chapter 11, but there are several basic mental techniques that you should understand at the beginning level of bodybuilding training.

Your mind is an extremely powerful force in determining your bodybuilding destiny. In fact, the key to your success lies in whether your mind is a friend or foe. Often people see their bodies in a negative way, focusing on their physical flaws or shortcomings. And that hard-to-overcome, negative mental image can really thwart your body-shaping efforts. But once that image is broken and replaced by a new, positive body image, bodybuilding becomes a wonderful trip filled with excitement, self-discovery, and success!

The mind also plays a vital role in the creation and preservation of motivation. Motivation starts you on the path to a fantastic body and sees you through to your destination. But where do you find motivation? How can you make it last?

Because motivation is a by-product of your mind, that's the place to look for it. Oh, you can be motivated by tape measures, mirrors, and the bathroom scale, but these things only spark the initial desire to get in shape. This desire—and the willingness to hunt and hurt for a super body—is fueled by your mind power.

To develop serious, long-lasting motivation, you must look deep inside your mind. You must ask yourself serious questions: "Don't I owe it to myself and the Creator to be the best I can be? Isn't life too short to spend it being fat and flabby? I have the tools to build a better body, but do I have what it takes to accept the challenge?" When you explore these thoughts and make up your mind to do something positive about the way you look and feel, *nothing* can stop you. You're on the way to a fit, healthy, fantastic body!

There is no question that the ability to concentrate, to focus fully mentally, on a working muscle as you train it improves your ability to contract the muscle and results in superior development and muscle quality. The first thing you must do in learning muscle concentration is to be absolutely certain of which muscle group—and even the exact part of the muscle itself —is being stressed by each exercise that you perform. Once you know which muscle to concentrate on, try to focus all of your mental energy on it; try to feel it contract and extend with every repetition throughout each set. The ability to concentrate on a working muscle this intensely can be practiced and eventually mastered.

BREAK-IN AND MUSCLE SORENESS

Since bodybuilding training is a much more intense form of exercise than you've probably experienced before, your muscles can become very sore if you try to jump right in by doing a full workout your very first day in a gym. So be sure that you break into bodybuilding training gradually.

Begin your break-in by performing only one set per exercise in your recommended beginning routine (see Chapter 3) during the first week, and then only after a thorough warm-up. Even though three sets may be recommended for a given routine, you should still do *only one set* per exercise in each workout during your initial week of weight training.

During the second week, do two sets of each exercise in which two or more sets are suggested (again, do not do three sets). Then, in the third week, you can start doing the entire recommended training program.

Be careful about adding weight to your barbell or dumbbells before your fourth week of training. During the first two or three weeks, you should use no more than the recommended poundages in each exercise, unless these weights feel exceedingly light to you. Normally you should add weight for each movement only when your body has become fully accustomed to the heavier work load. *The first few weeks*

of training with weights should be used to learn how to do the movements correctly, and this is more difficult to do if you are handling maximum poundages.

It's perfectly normal for your muscles to be slightly stiff and mildly sore the day after your first or second workout. However, your muscles can become *very* sore if you inadvertently push too hard in your initial workouts. In such a case the best remedy for muscle soreness is a long hot bath. You may also profit from a low-intensity aerobic workout, such as cycling, to help flush out body cell wastes that contribute to muscle soreness.

WARMING UP

Because weight training is an intense form of physical activity, it's essential that you warm up prior to a bodybuilding workout. Such a warm-up makes the muscles and joints more supple, which minimizes the chance of injury. A good warm-up also improves neuromuscular coordination and allows you to use slightly heavier weights than you would be able to handle without a warm-up.

I suggest that you spend at least ten minutes warming up before each training session. Begin by either cycling, running in place or jumping rope for three to five minutes to accelerate your pulse rate and get your body temperature elevated. (I personally prefer stationary cycling for this part of my own warm-up.) Then perform at least five to eight minutes of stretching and calisthenics. Only then should you start working out with the weights.

Later, when you are more experienced in bodybuilding and can handle heavier weights, you should also do a lighter set or two of a basic exercise for each muscle group prior to doing your main exercises for that body part. This extra warm-up will allow you to handle heavier poundages safely in your training sessions.

SAFETY RULES

As long as you follow certain commonsense safety rules, bodybuilding training is a totally safe form of exercise. The first of these rules is: Never attempt maximum lifts in the incline press, decline press, or squat without having an alert training partner standing by to spot you during a set. A spotter can rescue you whenever you are unable to finish a full repetition under your own power.

Never lift heavy weights without warming up, and don't allow yourself to cool down during a workout. Most weight training injuries occur when you have allowed your body to cool down during a workout by taking too much rest between sets, as you may when engaging in idle chitchat. Once your muscles and joints have cooled, they are more susceptible to injury.

You must be very careful to use proper biomechanical form in every exercise during a workout. Proper form for every exercise is fully explained in the exercise description chapters of this book. Learn the exercises correctly and perform them correctly, and you will not need to fear injuries resulting from bad training form.

Always use collars on a barbell, even though it may seem inconvenient to do so at times. If you are lifting a heavy barbell that doesn't have the collars fastened firmly in place, it's possible for the plates on one side to slip off the bar during an exercise. This in turn causes a whipping action of the bar when the heavier end suddenly dumps its plates. Under such circumstances it is easy to wreck your lower back, ankles, knees, shoulders, wrists, or elbows. Also, the bar can bash some innocent bystander.

Finally, I suggest that you wear a weight-lifting belt whenever you do heavy squats, back work, and overhead lifts. As mentioned earlier in this chapter, a weight-lifting belt keeps your lower back and abdomen warm and keeps you aware of maintaining tension in those areas, thus helping to prevent unnecessary injuries. However, you should never depend on a belt to *support* your back and midsection. Only powerfully developed muscles can effectively accomplish this function.

RECORD KEEPING

A training diary is essential to making some sense out of the mishmash of training and dietary methods that confront you. No two bodies respond alike to training and dietary stimuli, so you must try different types of workouts and diets, monitoring the results carefully to determine what works for you and what doesn't.

It's often difficult to see improvement trends over a short term, but you can easily put your finger on periods of time when you make good long-term bodybuilding gains. By keeping a detailed training diary, you can easily identify the factors that resulted in those gains.

The more detailed your diary, the greater its ultimate value to you. At the very least, record the date of each workout and the exercises, poundages, sets, and reps you performed. There are several ways to record this data in your training log. Here are three ways in which you can say the same thing in a diary entry:

Squat: 155 pounds, 3×15 reps

Squat: $155 \times 15 \times 15 \times 15$

Squat: 155×15
155×15
155×15

You should also record any factors that might have had a positive or negative effect on the outcome of a training session. Such factors include how long and how well you slept the night before, stressful situations that affected you, your general mood and preworkout energy level, anything that has particularly inspired you, and so forth.

Many bodybuilders neglect to record exactly what they eat at each meal; thus they don't learn everything they can about how their bodies react to various dietary stimuli. To assess your diet accurately over the years, you should record the time of day at which you ate each meal, how much of each food you consumed, and what supplements, if any, you took. At the end of the day you can total up your calories, grams of protein, grams of fats, and grams of carbohydrates.

There are commercially prepared bodybuilding training diaries available in bookstores and through advertisements in various bodybuilding magazines. Or you can use any type of bound notebook to record your workouts and meals. Most bookstores and stationery stores carry bound date books, which make ideal training diaries.

Once you have a couple of months of dietary and training entries, don't let your diary just sit on a shelf.

Review it regularly to identify the reasons behind progress trends. By doing that, you'll be miles ahead of those bodybuilders who don't maintain a training log. Virtually all of the best bodybuilders *do* keep detailed training diaries.

SELF-EVALUATION

Self-evaluation is an important ongoing process for all serious bodybuilders, as well as for women who are interested only in reshaping their bodies. A measuring tape has some value to beginning bodybuilders and the average person, but it's useless for a serious bodybuilder: For her the only thing that counts is the appearance of her body. Therefore your best evaluation tool will be a pair of mirrors set at angles that enable you to see clearly both the front and back of your body. You should use these mirrors at least once a week to assess your physical proportions and the relative hardness of your physique.

For a more permanent record—and one that will allow you to assess your progress over a long period of time—you should have photographs taken of your physique each month. These can be simple "instant" photos or high-quality 35mm pictures taken by an experienced bodybuilding photographer. In either case you should always have a wide variety of photos taken from all possible angles. One of the biggest mistakes made by the novice bodybuilders is to ignore lagging development of her back, calves, deltoids, or some other body part; it's very difficult to make this mistake when you're confronted by clear photographs of yourself that you've pasted into your training log.

OPTIMAL PHYSICAL FITNESS

To possess optimal physical fitness, you must have developed to a high degree three physical qualites: strength, cardiorespiratory endurance, and joint/muscle flexibility. If your goal is optimal physical fitness, then you must work out a combined conditioning program of weight training, aerobic activities, stretching, and diet.

Flexibility training is discussed in Chapter 6, and aerobics is discussed in both Chapter 6 and Chapter 9. Therefore, by reading this book, you will become familiar with methods of improving the three primary qualities of optimal physical fitness.

The best way to train for optimal physical fitness is to begin each weight-training or aerobic workout with a stretching session as a warm-up for these activities. You can also stretch after both weight training and aerobic work if you are particularly motivated. The key in developing flexibility, however, is almost daily stretching workouts.

Weight-training and aerobic workouts can be performed on alternate days of the week, but it's not crucial to do so at higher levels of the sport. For example, you can do your weight workouts on Mondays, Wednesdays, and Fridays, then do your aerobic sessions on Tuesdays, Thursdays, and Saturdays—perhaps even on Sundays as well. The choice of aerobic activity—be it cycling, running, swimming, whatever—is entirely up to you, but I think you'll find it easier to stay motivated in your aerobic program if you frequently vary your aerobic activities.

At my level of bodybuilding and body conditioning, I train with weights *and* do at least one aerobic workout virtually every day. For example, I'll train with weights in the morning, cycle in the afternoon, and perhaps take an exercise class in the evening. The closer I come to a major competition, the more aerobic work I perform and the faster my overall physical condition improves. I get into such incredible shape that it seems as though I could train twenty-four hours a day and not even need to sleep!

LOOKING AHEAD

In the next chapter you will learn exactly how to perform twenty beginning-level bodybuilding exercises. Then you will get right down to working out with weights in three training programs of graduated intensity. I'm sure that once you've mastered these exercises and then start using them in actual training routines, you'll be ecstatic with the way your body will begin to transform before your very eyes. I'm very happy for you, and in a few months—perhaps only in a few weeks—you'll know why. Go for it!

CHAPTER 3

beginning exercises and routines

Okay, this is it! We're really going to get down to business by learning twenty beginning-level bodybuilding exercises and then combining them into a training routine that you can immediately begin using to improve your strength, health, and beauty. In subsequent chapters I will teach you many more exercises, which will give you a wide selection of movements to choose from as you formulate your own personalized advanced-training routines.

A successful bodybuilder never stops seeking to learn new training techniques and exercises, so don't accept the movements presented in this book as the only bodybuilding exercises available to you. They are merely the sixty-five or so movements that I consider to be the best for a woman bodybuilder. I've done my best to present them to you in a way that will give you the best possible results from each exercise for every part of your body.

You will undoubtedly learn other good weight-training exercises by reading various bodybuilding magazines and other weight-training and bodybuilding books as well as by observing other men and women training in gyms. Add these new exercises to your basic collection of bodybuilding movements, apply the fundamental principles you will learn in this book to evaluate the worth of each exercise, and you will soon have at your disposal far more bodybuilding movements than you'll ever need to formulate superproductive workouts.

It is important that you carefully read the descriptions and study the exercise photos before trying each movement. You may even want to do the exercise with a broomstick before taking on an actual barbell. Since you will be using most of these exercises for the rest of your bodybuilding lifetime, it's vitally important that you master their correct performance.

If you have any doubt about perfect performance of a movement, don't hesitate to ask a more experienced bodybuilder to check out your exercise form. *Feel* the movement, the gratifying contraction of your muscles, as you deliberately perform each exercise. Don't cheat yourself out of the satisfaction you will receive from the correct performance and "feel" of your bodybuilding exercises. You're worth it!

ABDOMINAL EXERCISES

(1) BENT–KNEE SIT–UPS

(A) Emphasis. Bent-knee sit-ups stress the rectus abdominis muscle wall on the front of your abdomen. Sit-ups particularly stress the upper sections of the frontal abdominal wall.

(B) Starting Position. Lie on your back on an abdominal board with your feet toward the upper end of the board. Anchor your toes under the roller pads or strap provided at the top end of the board. Bend your knees to an approximate 45-degree angle and keep them bent throughout the movement. Doing sit-ups with your legs held straight can be injurious to your lower back. Place your hands behind your head or neck and keep them in the position throughout the movement.

(C) Exercise Performance. A correct sit-up movement should probably be called a curl-up. Begin it by lifting first your head and shoulders from the abdominal board, then sequentially your upper back, mid back, and lower back until your torso is in a position perpendicular to the floor. Return to the starting position and repeat the movement. Under no circumstances should you jerk your body into a sitting position by forcefully throwing your arms and head forward and upward.

(D) Movement Variations. If you don't have an abdominal board handy, you can simply anchor your feet beneath a heavy piece of furniture for your set of sit-ups. With an abdominal board you can progressively increase the intensity of the movement by raising the foot end of the board. Or you can hold a light barbell plate behind your head and neck as you perform the exercise. You can also do twisting sit-ups, in which you alternately twist your shoulders and torso from side to side as you sit erect.

Start.

Midpoint—note how body "curls up."

Finish.

Start.

(2) KNEE–UPS

(A) Emphasis. As with sit-ups, knee-ups directly stress the frontal abdominal wall, but knee-ups place more intense stress on the lower part of the rectus abdominis muscle group.

(B) Starting Position. Sit at the very end of a flat exercise bench. Incline your torso backward at about a 45-degree angle with the floor and maintain this body position throughout the movement by grasping the edges of the bench with your hands. Straighten your legs downward so your legs and torso make one long line, but keep your feet off the floor. Press your legs together and keep them together throughout the movement.

Finish.

(C) Exercise Performance. Simultaneously bend your legs fully and pull your knees up to the top of your forehead. To improve the contraction in your abdominal muscles at the top of the movement, you can move your upper torso a few inches forward to meet your knees. Reverse the procedure to return to the starting point and repeat the exercise.

(D) Movement Variations. You can add resistance to this movement either by holding a light dumbbell between your feet or by wearing iron boots (metal shoes that can be strapped to your feet; each iron boot usually weighs about 5 pounds). You can also do knee-ups in a twisting fashion, like sit-ups, by alternately pulling your knees up to opposite sides of your torso.

Start.

Finish.

(3) SEATED TWISTING

(A) Emphasis. Seated twisting firms and tones the external and internal obliques at the sides of your waist. It is also a good way to warm up your lower back and loosen it prior to a heavy torso workout.

(B) Starting Position. You will need a broomstick or unloaded barbell bar for this movement, since using weight for seated twists can actually build up your oblique muscles, giving your waist the illusion of greater width. Sit on a flat exercise bench and either place your feet firmly on the floor on either side of the bench, or interlace your feet and lower legs with the upright legs of the bench to keep your lower body from moving during the exercise. Place the broom stick across your shoulders behind your neck (or, better yet, across your lower trapezius muscles) and wrap your arms around it throughout the movement.

(C) Exercise Performance. Twist forcibly at the waist as far to the left as possible, then back as far to the right as you can. Make the movement rhythmic

and vigorous. Count one full cycle to the left and right as a single repetition.

(D) Movement Variations. You can also do twisting in a more concentrated manner by projecting your elbow, although you must take special care to keep your hips from moving with your torso as you twist to each side (they should remain stationary, which is easy to accomplish when doing the exercise in a seated position). You can also do bent-over twists by standing with your feet about shoulder width apart and bending over with your torso parallel to the floor before beginning to do your twisting movement. Again, keep your hips and legs stationary as you do bent-over twists. I like to do two or more twists per side before twisting all of the way back to the other side. This enables me to control and direct more of a contraction to the muscles at the sides of my waist. In a movement like this it's easy to get carried away with momentum rather than with powerful muscle contraction, hence my practice of doing several short twists to one side before shifting back to the other.

CHEST EXERCISES

(4) PEC DECK FLYES

(A) Emphasis. Pec deck flyes stress the entire pectoral muscle mass, particularly the inner edges of the pecs, where they originate from your sternum (breastbone). Minor secondary stress is placed on the anterior heads of your deltoids.

(B) Starting Position. Adjust the height of the seat to a position in which your upper arms are parallel to the floor when you are performing the movement. You can rotate the seat to adjust the height on most pec deck machines; others feature a seat that is adjusted with either a pin or a spring-loaded lever. Sit in the seat and force your elbows behind the two rotating pads of the machine. Your forearms should be held perpendicular to the floor and your fingers should be resting over the top edges of the pads. Allow your elbows to move as far to the rear as comfortably possible.

(C) Exercise Performance. Use your pectoral strength to push against the pads with your elbows, moving the pads forward and inward toward each other until they touch directly in front of your chest. Hold this peak contracted position for a moment to stress your pectorals fully, then return to the starting position and repeat the movement.

(D) Movement Variations. To get somewhat different effects on your pectorals from pec deck flyes, adjust the seat to positions higher and lower than normal. With many pec deck machines you can also do this movement with one arm at a time, which automatically makes it a more intense exercise for your pectorals. When you do one-armed and one-legged movements, you needn't split your attention between two limbs. Therefore you can put greater concentration into one-armed and one-legged movements and more intensely stress the working muscles. This is particularly true when you are an advanced bodybuilder and can use partial movements with one arm or leg at a time.

Start.

Finish.

Start.

your chest. Bend your arms slightly and keep them rounded like that throughout the movement.

(C) Exercise Performance. Slowly lower the dumbbells in semicircular arcs directly out to the sides until they are a bit below shoulder level. The key point in this movement is more the depth to which you lower your elbows without bending them, rather than how low the dumbbells themselves travel. Return the weights to their starting points and repeat the movement. Be sure to feel a stretching sensation in your pectorals at the low point of the exercise, a sure sign that you've lowered the dumbbells far enough.

(D) Movement Variations. Incline flyes can also be performed on benches that aren't angled as steeply. For instance, many champion women bodybuilders favor the 30-degree incline bench. You can also perform incline flyes with cables running through floor pulleys on each side of the bench, an exercise described in Chapter 5. And if you perform decline flyes (lying back on a bench that places your head in a position below the level of your hips), you will shift primary emphasis in the movement to your lower and outer pectorals.

Finish.

(5) INCLINE DUMBBELL FLYES

(A) Emphasis. Incline flyes stress the pectorals, expecially the upper section of the muscle group. Secondary stress is placed on the anterior deltoids. I feel that women bodybuilders get more out of performing flyes and bench presses on incline and decline benches rather than on a flat bench. It's also much easier on your shoulder joints to do incline and decline movements rather than flat-bench chest exercises.

(B) Starting Position. Grasp two light dumbbells in your hands and lie back on a 45-degree incline bench. If there is a seat attached to the bench, you can sit on it. Otherwise you should stand on the foot platforms provided with those benches without seats. Extend your arms directly upward from your shoulders and rotate your hands so your palms are facing each other. Touch the dumbbells together directly above

Start.

ing the movement. Take a grip on the lat machine bar with your palms facing forward and your hands set four to six inches outside shoulder width on each side. Sit on the bench and wedge your knees under the restraining bar. Fully straighten your arms.

(C) Exercise Performance. Making sure that your elbows travel both downward and backward, slowly bend your arms to pull the lat machine handle down to touch your trapezius muscles at the base of your neck behind your head. In this contracted (bottom) position of all lat exercises, it's important that you arch your back; you won't be able to contract your latissimus dorsi muscles fully without this back arch. Return the handle to the starting point of the movement and repeat the exercise.

(D) Movement Variations. There are many variations and combinations of variations of lat machine pull-downs. You can change the width of your grip on the lat machine handle, and you can do the movement

Finish.

BACK EXERCISES

(6) LAT PULL–DOWNS (BEHIND NECK)

(A) Emphasis. Pull-downs place primary stress on the lats, the biceps, and the brachialis muscles lying beneath the biceps. Secondary stress is on the posterior deltoids and the gripping muscles of your forearms. Lat pull-downs and chins tend to develop lat width, while bent rows and seated pulley rows are normally used to build upper back muscle thickness.

(B) Starting Position. Most gyms have lat machines with a seat and knee restraint bar. A few gyms don't have machines with this seat and bar, however, and when you are using such a lat machine you must either kneel or sit on the floor beneath the pulley dur-

with your palms facing toward you instead of away from your body. There is also a lat machine handle that allows you to take a parallel grip (one in which your palms face each other), either a shoulder-width grip or one with your hands about six inches apart. And you can pull all lat bars down to your upper chest in front of your neck rather than to a position behind your neck. It's essential that you *experiment*! Remember to feel the satisflection (my term for an extremely gratifying contraction in the working muscles of your choice, resulting in even more satisfying results) in your back muscles.

(7) SEATED PULLEY ROWS

(A) Emphasis. This is an excellent all-purpose back exercise that is almost always included in my routines. While it is primarily intended to develop upper back thickness, it also adds significantly to lat width. In addition, you place major stress on your trapezius and erector spinae muscles during the movement, and secondary stress on your biceps, brachialis, posterior deltoid, and forearm gripping muscles.

(B) Starting Position. Attach a handle to the cable that allows a parallel grip with your hands close together and grasp the handle with your palms facing each other. Sit down on the padded surface of the machine bench and place your feet against the restraining bar at the front of the bench. Bend your legs slightly and keep them bent throughout the movement. Straighten your arms completely and lean forward with your head between your arms to stretch fully your lats and lower back muscles.

Start.

(C) Exercise Performance. From this position, simultaneously sit erect and pull the handle toward your torso to touch against your upper abdomen. As you pull the handle in toward your body, keep your elbows close to your sides. Arch your back at the completion of the movement, holding the contraction for a moment, but don't make the mistake of leaning back to finish the rep. Leaning back just removes stress from your lats and places it more on your trapezius muscles. Reverse the procedure just described to return to the starting position and repeat the movement.

(D) Movement Variations. There are a variety of handles that you can use on this machine, each of which hits the back muscles a little differently. Most frequently you can attach the shoulder-width parallel-grip handle used for lat machine pull-downs. You can also use a normal straight lat machine handle with your palms facing either downward or upward at various grip widths during the movement. There is also a special type of handle arrangement in which you use two loop handles that run via individual cables to the main cable of the apparatus.

Finish.

SHOULDER EXERCISES

(8) STANDING DUMBBELL SIDE LATERALS

(A) Emphasis. Side laterals stress primarily the medial heads of the deltoids, lending width to your shoulders. Minor secondary emphasis is placed on the trapezius muscles of the upper back.

(B) Starting Position. Grasp two light dumbbells and stand erect with your feet set about shoulder width apart. Bend slightly forward at the waist and maintain this torso position throughout the movement. Turn your wrists so that your palms are toward each other at the start of the movement. Bend your arms slightly and keep them bent thoughout the exercise. Press the dumbbells together about six inches in front of your hips.

Start.

Finish.

(C) Exercise Performance. Making certain that your palms face toward the floor during the movement, slowly raise the dumbbells out to the sides and slightly forward until they are a bit above shoulder level. At the top of the movement you should consciously rotate your wrists so your pinky fingers lead the movement right along with the elbows. It's tempting to cheat at the top of this movement by swinging the dumbbells or bending your knees. However, you must maintain strict form to get maximum benefit from the movement. Lower the weights back to the starting point and repeat the exercise.

(D) Movement Variations. You can do side laterals while seated at the end of a flat exercise bench or with one arm at a time while holding on to a sturdy upright with your free hand. The exercise can also be done with floor pulleys, either one arm at a time or with both arms simultaneously. The cable variation of side laterals can be done with the cables passing either in front or in back of your body.

(9) ALTERNATE DUMBBELL PRESSES

(A) Emphasis. All forms of overhead presses with a barbell, two dumbbells, or a pressing machine directly stress the anterior heads of the deltoids and the triceps. Secondary stress is placed on the medial and posterior deltoids as well as on the trapezius muscles.

(B) Starting Position. Grasp two dumbbells of moderate weight, place your feet about shoulder width apart, stand erect, and pull the dumbbells up to your shoulders. Rotate your hands so that your palms are facing forward throughout the movement.

(C) Exercise Performance. Push the dumbbell in your left hand directly upward until it is at arm's length above your shoulder joint. As you begin to lower the dumbbell, start to press the other one to arm's length. Continue alternately pressing and lowering the dumbbells until you have performed the required number of repetitions with each arm.

(D) Movement Variations. Many bodybuilders do their dumbbell presses with their palms facing toward

each other, while I get an interesting deltoid contraction when I do my dumbbell presses with my palms facing *away* from each other. You can also press the dumbbells upward simultaneously rather than alternately with any of these hand positions. You can also do all two-armed variations of dumbbell presses while sitting at the end of a flat exercise bench, which stabilizes your torso and prevents you from bending backward during the movement. A final variation is to do dumbbell presses with one arm at a time while holding on to a sturdy upright with your free hand for support.

(10) BARBELL UPRIGHT ROWS

(A) Emphasis. All variations of upright rows strongly stress both the deltoid and trapezius muscle groups. Secondary emphasis is placed on the biceps and the gripping muscles of the forearms.

(B) Starting Position. With your palms toward your body, take a narrow grip (four to six inches of space should be showing between your index fingers) in the middle of a moderately weighted barbell. Place your feet a comfortable distance apart and stand erect with your arms straight down at your sides and your hands and the barbell resting across your upper thighs.

(C) Exercise Performance. Keeping the barbell as close to your torso as possible during the movement, slowly pull the weight upward until the backs of your hands touch the under side of your chin. Throughout the movement you must keep your elbows well above the level of your hands on the bar. You can squeeze your shoulder blades together momentarily in this top position before returning the barbell to the starting point to repeat the movement.

(D) Movement Variations. You can do upright rows with a bar handle attached to the cable running

Start.

Finish.

through a floor pulley. You can also perform upright rows while holding two dumbbells rather than a barbell. However, be sure to get a full stretch in your trapezius muscles at the bottom of each rep of these movements before beginning another repetition.

ARM EXERCISES

(11) TRICEPS PUSH–DOWNS

(A) Emphasis. Often called pulley push-downs, the exercise directly stresses the triceps muscles, particularly the outer head of the triceps muscle complex.

(B) Starting Position. Place your feet about shoulder width apart, your body facing the handle attached to an overhead pulley. Bending your arms fully, grasp the pulley handle with your index fingers no more than three or four inches apart. Your palms should be facing away from your body. Keep your upper arms pressed against the sides of your torso throughout the movement.

(C) Exercise Performance. Slowly straighten your arms to move the handle in a semicircular arc from the starting position to a finishing point across your upper thighs. Return the handle to the starting position and repeat the movement for the required number of repetitions.

(D) Movement Variations. There are quite a number of different handles that you can use for triceps push-downs. The regular long lat machine handle is probably most often used, but there is a much shorter handle designed specifically for push-downs that is angled downward slightly at each end. With either of these handles you can do the movement with your palms facing upward rather than downward. By at-

Midpoint.

Finish.

taching a rope handle to the end of the cable, you can do triceps push-downs with a parallel grip. Finally you can attach a loop handle to the cable and do push-downs with one arm at a time, your palm facing either downward or upward.

(12) TRICEPS DIPS BETWEEN BENCHES

(A) Emphasis. This is a very direct movement for both the inner and outer heads of your triceps.

(B) Starting Position. Place two flat exercise benches parallel to each other and about three feet apart (the distance between benches depends on your height and limb length, so you'll need to experiment with it). Stand between the benches with your back near one of them. Bend your legs and place your hands on that bench about six to eight inches apart, your fingers curling around the edge of the bench and toward your body. Walk forward and place both heels on the opposite bench. Stiffen your legs and torso so that they make a 90-degree angle during the movement. Totally straighten your arms.

Start, with dumbbell for resistance.

(C) Exercise Performance. Bend your arms as fully as possible and lower your bottom as close to the floor as you can. Straighten your arms to push yourself back to the starting point and repeat the exercise.

(D) Movement Variations. You may find it more comfortable to perform this exercise with your heels on a bench and your hands on the restraining bar attached to a lat machine. Regardless of whether you use one or two benches, you can vary the width of your hand placement: Your hands can be so close that they touch each other, or they can be as far apart as shoulder width. You will quickly become strong at this movement and will need added resistance. This is best provided by a training partner standing behind you and pushing down with sufficient force on your shoulders. Alternatively you can have your training partner place a light dumbbell or loose barbell plate in your lap at the beginning of your set.

(13) STANDING BARBELL CURLS

(A) Emphasis. This is the most basic biceps movement. It places very intense stress on the biceps muscles and secondary emphasis on the brachialis muscles and flexor muscles on the inner sides of your forearms.

(B) Starting Position. Bend over and take a shoulder-width grip on a moderately weighted barbell, your palms facing away from your body. Place your feet a comfortable distance apart and stand erect. Straighten your arms down at your sides with the barbell resting across your upper thighs. Keep your upper arms pinned against the sides of your torso throughout the movement.

(C) Exercise Performance. Using biceps strength, curl the barbell in a semicircular arc from the starting

Finish.

Start.

position across your thighs up to a point beneath your chin. Begin the movement with your wrists held straight and finish it that way as well. Lower the barbell back along the same arc to the starting point and repeat the exercise.

(D) Movement Variations. You can use myriad grip widths on the barbell, from a narrow one with your hands touching each other to one as wide as the length of the bar permits. Try using a false grip (one with your thumbs under the bar rather than around it); this type of curling grip gives me greater satisflexion in my biceps muscles. If you have trouble with your torso moving forward and backward during the exercise, you can make the movement more strict by performing it with your back resting against a wall. Advanced bodybuilders will do cheating curls, in which they purposely use torso movement to swing the bar upward, but for now you should aim to use the strictest possible exercise form, since that places maximum stress on your working biceps muscles.

Start

Finish.

(14) ALTERNATE DUMBBELL CURLS

(A) Emphasis. All dumbbell curl movements place primary stress on the biceps muscles. Secondary emphasis is on the brachialis muscles and the powerful flexor muscles of the forearms.

(B) Starting Position. Grasp two dumbbells of moderate weight, place your feet a comfortable distance apart, stand erect, and hang your arms straight down at your sides. Be sure that your upper arms are pressed against the sides of your torso during the movement. At the beginning of each repetition your palms should be facing inward toward your body.

(C) Exercise Performance. Slowly bend your right arm and curl the dumbbell in a semicircular arc forward from the position at the side of your leg up to your shoulder. As you curl the dumbbell upward you must rotate your wrist so that your palm ends up facing upward during most of the movement. This

wrist-twisting movement is called *supination,* and it's a very important concept in building high-quality biceps development. Since you can't supinate your hands when you do barbell curls, you can actually get more out of your dumbbell curls when training biceps. As you begin to lower the dumbbell in your right hand, start to curl (or raise) the weight in your left hand. Continue curling the dumbbells alternately in this manner until you have done the suggested number of repetitions with each hand.

(D) Movement Variations. You can also curl the dumbbells upward simultaneously, or do the curls with one arm at a time using a single dumbbell. All three variations of dumbbell curls can be done while seated at the end of a flat exercise bench, which isolates your legs from the movement and makes it more strict. Or, better yet, you can do your dumbbell curls while lying back on an incline bench, which puts your legs and torso in a position that makes it impossible to cheat on the exercise. This variation of dumbbell curls is referred to as incline dumbbell curls.

THIGH AND HIP EXERCISES

(15) LEG PRESSES

(A) Emphasis. This movement can be performed on a wide variety of leg press machines. The original leg press machine allowed you to do the movement while lying on your back and pushing directly upward against the weight. Nautilus and Universal Gym machines, as well as a few others, allow you to sit erect and push directly forward against the weight.

And most recently a leg press machine has evolved in which you push the weight up a track set at a 45-degree angle with the floor. Regardless of the machine used, leg presses strongly stress the quadriceps (or frontal thigh muscles). Secondary emphasis is placed on the hip and buttock muscles, the hamstrings, and most of the upper body muscle groups.

Start.

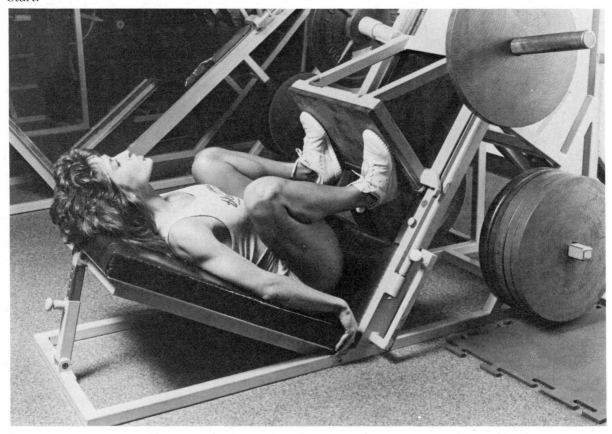

(B) Starting Position. Let's use the Nautilus leg press machine to illustrate this movement because from its description you can easily learn leg presses on the other types of machines. First shift the seat forward by moving the lever at the right side of the seat. (On some less adjustable machines you'll have to place pads between the seat back and your own back to position your hips as close to the movement pedals as possible.) Sit on the seat and place your feet on the pedals attached to the lever arm of the machine. Grasp the handles at the sides of the seat and keep your arms and spinal column straight throughout the movement.

(C) Exercise Performance. Slowly straighten your legs until your knees are nearly locked out, then bend your legs and return to the starting point of the movement. Repeat the exercise for the suggested number of counts.

(D) Movement Variations. Depending on the leg press machine, you can vary the width of your foot placement on the movement pedals or platform. You can also angle your toes a bit outward, a little inward, or straight ahead. Each variation of foot placement puts a slightly different type of stress on your quadriceps muscles.

Finish.

(16) LEG EXTENSIONS

(A) Emphasis. When you do leg extensions, you isolate virtually all of the stress directly on your quadriceps muscles.

(B) Starting Position. Sit on the padded surface of the leg extension machine with the back of your knees against the edge of the seat or padded surface. Hook your insteps under the lower set of roller pads (if there are two sets) attached to the lever arm of the machine. You may wish to place one or two pads between the seat back and your own back if your limbs are short and the seat back is not adjustable. Grasp either the edges of the seat or the handles of the machine to steady your body in position during the movement.

(C) Exercise Performance. Slowly straighten your legs. When your legs are locked straight, hold the position for a count of two to guarantee that you have achieved an optimal peak contraction in your quads. Lower back to the starting point and repeat the movement.

(D) Movement Variations. One good way to place different stresses on your quads is to change your toe angle during the exercise, much as you can do with calf exercises. Do one set with your toes angled outward about 45 degrees, the next with your toes pointed directly forward, and a third with your toes angled inward. You can also do leg extensions one leg at a time. As mentioned earlier, this allows you to contract the working muscles harder because you don't have to divide your attention. When doing leg extensions with one leg you can use the other to give you a bit of a forced rep boost in order to exercise with an even heavier weight. You might also try doing some sets with your toes pointed and others with your feet flexed (your toes pulled as far toward your upper body as possible).

(17) LEG CURLS

(A) Emphasis. Leg curls place direct stress on the biceps femoris muscles (also called the hamstrings, or thigh biceps) at the back of your thighs.

(B) Starting Position. Lie facedown on the padded surface of a leg curl machine, your knees at the edge of the pad toward the machine's lever arm. Hook your heels under the upper set of roller pads (if there are two sets provided) and fully straighten your legs. Grasp either the edges of the pad or the handles provided on some leg curl machines to steady your upper body in position during the movement.

(C) Exercise Performance. Making sure that your hips do not rise from the padded surface of the machine, slowly bend your legs as fully as possible. Hold this contracted position for a moment, then lower your feet back to the starting point. Repeat the exercise.

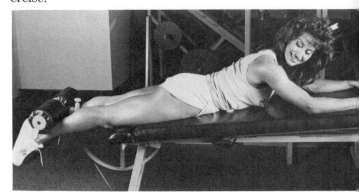

Finish.

(D) Movement Variations. Try doing some sets with your toes pointed and others with your feet flexed. You should also vary the angle of your toes, as explained in the description of leg extensions. You can perform leg curls, too, one leg at a time. In many large commercial gyms there is a special leg curl machine that allows you to do the movement one leg at a time in a standing position.

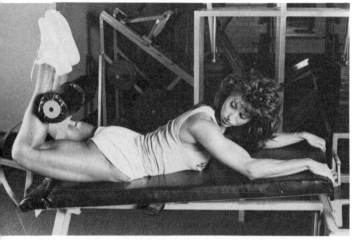

Advanced variation with a peak contraction.

At the advanced level of training, you can get a much more intense contraction in your thigh biceps by doing leg curls in one of my favorite variations. With a slightly lighter weight loaded on the machine, I arch my back and lift both my thighs and hips from the padded surface of the machine at the conclusion of the leg curl movement. This is a very intense hamstring exercise, however, so don't try it until you have at least eight months of steady, hard training under your belt.

(18) PULLY LEG/HIP MOVEMENT

(A) Emphasis. There are four of these movements, and in combination they stress the hip, buttock, and the upper/inner/outer thigh muscles. There are countless state-of-the-art machines designed to stress these areas, which seem to be a problem with 99.9 percent of most women. Unfortunately most of us don't have access to high-tech gyms featuring these space-age apparatus, which is why I'm including these movements in this book. Most gyms have a floor pulley, and the movements are simple to do (simple but *difficult*), and most important, they work.

Movement One: Buttocks Extension. A padded cuff is attached to a floor pulley. Fasten this cuff to your ankle and stand facing the pulley. Grasp a sturdy upright to keep your body in position during the movement. Keeping your torso upright and your working leg straight, slowly raise your foot backward and upward as high as you can. Contract your buttocks strongly at the top position of the movement,

Start.

Finish.

making sure that your upper body does not lean forward, then return to the starting point. You can also do this movement with your leg slightly bent. With either variation you may find it especially beneficial to do many partial movements just in the contracted position of the exercise. As with so many exercises, concentration is the key in this movement.

Movement Two: Inner Thigh Pull. Standing sideways next to the weight stack, grasp a sturdy upright to steady your body in position during the movement. Allow the weight to pull your exercising foot (the one closest to the weight stack) away from your body until your leg makes an approximate 45-degree angle with the floor. From this basic starting position, slowly move your foot toward and slightly across the midline of your body. This won't be a very long-range movement, but it strongly stresses your inner thigh muscles nonetheless.

Start.

Finish.

Movement Three: Outer Thigh Push. Face in the direction opposite the one you faced in the inner thigh pull exercise. Keep your working leg straight and your working foot ahead of your body throughout the movement. Allow the weight to pull your working foot exactly at the midline of your body, then slowly move your leg outward and upward as high as possible while keeping your torso in as erect a position as you can. Granted, this is a really tough movement, but it is a very effective one for your hip and thigh muscles. And if you bend your torso to the side toward the leg you are raising, you can even stress the external oblique and intercostal muscles at the side of your waist.

Start.

Finish.

Start.

Finish.

Movement Four: Forward Leg Push/Kick. This exercise is a little too complicated and intense for most beginners to learn and utilize, so you should save this exercise until you have been training steadily for two or three months. To stress your upper quads and hip flexors, stand facing away from the machine and brace your body in position for the movement by grasping a sturdy upright. Allow the weight to pull your foot to the rear. With your leg held relatively straight you can simply raise your foot directly forward and upward to hip level. Or you can start the movement with your leg bent and finish it as though you are kicking a football.

CALF EXERCISES

(19) STANDING CALF–MACHINE TOE RAISES

(A) Emphasis. This is a very direct movement for the gastrocnemius muscles of your calves.

(B) Starting Position. Face the calf machine and bend your legs so you can position the yokes attached to the lever arms of the machine across your shoulders. Place your toes and the balls of your feet on the toe block attached to the machine; set your feet ten to twelve inches apart with your toes pointed directly forward. Straighten your legs and torso to bear the weight of the machine. Relax your calves and allow your heels to sink as far below the level of your toes as possible to stretch all of your calf muscles fully.

(C) Exercise Performance. Slowly extend your feet and rise up as high as you can on your toes and the balls of your feet. Return to the starting position with your calves fully stretched and repeat the movement.

(D) Movement Variations. In doing any calf exercise you should alternate between three toe positions in order to attack your calf muscles from a maximum variety of angles. In addition to doing toe raises with your feet pointed directly forward, you can perform them with your toes pointed outward at 45-degree angles on each side, or with your toes pointed inward at 45-degree angles. You can vary the distance between your feet on the toe block. I also occasionally do this movement with one leg at a time, which allows me to concentrate better on the movement of my calf muscles.

An advanced calf movement, described in Chapter 5, allows rotational movement of the ankle joint to render a much fuller contraction in your calf muscles. The "fixed" position of the foot, even though your feet are pointed at different angles, gives you the same "fixed" contraction *unless* you include this rotational movement from time to time. Don't worry about it at this point, however, because I just want you to be aware of this technique when you outgrow your beginning-level calf exercises.

Start.

Finish.

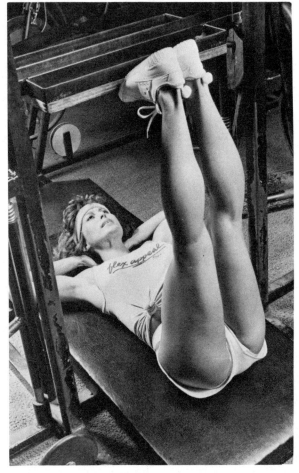

Start.   *Finish.*

(20) CALF PRESSES

(A) Emphasis. This movement can be done on any type of leg press machine. It strongly stresses the gastrocnemius muscles of your calves. As with leg presses, this movement can be done on vertical, horizontal, and angled leg press machines.

(B) Starting Position. Assume the same starting position as for a leg press, but this time fully straighten your legs and hold them straight throughout the movement. Slide your feet off the machine's pedals or platform until only the balls of your feet and your toes are in contact with the platform or pedals.

Relax your calves and allow your toes to come back as far as possible toward your torso.

(C) Exercise Performance. Push out with your toes as far as possible, then come back to the starting point (to the fully stretched position). Repeat the movement for the suggested number of repetitions.

(D) Movement Variations. As with toe raises on a standing calf machine, you should vary your foot angle from set to set. And as I mentioned, when you become more experienced with these calf movements you can actually rotate your feet at the ankle from one toe position to another in the middle of a repetition of calf presses and all other calf movements.

YOUR BEGINNING–LEVEL TRAINING PROGRAMS

There are three intensity-graded programs in this section, but they are all based on the same routine formulated from the preceding twenty bodybuilding exercises. In sequence these three routines will safely take you through your first two or three months of bodybuilding training and fully condition your body for the more intense workouts presented in later chapters.

Your beginning-level workouts are divided into three modules—one each for your abdomen, upper body, and lower body—and you will perform one or more circuits of each module before moving on to the next one in your program. After a two- or three-week break-in period, you will be performing more than one set of every exercise. In this case you should sequentially perform one set of every exercise in each module, then return to the start of that module to begin another, and later a third, trip through the module. Only then can you proceed to do exercises in your second module.

The following is the basic program that newcomers to bodybuilding training should follow on Mondays, Wednesdays, and Fridays, or any other three nonconsecutive days of your choice, for the first two or three weeks of training:

Exercise	Sets	Reps	Suggested Starting Weight
ABDOMINAL MODULE			
1. Bent-knee sit-ups	2	15	no weight
2. Knee-ups	2	20	no weight
3. Seated twisting	2	two minutes	no weight
UPPER BODY MODULE			
4. Pec deck flyes	1	12	10–20 lbs.
5. Incline dumbbell flyes	1	12–15	10–15 lbs.
6. Lat pull-downs (behind neck)	1	15	30–40 lbs.
7. Seated pulley rows	1	15	40 lbs.
8. Standing dumbbell side laterals	1	15	5–7½ lbs.
9. Alternate dumbbell presses	1	12–15	10–15 lbs.
10. Barbell upright rows	1	15	20–25 lbs.
11. Triceps push-downs	1	15	20 lbs.
12. Triceps dips between benches	1	15	no weight
13. Standing barbell curls	1	15	20–25 lbs.
14. Alternate dumbbell curls	1	15	7½–10 lbs.

Exercise	Sets	Reps	Suggested Starting Weight
LOWER BODY MODULE			
15. Leg presses	1	15	100–120 lbs.
16. Leg extensions	1	15	30–40 lbs.
17. Leg curls	1	15	10–20 lbs.
18. Leg/hip movements (three ways—no front kick)	1	12–15	5–10 lbs.
19. Standing calf-machine toe raises	1	15	80–100 lbs.
20. Calf presses	1	15	100–120 lbs.

Note Number One: On machines with selectorized plates (e.g., the pec deck machine, many leg curl/leg extension machines), count one plate as 10 pounds unless the machine is otherwise marked.

Note Number Two: On dumbbell movements (e.g., alternate dumbbell curls, alternate dumbbell presses) I have listed only the weight of one dumbbell. You will, of course, need two dumbbells of the weight listed for your dumbbell exercises in this beginning-level program.

Note Number Three: Go through your abdominal module doing one set of each movement, then repeat it before proceeding on to your upper body module.

Your Next Step Up in Intensity

After you have followed the break-in routine for two or three weeks, you should increase your abdominal module to the following levels:

Exercise	Sets	Reps
1. Bent-knee sit-ups	3	25
2. Knee-ups	3	30
3. Seated twisting	3	3–4 minutes

Repeat this module three times before moving on to your upper body module.

You will go through your upper body module and lower body module two times at this level—twice through the upper body part and then twice through the lower body section. On your second circuit through each module, you can increase the weight a bit and drop your reps from 15 to 12.

You can stay at this intensity level for another two or three weeks. Also, feel free to begin increasing training poundages in those exercises that are easiest for you to complete.

A Third Step Up

Finally you can do three cycles for each of your three modules. The third trip through an upper body or lower body module should involve another moderate weight increase and a drop in reps to something in the range of 8 to 10. You can stay on this program for four to six weeks before moving on to the more intense intermediate-level workouts in Chapter 5.

Congratulations! You're now ready to get into the gym and start expecting radical improvements in your body, beauty, strength, health, and overall fitness, as well as the development of a wonderful state of well-being. Keep going!

CHAPTER 4

intermediate training

Now that you've gotten a taste of what bodybuilding is all about, it's time to increase your knowledge of resistance training techniques and procedures by discussing a variety of intermediate-level training topics. These topics include assessment of competitive potential, the pros and cons of training partners, the concept of training to failure, five methods of training past the point of failure, three other intermediate-level training techniques, split routines, when to change training programs, overtraining, injuries, individualizing routines, muscle priority training, bodybuilding drugs, how to vault over sticking points in your progress, building workout enthusiasm, heavy versus light training, outdoor workouts, and specific female factors in bodybuilding.

COMPETITIVE POTENTIAL

Rather than thinking of genetic potential as a limiting factor in my bodybuilding, I prefer to think of it as an enabling factor. Much has been written and said about champion bodybuilders being genetically suited for their sport and about how women who haven't been blessed with great potential won't succeed at bodybuilding. I agree that a bodybuilder with optimal potential will make the fastest progress, but in my experience any woman who is completely dedicated to the sport and highly motivated to succeed will indeed become a successful competitor *if* that's what she truly desires.

Every woman has naturally strong and weak muscle groups—those that respond either more or less quickly than normally; the beauty of bodybuilding to me lies in the challenge of improving weak areas to balance my physical proportions. It may be difficult for you to look at a photograph of my physique and understand how hard I've had to train to develop weak areas, but it's true. For example, my thighs grow in size fairly rapidly from hard training, while my abdominals are relatively slow to respond, so I have had to work my thighs less intensely than I'd like while *doubling* the intensity of my abdominal training in order to keep my body proportionately balanced from top to bottom.

Don't shed tears if you appear to have particularly weak body parts. Instead, dig in and work them so hard that they are forced to respond favorably and proportionately—the way *you* want them to. There isn't a single champion bodybuilder competing today who hasn't had to overcome the same obstacle that you have ahead of you, and some have overcome seemingly abysmal physical potential.

To give you a yardstick against which you can compare yourself, here are three physical qualities that a woman with optimal potential would display:

(1) A relatively low degree of natural body fat. This factor is an indication that a bodybuilder has a good basal metabolic rate (BMR), which will allow her to achieve a high degree of muscularity with relative ease.

(2) An obvious degree of natural muscle mass. This quality will be most evident when viewing an untrained woman's legs or back, but it may be equally obvious in other parts of the body. Most "natural" bodybuilders have a relatively large percentage of muscle mass in comparison to body fat before they even begin training.

(3) Relatively small knees, ankles, and wrists. For optimal aesthetic development, it's best to have small joints surrounded by large muscle volumes. While it's a disadvantage to have an extremely small pelvic structure, many of the best women bodybuilders have relatively narrow hips and broader-than-average shoulders. Unfortunately, I'm not one of this group. I was born with a yucky pear-shaped body! It's also an advantage to have a very narrow waist.

It's difficult for an inexperienced bodybuilder to assess her own potential, so it may be best for you to have a knowledgeable gym owner or competition judge give you an idea of where you stand in terms of genetic potential for bodybuilding. Probably less than 5 percent of all women entering the sport have ideal potential. The rest must work hard to overcome structural and metabolic disadvantages.

After six months to a year of training, you will be able to reassess your potential. At that point you can also decide if you genuinely love the sport of bodybuilding and prefer above all else to be in the gym, pumping iron. If you don't have this degree of enthusiasm for the sport, you probably won't succeed as a bodybuilder.

In addition to having physical potential, most high-level bodybuilders these days are relatively intelligent. While it's possible that a less intelligent woman may one day win the Miss Olympic title, it's highly unlikely. To get the most out of your training and diet, you must have the intelligence to understand and apply to your workouts information derived from such diverse scientific disciplines as exercise physiology, biomechanics, biochemistry, anatomy, kinesiology, psychology, and physics.

Above and beyond the concept of genetic potential in bodybuilding, there *are* secrets to success in the sport. They are such old-fashioned virtues as dedication, persistence, and patience. So even if your potential appears to be quite bad, you can overcome this disadvantage through your own efforts. That's another aspect of bodybuilding that I like: You succeed or fail largely on your own merits, and no one but you can take credit for your successes. However, I am also a firm believe in giving credit where credit is due. I have never claimed to have won world championships or built a world-class physique on my own. I *never* could have done it without the support of others and my faith in God, Who enabled me to be where I am today. Don't fool yourself; you can't and shouldn't isolate yourself from all the enabling factors and individuals that surround you.

TRAINING PARTNERS

Champion bodybuilders are equally divided over whether or not to use training partners. For the past year I have been training with a very motivated male bodybuilder named Christian Janatsch, but in the past I trained extensively on my own. As a result, I can probably give you a good perspective on both types of training, with and without a partner.

When you train alone you need never worry about compromising your own training methods to suit those of a partner, nor do you have to worry about coordinating your time schedule to fit that of another person. However, you will be forced to scramble around from time to time for an exercise spotter, and you often won't be able to train as hard on your own as you would with a good partner.

It takes a certain type of personality to train alone. Most of the top women bodybuilders who train by themselves are self-reliant and at times somewhat introverted. They're rugged individualists who often like to change workout schedules from one training session to the next. Working out with a partner would slow this type of bodybuilder down and keep her from making optimal gains in her workouts.

During the period that I trained alone I was conducting hundreds of experiments on my body to determine which training techniques, exercises, and routines worked best for me. It would have been impossible to carry out these experiments and also satisfy the needs of a training partner. So I got deeply into the mental side of bodybuilding training. The knowledge and angle from which I learned and absorbed information had a snowballing effect in terms of my motivation and enthusiasm for bodybuilding and all it entails, from personal goals to career goals. At that point in time it was best for me to train alone.

The primary advantage of training with a partner is in having someone to push you to work out even harder than you will on your own. Sometimes a healthy competition develops between training partners that spurs each to try to outdo the other. Sometimes a training partner can verbally push you to greater heights of workout intensity. "Do another rep," your partner says, and you go for that additional rep. And if you don't or can't do the extra repetition, your ever-present partner is there to enable you to force out the rep anyway.

You can more easily perform forced reps, descending sets, and other training intensification techniques when you have a training partner standing by. Also, you'll find it much more difficult to miss a workout when you know that your training partner is down at the gym, waiting for you to show up.

About half of the women I know who use a partner train with other women, while the rest of us work out with men. Training with Christian has convinced me that men and women can train very profitably as workout partners. Men have much greater strength than women, which tends to push us to blast away with heavier iron. On the other hand, women have naturally higher pain thresholds and greater endurance than men, which allows us to push them to train longer, differently, and more intensely. Consequently both partners end up getting in better workouts and make remarkably greater gains in muscle mass and quality. It's also quite fulfilling to witness the progress that your partner is making and to know you are an integral part in helping him or her reach his or her goal.

TRAINING TO FAILURE

Most unsuccessful bodybuilders fail either to train consistently or to train hard enough to make good gains. To be sure that you make good gains, you should always push post–warm-up sets to failure, or to that point at which you can no longer complete a full repetition under your own power. This will push your muscles quite hard, but you can actually train past the point of failure by using five techniques—cheating, forced reps, descending sets, burns, and negative reps—discussed in the next section of this chapter.

To illustrate how to train to the point of failure, let's use standing barbell curls. Let's say that you have already thoroughly warmed up your biceps muscles with one or two lighter sets of the movement. Load up the bar with a poundage that you can use for 6 to 8 full, strict reps, then go to the limit in strict form until you can't finish a rep, regardless of how hard you try. Perhaps you still have enough strength to curl the barbell a third of the way to the finishing position, but you won't be able to complete the movement. This is what I mean by training to failure.

TRAINING PAST FAILURE

If you can force your muscles to keep working past the point at which they would normally fail—that is, if you push them past failure—you can force them to grow in mass and power much more quickly than if you merely take the set to failure. The five main ways in which you can train past the failure point are cheating, forced reps, descending sets, burns, and negative reps.

Cheating

In Chapter 2 you were urged to use strict form and avoid cheating in all of your exercises. This was because most beginning bodybuilders cheat during an exercise to remove stress from the working muscles. Now that you are an intermediate bodybuilder, however, you are experienced enough in your training to use cheating movements to place greater stress on the working muscles.

Cheating is used to remove only enough weight from the working muscles to allow them to continue a set past the failure point. Just because you fail to complete a repetition of barbell curls with 60 pounds doesn't mean that your muscles are incapable of lifting any more weight. In reality you can no doubt still do a barbell curl with 50 pounds, and perhaps another with 40 or 45 pounds. So the object of the cheating principle in bodybuilding training is to use just enough extraneous body movement to remove 10 or 15 pounds from the barbell, which forces your working muscles to continue exerting against resistance long past the point at which you would normally terminate a set.

Using the barbell curl movement as an example, let's say that you can do 7 strict reps with 60 pounds before reaching failure. Only then do you use just enough torso swing to boost the bar past the point at which it would normally stall out. Then you slowly lower the weight back to the starting point, strongly resisting its downward momentum. Naturally your working muscles grow progressively more fatigued with each repetition, so you must use a little more of a cheat on each extra rep.

In normal bodybuilding training you won't have to do more than 2 or 3 cheating reps past the point of failure. Your muscles will simply grow too fatigued past the second or third cheating rep to achieve any additional benefit from more cheating reps.

Forced Reps

The forced reps technique is a much more precise means of removing just enough weight from the barbell or exercise machine that you are using to allow you to push out 2 or 3 reps past the point of normal muscular failure. In this case your training partner pulls up on the barbell you're using just enough to let you force out your extra reps. And your partner can remove this amount of weight much more precisely than you can do it on your own with extraneous body movement.

You will discover that it's difficult for a spotter unused to your training style and abilities to remove just the right amount of weight to make forced reps profitable. That's the reason why it's better to work out with the same training partner for an extended period of time. Together you can become totally familiar with each other's ability for hard physical exercise, and thus you can best assist each other with the use of forced reps.

As with cheating reps, you will not profit from doing more than 2 or 3 forced reps at the end of a set that has already been carried to failure in strict exercise form.

Descending Sets

If you have two training partners available, you can have them actually strip plates from the barbell you are using to make it lighter as your muscles grow more fatigued. This third method of extending a set past failure is called descending sets.

To illustrate descending sets in action, let's again use barbell curls for our example. Load up the barbell with plenty of 2½- and 5-pound plates, but leave the collars off the bar. Be sure the weight is appropriate for use for about 6 reps. Stand up with the barbell in your hands for your curls and station your training partners at each end of the bar.

Start with a set of strict barbell curls to failure at about 6 reps. But at the end of the set, don't put the bar back on the floor. Stand erect with it across your upper thighs while your partners quickly strip a total of 5 or 10 pounds from the ends of the bar. Immediately try to force out 3 or 4 more strict reps with the decreased poundage. Have more weight stripped off the bar at the end of this set and force out a final 3 or 4 reps.

You will find that this descending-sets training is quite grueling work, but it's very productive in terms of increasing muscle mass and quality. In fact, you will discover that one of these extended descending sets is equal to three or four normal sets carried to failure.

Burns

Short, quick partial reps called burns also allow you to force a muscle group to continue working past the point of normal muscular failure. Eight to 10 of these partials at the end of a normal set causes a greater-than-normal buildup of fatigue toxins in the working muscle. This causes a burning sensation in the muscle, which explains why such reps are known as burns.

To illustrate how this technique is applied, let's use seated pulley rows as an example. Suppose you can do 8 full, strict reps with a given resistance before failing on the ninth repetition. At that point you merely continue to pull the pulley handle quickly and forcefully as far from the starting point as possible for 8 to 10 partial reps, or burns. Your lats and biceps will scream for mercy at the end of such a set.

I use my own special modification of the burn technique. It involves performing 5 to 10 slow partial reps in *the most productive part of the movement's range of motion.* You can feel this range of motion in an exercise at the point where the working muscles contract most forcefully.

Using this technique, I might perform 4 to 5 normal full-range reps of seated pulley rows and then do 6 to 8 partials with a slow cadence in the middle part of the exercise's normal range of motion. To get the most out of these partial reps, I find it's essential to concentrate mentally as intensely as possible on the muscle contractions. Once you're used to doing normal burns, give this technique a try. You'll find it particularly productive!

Negative Reps

There are two variations of negative reps that I use more frequently in the off-season, and you should experiment with them during an off-season cycle too. It has been scientifically demonstrated that the negative (downward) half of a repetition of any exercise offers tremendous potential for muscle mass and power development. In pure negative reps, two partners grasp a weight 20 to 30 percent heavier than you can use for a full single rep in an exercise and they lift it up to the finish position of the movement. From that point you lower the weight as slowly as possible, mightily resisting its downward momentum. Sets of 5 to 8 pure negative reps can be quite valuable in building additional mass power, but pure negatives wear out training partners so quickly that it's usually not feasible to use this technique.

You can, however, benefit from doing the negative-rep variations I use in my own workouts. The first of these is called *negative emphasized reps.* These can only be done on exercise machines that allow you to do the positive (upward) part of the rep with both arms or legs and the negative phase of the repetition with only one arm or leg. Obviously you couldn't do this with barbell military presses, since gravity would rip the bar from your hand during the negative cycle of a rep. But you can easily do the same movement on a Nautilus double-shoulder machine.

I like to do calf presses on the leg press station of a Universal Gym machine, so let's use this exercise to illustrate negative emphasized reps. With the machine loaded to 300 pounds, I perform 8 to 10 full positive-negative reps. Then I push the machine pedals all of the way out with both feet, shift the weight to the ball of my left foot, and lower the weight, resisting it with only the calf of that leg. On the next rep I again go up with both feet, but come down resisting the weight with the strength of my right calf. By alternating legs in the negative portion of the movement, doing 5 or 6 negative emphasized repetitions with each leg, I can blast my calves to the limit!

The other variation of full negative reps that you can try is called *forced negative reps.* This technique requires the help of a training partner, it can be used with free-weight movements, and both arms or legs are involved throughout the movement.

In forced negatives you should do 5 or 6 normal positive-negative reps of an exercise to warm up your muscles and joints fully. Then you raise the weight on your own to the finish position of the movement and resist the lowering of the weight as your partner pushes down on it to add to the resistance. Your partner should push down with a degree of force that prevents you from stopping the weight yet allows you to resist powerfully its full downward momentum for three or four seconds.

I especially like to include forced negatives during my off-season cycle in a set or two of such exercises as leg extensions, leg curls, barbell curls, pec deck flyes, Nautilus presses, pulley push-downs, and seated calf raises. I'm sure that you'll develop your own favorite exercises for using forced negative reps.

OTHER INTERMEDIATE–LEVEL TECHNIQUES

As you mature as a bodybuilder you must put greater and greater intensity on your muscles to keep them increasing hypertrophically. Therefore you must continually search out better training intensification techniques. Two of these techniques are supersets and the more intense pre-exhaustion supersets. And to understand the pre-exhaustion technique, you must know the difference between basic and isolation exercises.

Supersets

Supersets are groups of two exercises performed with minimal rest between the movements and a normal rest interval between the supersets. The least intense form of superset includes two exercises for antagonistic muscle groups, such as the biceps and triceps or quadriceps and hamstrings. The following are several examples of supersets for antagonistic muscle groups:

Biceps + Triceps = Barbell curls + Triceps
push-downs
Quads + Hamstrings = Leg extensions + Leg curls
Lats + Pecs = Pull-downs + Barbell incline presses

A more intense form of superset involves performing two exercises for the same muscle group with minimum rest between movements. The following are examples of supersets for the same muscle group:

Chest = Incline presses + Cable crossovers
Lats = Pull-overs + Lat machine pull-downs
Delts = Alternate dumbbell presses + Side laterals
Thighs = Leg presses + Leg extensions

If you recall the discussion of resistance progression from Chapter 2, one of the several ways to increase training intensity is to reduce the amount of rest between sets. By doing supersets, you effectively reduce the average amount of rest between exercises. As a result, supersets add greatly to your training intensity.

Basic Versus Isolation Exercises

In order to understand pre-exhaustion supersets, you need to know the difference between basic and isolation exercises. Basic movements are those that work the large muscle groups of the body in conjunction with other muscle groups (e.g., the squat, which works the frontal thighs in conjunction with the hamstrings, buttocks, lower back, abdominals, and virtually every other muscle group of your body). Isolation exercises stress single muscle groups—and sometimes only a part of a muscle—in relative isolation from the rest of the body (e.g., leg extensions, which work the quadriceps on the front of your thighs in isolation from the rest of your body).

Generally speaking, basic exercises are intended to add muscle mass to your physique, and isolation movements are primarily intended to bring out muscular detail in your various body parts. If you are a competitive bodybuilder, you will use primarily basic exercises in the off-season and primarily isolation movements prior to a competition. Still, you will use at least one basic exercise per muscle group during a precontest cycle.

In Table 4-1 you will see a chart of the most common basic and isolation exercises for each muscle group.

Pre-exhaustion supersets involve primarily basic and isolation movements for the torso muscle groups, so it's essential that you understand the more common basic and isolation movements for your chest, back, and shoulder muscle groups.

Pre-Exhaustion Supersets

When you perform a basic exercise for a torso muscle group, you are not only stressing that torso group but also the smaller biceps or triceps muscles of your upper arms. For example, when you do bench presses, you work your pectorals and anterior deltoids in combination with your triceps muscles. And since your triceps are much smaller and weaker than your chest and shoulder muscles, they will fatigue and fail long before your pectorals have been fully stimulated. Therefore you won't have too much success in developing your torso groups by simply doing basic exercises.

Table 4-1: Common Basic and Isolation Exercises

BODY PART	BASIC EXERCISES	ISOLATION EXERCISES
Thighs	Squats, leg presses, lunges, stiff-legged deadlifts	Leg extensions, leg curls, cable adductions, cable abductions
Trapezius	Barbell upright rows, cable upright rows	Barbell shrugs, dumbbells shrugs, machine shrugs
Spinal Erectors	Deadlifts, stiff-legged deadlifts	Hyperextensions
Pectorals	Incline barbell/dumbell presses, barbell/dumbbell bench presses, decline presses, parallel bar dips	Pec deck flyes, Nautilus flyes, dumbbell flyes (all angles), cable flyes (all angles)
Deltoids	Military presses, presses behind neck, dumbbell presses	Front, side and bent laterals with dumbbells and cables
Biceps	Standing barbell curls, dumbbell curls	Concentration curls, cable curls, Nautilus curls
Triceps	Barbell triceps extensions, dips, narrow-grip bench presses	Triceps push-downs, dumbbell kickbacks

By supersetting an isolation exercise for a particular torso muscle group with a basic movement for the same body part, you can "pre-exhaust" the torso muscle with the isolation exercise before doing the basic movement. This makes the torso muscle group briefly weaker than the arm muscles, which allows you to push your torso muscle group to the limit with the basic exercise. You simply won't believe how hard you can push your chest, back and shoulder muscles with a basic exercise once you have done a pre-exhaustion superset.

It's essential that you rest as little as possible between the exercises of a pre-exhaustion superset, because your torso muscles will recuperate very quickly following an isolation exercise, thereby spoiling the pre-exhaustion effect. In only fifteen seconds you can recover 50 percent of the strength and endurance of a pre-exhausted muscle.

The following are sample pre-exhaustion supersets for each aspect of your torso muscle groups:

Upper pectorals = Incline flyes + Incline presses
Lower pectorals = Decline flyes + Decline presses
Deltoids = Dumbbell side laterals + alternate dumbbell presses
Latissimus dorsi = Pullovers + Lat machine pulldowns

You can also do pre-exhaustion for your thighs before performing a set of squats. This is necessary for many bodybuilders because the lower back muscles often fail before the quadriceps have been completely exhausted by a set of squats. The easiest way to pre-exhaust the thighs would be to perform a set of leg extensions to failure before doing squats. However, your thigh muscles are very large and powerful, and you can better pre-exhaust them by doing two exercises—leg presses plus leg extensions— in rapid succession prior to your set of squats. This series of three thigh movements is extremely intense training, so you must work up to doing an all-out series of three movements gradually and slowly. But once you are doing the three exercises with maximum effort and determination you will find a single series of three movements equal to 6 to 10 normal sets of thigh training.

Since your arm muscles are so much smaller and weaker than your torso muscle groups, it would be folly to train biceps and/or triceps before the back, chest, and/or shoulder muscle groups. Still, I see many women bodybuilders training their upper arms early in their workouts. In order to make optimal bodybuilding progress, you should always train your upper arm muscles after you have finished your torso training, and you should train your back, shoulder, and chest using the pre-exhaustion technique.

SPLIT ROUTINES

For the first few months of your bodybuilding training you will also increase workout intensity by gradually doing more total sets for each muscle group. Eventually you will be doing so many sets that you won't have enough energy available to complete your entire workout at full intensity. This usually occurs at the point where you are training for approximately an hour. Indeed, I have found that very few women can train consistently hard for more than sixty minutes at a time.

The best way to solve the problem of waning energy reserves toward the end of a workout is to split your muscles groups into more or less equal halves and train half of your body Mondays and Thursdays and the other half on Tuesdays and Fridays. This method is called a *split routine,* and it is followed by virtually all champion bodybuilders, men and women alike.

Since you are allowing at least two days of rest between workouts for each muscle group—and keep in mind that a body part can be resting while another is being trained—you can work out more frequently than three days per week. In reality your muscles can fully recuperate and grow much larger on a four-day split routine than they can if you are training three nonconsecutive days per week. Also you will ultimately find that your muscles grow in mass and strength much quicker on a split routine than they do if you're working your entire body in one training session.

The following are two alternative methods of splitting up your body for a four-day split routine:

ALTERNATIVE # 1

Monday and Thursday	Tuesday and Friday
Abdominals	Abdominals
Chest	Thighs
Shoulders	Upper arms
Back	Forearms
Calves	Calves

ALTERNATIVE # 2

Monday and Thursday	Tuesday and Friday
Abdominals	Abdominals
Chest	Back
Shoulders	Thighs
Triceps	Biceps
Calves	Calves

In the final analysis, the main value of using a split routine is that it allows you to stress each muscle group with the maximum intensity every time it is trained. You can also follow a five-day or six-day split routine, which are discussed in Chapter 6. Five-day and six-day split routines are particularly valuable to a competitive bodybuilder during her precontest training cycle.

WHEN TO CHANGE TRAINING PROGRAMS

Anyone will become bored with a routine and cease to make gains on it if the program is followed for too long a period of time. As a result, you must change your training schedules occasionally in order to continue making good bodybuilding gains. The frequency with which you change training schedules, however, depends on your mental temperament.

Stoic and methodical women can follow a training program for several months and still be making good gains, while more excitable and easily bored women can seldom use a routine for more than one or two weeks before losing momentum. Most bodybuilders make good gains following a program for four to six weeks before switching to another one. Once you are fully into your bodybuilding training, you should initially change routines every four to six weeks while noting your mental and physical reactions to both your old and new routines.

Ultimately you will learn to tell when to change routines on the basis of how your body feels and how mentally interested you are in a training schedule. As soon as you become bored with a routine or no longer look forward to each workout, you are mentally ready to switch to a new program. And as soon as you notice that you are no longer making good bodybuilding progress on your current routine, it's time to move on to another. Whether this takes you one day or one year, it makes little difference when you change training schedules as long as you do so precisely at the point when your old program no longer gives you optimal progress.

OVERTRAINING

It is possible to overwork your body to the point where you can no longer fully recuperate between workouts. This leads to an overtrained state in which you are unable to make good bodybuilding gains. And when you are overtrained, you will frequently become ill, which further inhibits progress.

Since it is counterproductive to overtrain, you should learn how to recognize when your are beginning to overtrain. The following are the ten most common symptoms of an impending overtrained state:

(1) Lack of interest in training
(2) Chronic physical and/or mental fatigue
(3) Persistent joint and/or muscle soreness
(4) Loss of appetite
(5) Insomnia
(6) Irritability
(7) Illness and/or injury
(8) Deteriorization of motor coordination
(9) Increase in resting pulse rate
(10) Increase in blood pressure.

If you notice more than one of these symptoms, you are entering an overtrained state. The best remedy for this is to take a four-to-seven-day layoff from bodybuilding training—and possibly from aerobic workouts as well—and then switch to a new training program once you are back in the gym.

I have found that training at different gyms helps me to avoid overtraining. Any new environment—even if I work out in a gym for only a single day—brings a wealth of new mental and physical stimuli. No two pieces of equipment feel the same, and the new stresses of training on a different lat rowing machine hit my back from a new angle and keep my body fresh and open to greater bodybuilding gains. Each new gym has different pieces of equipment and new bodybuilders to train with, all of which helps me to keep from overtraining.

I also avoid overtraining by doing short, high-intensity workouts. Many bodybuilders overtrain simply by doing too many total sets each workout. With too lengthy workouts your body is unable to recover fully between training sessions. Your energy reserves grow more and more depleted until you become overtrained. So if you do become overtrained from doing too lengthy workouts, you should take a short break and switch to a shorter and higher-intensity training program once you're back in the gym.

TRAINING INJURIES

Training injuries are the bane of any competitive bodybuilder's existence because they slow, and at times completely halt, a woman's progress to the top as an amateur and professional athlete. Therefore you must know how to avoid injuries in your workouts, how to recover most quickly from your injuries, and how to train around an injury.

Obviously it would be best to prevent all training injuries from occurring. There are three ways in which you can prevent injuries: (1) Warm up thoroughly and keep warm during your workout; (2) use good exercise form at all times; and (3) avoid using training poundages that are beyond your capabilities.

The proper way to warm up was discussed in Chapter 2. A thorough warm-up helps you to avoid both traumatic injuries (e.g., strained muscles) and microtraumatic injuries (e.g., those small connective-tissue injuries that eventually cause chronic joint pain). Also it's essential once you have thoroughly warmed up and started your workout that you keep warm until you have finished your training session. This is accomplished by wearing sufficient clothing and keeping your workout moving along at a good pace. Most training injuries occur when you have spent too much time between sets gabbing with someone in the gym, which allows your body to cool down, and then attempt to use a heavy training poundage in a basic movement, often with poor biomechanical form.

Using perfect exercise form at all times, even when you're doing forced reps, is essential when training with heavy poundages. Even if you are warmed up, you can injure yourself by using poor biomechanics with a heavy poundage in an exercise. You should not only maintain optimal form but also avoid jerking or bouncing a heavy weight in any exercise. Bouncing, jerky, short movements are the main culprit in causing microtraumatic injuries.

The best way to avoid bouncing or jerking a weight is to stay within your strength capabilities during each workout. No one can perform a repetition in perfect form if she is using a weight too heavy for her strength levels. Inevitably your biomechanical form and exercise style will deteriorate when you use a weight that's too heavy for you, and that leaves you open to injury.

If you sustain a major injury (e.g., a joint dislocation, a torn muscle, or torn connective tissue), you should immediately consult a physician. However, you can treat less serious injuries safely on your own.

As soon as you incur a minor injury, you should initially treat it with ice, which decreases swelling at the injury site and speeds recovery time. Every half hour you should rub an ice cube directly on the skin over the injured area for five or ten minutes. These ice massages should be administered during waking hours for the first twenty-four hours following an injury. You must also totally rest the injured joint or muscle for at least seventy-two hours after your injury.

Twenty-four to thirty-six hours after your injury was sustained, you can begin heat treatment of the injured area. This is best done by wrapping a hot-water bottle with a damp towel and holding it against the site of the injury. Damp heat is most efficiently conducted into your body. Continue heat treatments for ten to fifteen minutes every hour or so for forty-eight hours. The heat treatment after icing an injury helps to speed healing of an injury.

After two days of heat treatment you can begin active rehabilitation of the injury with light stretching and movement of the injured muscle or joint. Gradually increase the intensity of your stretching resistance movements. Back off on training intensity if you feel undue pain in the injured area. Slowly build up resistance until your injured area is stronger than it was before it was hurt. Then you can safely train the injured area with 100 percent intensity without fear of further injury.

If you are injured, you should still train the rest of your body until the injury has healed and you can again work your entire physique with maximum intensity. But you should avoid exercises that stress the injured joint or body part. For example, you should avoid leg exercises if you have an injured knee.

The most common chronic injury among bodybuilders is a sore lower back. This is the type of injury that can remain dormant for a year and then flare up for a few weeks. With a sore back you can still train hard if you avoid deadlifts, heavy squats, and other exercises that unduly stress your lower spine. You can still work your upper back quite hard without doing rowing movements if you perform plenty of chins and lat-machine pull-downs. For your lower back you can do hyperextensions even when your lower back is sore, and for your thighs you can safely do leg presses and hack squats in place of squats with a barbell.

INDIVIDUALIZED ROUTINES

I can't keep making up training programs for you, so it will be necessary for you to learn to formulate your own individualized routines. And since you will ultimately know much better than I how your body reacts to each training stimulus, the routines you make up for yourself will be much more fruitful than the ones I could give you or routines that you find when reading a weight-training or bodybuilding magazine.

Initially the programs that I give you or that you read in a magazine should serve as models on which to construct your own training schedules. The basic structures of all bodybuilding routines are somewhat similar, and you needn't vary them much. As you know from reading the section on pre-exhaustion earlier in this chapter, for example, during each workout you should always schedule work for your upper arm muscles after you've trained your torso groups.

The following are ten other considerations that you must accept when formulating your individualized routines:

(1) Generally, try to train larger muscle groups early in your routine, when you will have more energy to expend in training them. It's far easier to work a small

muscle group, like your biceps, than a larger one, like your quadriceps, when your energy reserves are waning. Here is a listing of your body's major muscle groups from largest to smallest: thighs, back, chest, calves, shoulders, upper arms, forearms, and abdominals.

(2) Try to work your weaker groups early in your training session, when you have maximum energy to devote to stressing them. This is called *muscle priority training,* and it is discussed in greater detail in the next section of this chapter.

(3) Train each major muscle group no more often than twice a week in the off-season and three times each week prior to a competition. Your calf, forearm, and abdominal muscles can be trained from two to six times a week. It is best to use a four-day split routine in the off-season and either a five-day or six-day split during a precontest cycle.

(4) In the off-season you should do no more than eight to ten total sets for large muscle groups (e.g., the thighs, back, chest, and shoulders) and no more than four to six sets for smaller muscle groups (e.g., the biceps and triceps) during each training session.

(5) Prior to a competition you can do up to 50 percent more sets per muscle group each workout than in the off-season.

(6) In the off-season you should keep your reps for each set relatively low. For upper-body muscle groups do 6 to 8 reps per set, and for lower-body parts do 8 to 12 reps per set.

(7) During a precontest cycle you can do 8 to 12 repetitions for each set for upper body muscle groups and between 10 and 15 reps per set for lower body groups. For abdominal exercises—regardless of the training cycle you are in (off-season or precontest)—you can do between 25 and 100 reps in each set.

(8) Try to program your forearm exercises last in your routine. It will be very difficult to do exercises for any other muscle group after you've done your forearms; your forearm muscles become simply too pumped up to allow you to grip a barbell or dumbbell securely for other movements.

(9) Remember that there aren't any secrets in bodybuilding in terms of formulating a routine for a particular muscle group. There are no magic routines, only programs that you have experimented with and found to work for your own body. Never lose the urge to experiment in your workouts to discover those variables that work best for your physique.

(10) In each routine for an individual body part, be sure that you include at least one basic exercise for the muscle group involved in order to develop additional muscle mass. Also, be sure to include at least one isolation movement to shape and harden the individual muscles.

MUSCLE PRIORITY TRAINING

I mentioned earlier that individual muscle groups increase in mass and muscle quality unequally. Since equal body proportions will help you a great deal to win bodybuilding competitions, you should always seek to maintain the development of good body parts and increase the development of lagging muscle groups to bring them up to the level of the rest of your body. The best tool you have at your disposal to even up your physical proportions is a technique called *muscle priority training.*

In muscle priority training you work your lagging body parts *first* during your workout, when you have the most physical energy and mental drive available to train a weak group with maximum intensity. When using this training principle, you will also spend less time and energy on training your more dominant muscle groups. This combination of intensity factors ultimately helps you to balance your physical proportions and create a winning physique.

When you use muscle priority training, the object is, not to overburden a lagging muscle group with more sets, but to place greater stress on it by *increasing workout intensity to the limit.* You will simply blast the lagging body part with forced reps, descending sets, and every other intensity-increasing workout technique at your disposal.

If you have an exceedingly weak muscle group, you can train it separately. For example, if your thighs are lagging, you can work all of your physique but your thighs on Mondays and Thursdays and then only your thighs on Tuesdays and Fridays. This will help you to place the highest degree of training intensity on your lagging thighs, which will literally force them to increase hypertrophically.

I personally don't like to cut back on my training for a strong muscle group because it causes me to lose muscle tone in the body part I'm neglecting. Even when I'm using priority training to bring up a weak muscle group, I don't slack off that much on my strong points. Instead, I tend to train my dominant body parts with a higher number of reps (in the range of about 15 repetitions per set). This helps me to maintain overall muscle tone quite effectively.

Keep in mind that you will probably end up rotating your use of muscle priority training from one body part to another. It always seems that as soon as I get one lagging muscle group up to par, I have to turn my attention to another body part that has become a weak point by comparison. As a result, no champion bodybuilder is ever happy with her physical development, and she is always seeking to improve the proportional balance of her physique.

BODYBUILDING DRUGS

If you haven't already heard about anabolic steroids, you soon will. These bodybuilding drugs are male hormone derivatives taken by male bodybuilders and other athletes to increase muscle mass and strength. Even though these drugs all have disastrous side effects—as well as negative ethical consequences—many women bodybuilders are using them to make their physiques more impressive.

I strongly believe that no woman bodybuilder should use drugs to add to her muscle mass or to improve her physique. Steroids are simply too masculinizing and dangerous for any body, and I don't believe in their use by any woman athlete. Among the hazardous side effects of anabolic steroid use are masculinization, increased water retention, elevated blood pressure, clitoral enlargement, liver disorders, kidney function problems, a deepened voice, and greater growth of body hair, all of which are irreversible side effects.

Even if it were safe to use anabolic steroids, would it be fair to use them to gain an edge over your competition? This is a question that is being hotly debated today in both men's and women's bodybuilding, and most male bodybuilders have testified that they would prefer not to use drugs if they could be avoided, but that they continue to use them because all of their competitors are on steroids and other bodybuilding drugs. I feel that it is morally objectionable to use drugs of any kind, particularly if they damage your body.

Put simply, I'm vitally interested in *women's* bodybuilding. Once a woman begins tampering with the hormonal-chemical balance of her body by using steroids, she has to question whether or not she is chemically still a woman. Bodybuilding drugs are ruining our sport, and we *must* draw the line somewhere. Drug use is the one well-defined factor that must be dealt with immediately, *before* it gets out of hand, as it has in men's competition.

Without question, there will be unique women who naturally possess an abnormally high level of male hormones in their bodies. Fine. But is this a valid reason for glorifying this person or her type or physique? Is this really what competitive bodybuilding is all about? For the shock value? Some women feel good when people see them at a competition and comment, "Look at that! Freaky! Unbelievable!"

I guess this is one crucial area in which I am different, because I *want* to be believable. I would like to contribute my physique to the self-fulfilling dreams of everyday, average people who want to improve themselves. I prefer to give these women a hope that they can one day look as good as I do. Yes, it will be difficult. Yes, it will take time to achieve this goal. Yes, you will, for it is a believable goal, unlike the standard of muscular development set by steroid-popping women.

This is a highly personal and extremely touchy subject, and I wish to make it clear that I am *not* insinuating that any of my fellow competitors are or have ever been on drugs. I believe in a person's innocence until that person is proven guilty. *Proven guilty*—that's the key. Competitive women's bodybuilding will flourish and grow—indeed, lead the world in physical excellence—if and only if we have comprehensive drug testing of every athlete entered in national and international amateur and professional competitions.

By *comprehensive* I mean testing during the actual training period *prior* to an event, as well as at the event itself. How else will we know who's guilty and who's not? We won't until we have documentary proof. We can suspect, wonder, and accuse all we like, but it's meaningless unless we have conclusive proof that a woman bodybuilder is taking steroids. And conclusive evidence demands a verdict!

When our sport is free of drugs, the world can look to us with confidence, admiration, and respect. They can witness what is humanly possible to accomplish in bodybuilding. I have great care and interest in fulfilling the potential that God has given me, and I have absolutely no interest in any potential that is achieved through the use of drugs. Period.

STICKING POINTS

It is normal for you to have natural cycles or periods of fast gains followed by periods of slower—and occasionally no—gains. When you reach a progress plateau, or sticking point, there are several strategies that you can use to overcome this obstacle.

First, sticking points often occur as a result of overtraining, so check for symptoms of an overtrained condition; if you are overtrained, take appropriate steps to counteract this state. You may also reach a sticking point by not changing your training programs frequently enough, so be sure that you change to a new routine often enough to ensure continued progress.

You may also reach a progress plateau by training with an insufficient degree of workout intensity. You must be honest with yourself. Ask yourself: Am I training as hard as I can? If you are unable to answer this question affirmatively, make the necessary adjustments in your workouts.

Finally you might not have enough training enthusiasm to maintain fast gains. I will discuss how to build up enthusiasm for your workouts in the next section of this chapter, and you can use my suggestions to increase your gains through improved training enthusiasm.

Keep in mind that your body requires a two- or three-week consolidation period following a cycle of heavy growth before a new growth cycle can be initiated. Therefore you should accept an occasional progress plateau as a normal occurrence in a bodybuilder's life. But if you are stuck in your bodybuilding progress for more than a month, you should begin to look for a way to smash through the barrier erected by your sticking point.

BODYBUILDING WORKOUT ENTHUSIASM

Unless you can remain enthusiastic about maintaining a bodybuilding life-style, you won't make optimal progress in your training. There are many ways to build workout enthusiasm, including attending bodybuilding competitions, reviewing your training diary, and reading the articles and looking at the marvelous photographs in bodybuilding magazines.

Although I had been training steadily for about three years prior to my first bodybuilding competition, I hadn't actually thought about competing until Lisa Lyon promoted the first and biggest national championships in America. To tell you the truth, I was "bodybuilding" long before I knew that the activity was *called* bodybuilding.

When I made the decision to compete, I thought it might be a good idea to attend a local competition that was being held at my university, just to make sure I had an idea of what I was getting myself into. Well, to say the very least, the experience of attending the Mr. Pan American University show totally elated me. The event ended at around nine-thirty P.M. and I still had a thirty-minute drive home, but I had enough time to open up the Sport Palace, where I worked, get in a great workout, and still get home by midnight. I was so supercharged with enthusiasm after seeing the competition that I just couldn't wait to begin my workout. My friend Jeanine was affected the same way. Everyone else thought we were nuts, but such is the power of viewing a major bodybuilding show for building workout enthusiams.

Attending a bodybuilding competition can be both a learning experience and a source of greater enthusiasm for your workouts. By attending a show you can learn how to compete in one, and you can compare your current level of development with that of the winner and other competitors. Once you come close to having the looks of a successful woman bodybuilder, you will find your desire to exceed her level of excellence growing by leaps and bounds.

Many show promoters engage a high-level woman bodybuilder to give a posing exhibition as part of the show, and watching this great athlete sweep through her routine can be tremendously inspiring. When I am engaged to give a posing exhibition, I always present a bodybuilding seminar in conjunction with it. (Actually, I prefer the personal touch of a seminar and give many more of them than I do exhibitions.) If the guest poser will be giving a seminar, you can greatly increase your workout enthusiasm by attending it, meeting her, and learning exactly how she trains and diets.

Nothing builds greater enthusiasm for bodybuilding than graphically seeing personal progress in your physical development, and nothing *reveals* this progress as clearly as a detailed and meticulously maintained training diary, particularly if it also contains progress photos of your physique. Even if you can't see improvement in muscle mass, physical proportions, and muscle quality, you can easily note increases in training poundages from one month or one year to another. You can be satisfied that your physique is improving if you note a marked increase in your workout poundage as well.

In the beginning I gained a great deal of inspiration from reading about bodybuilding in various muscle magazines and books. I used to go by my local newsstand every day to see if the latest issue of *Muscle & Fitness* had arrived, and I read every new issue from cover to cover. Studying the sport improves your knowledge of bodybuilding, and that in turn increases your training drive. Today, I still gain a great deal of workout enthusiasm from reading about the men and women at the highest levels of the sport and by studying their photographs in various magazines.

I save every book and magazine related to bodybuilding that I purchase, and it would be a good idea for you to do the same. These books and magazines form a valuable reference library that you can consult whenever you run into a training problem that you can't handle. And if you are facing an upcoming workout with a low level of enthusiasm, simply leafing through your collection of books and magazines is guaranteed to push your workout enthusiasm to new heights!

This photo of me was taken just prior to entering my first bodybuilding competition.

Photo by Julian Mendoza

©Harry Langdon

This is a very recent photograph—look at the difference!

HEAVY VERSUS LIGHT TRAINING

There is considerable debate in bodybuilding circles about the merit of training consistently with very heavy weights versus more moderate poundages. Both schools of though have merit, and my own personal philosophy combines both types of training in a single workout.

There is no question that heavy training increases muscle mass. Indeed, there is a direct relationship between the weight of the barbells and dumbbells you use and the relative mass of the muscles that move a heavy weight in each exercise. Every woman bodybuilder needs increased mass in at least one muscle group, so she should work that group with heavy weights for low repetitions, primarily in basic exercises. There is an increased risk of injury when you train consistently heavy, however.

Lighter, higher-rep workouts don't build as much mass, but they consistently improve the quality—the shape, hardness, and muscular detail—of a muscle group. Lighter training with higher reps is also good for maintaining the muscle mass of any body part.

In my own training philosophy I do plenty of heavy workouts for those muscle groups that I feel need additional mass and contour. But I don't push the really heavy weights in any exercise for one of these body parts until I have completely warmed up both the working muscles and involved joints with plenty of sets of lighter work, and I am always careful to maintain scrupulously correct biomechanics (form) during every heavy set.

For my stronger muscle groups I will generally do lighter, high-quality sets of each exercise. While I may do only 6 to 8 reps with maximum poundages for weak body parts, I'll often do 15 to 20 repetitions while working out with lighter weights for strong muscle groups. I have time-tested and proved this sytem on my own body, and I'm sure that you will find it an effective addition to your personal training philosophy.

OUTDOOR WORKOUTS

For the past year I have done most of my training when not on the road at Joe Gold's World Gym in San-

ta Monica, California. Part of the World Gym is contained on an outdoor sun deck, which makes it nice to train outdoors on sunny days. I've noticed that whenever the weather is particularly nice, I tend to gravitate to the outdoor section of the gym during my workouts.

Outdoor workouts can be very pleasant experiences as long as you don't train outdoors when it's excessively hot or there are overly high levels of air pollution. If you live in a hot climate, you will find it much better to work out prior to ten A.M. The morning hours are also less smoggy than later in the day. At the World Gym, however, I seldom need to worry about the heat or smog. The gym is situated within two hundred yards of the Pacific Ocean, which moderates the temperature and keeps air pollution to a minimum.

If you work out in a home gym, there is no reason why you shouldn't cart some of your equipment out into the backyard for an occasional sun-drenched workout. You will find outdoor training to be quite invigorating, and you can even improve your tan at the same time.

SPECIFIC FEMALE FACTORS IN BODYBUILDING

The bodybuilding life-style has positive effects on menstruation, pregnancy, and childbirth.

Regular exercise and proper diet can help to ease menstrual difficulties. Exercise in particular can help to relieve menstrual cramping, although too much exercise and too strict a diet can lead to amenorrhea, or a cessation of menstrual discharge. It appears that amenorrhea is caused by a low degree of body fat and high levels of general stress, both of which can be evident in a bodybuilder's precontest life-style.

Medical researchers disagree about whether or not an amenorrheic woman still ovulates, so amenorrhea should not be considered a reliable form of birth control. If you are amenorrheic, you needn't worry about the condition, which is common among bodybuilders, runners, dancers, gymnasts, and other athletes who maintain low levels of body fat. You can induce a resumption of menses simply by increasing your body-fat levels and decreasing the amount of stress you bear.

Many competitive women bodybuilders have become pregnant and borne children. They are able to train relatively hard until the last month of their pregnancies, and all have reported a decrease in pregnancy and childbirth complications. The more physically active you are, the easier your pregnancy and childbirth will be. What's more, there are many who have returned to bodybuilding competition after giving birth and reached even better physical condition than before they became pregnant.

LOOKING AHEAD

In Chapter 5, I will present twenty-six more intermediate-level weight-training exercises and three more intensity-graded training programs that will greatly improve your health, fitness, physical appearance, mental well-being, and sense of accomplishment.

CHAPTER 5

intermediate exercises and routines

Now that you've acquired a good feel for how a variety of bodybuilding exercises affect your muscles, I'm sure the twenty-six new movements presented in this section will be no problem for you to master. Well, there *could* be a slight problem. Let me explain.

With the exercises presented in Chapter 3—as well as the large number of variations on movements in Chapters 3 and 5—you will have more than 150 bodybuilding exercises at your disposal once you master the movements presented in this chapter. The problem is that you'll probably enjoy doing all of these exercises so much that it'll be difficult to choose only a handful of the movements to do in each workout. Don't let this get you down, however, because as an advanced bodybuilder, you can do a different workout every day, rotating new exercises into your program until you have done all of your favorite movements.

ABDOMINAL EXERCISES

(1) ROMAN CHAIR SIT–UPS

(A) Emphasis. This is an excellent movement for stressing the entire frontal abdominal wall (rectus abdominis), particularly the uppermost portion of your waist.

(B) Starting Position. Sit on the seat of a Roman chair and wedge your toes beneath the toe bar to restrain your body during the movement. During the movements, cross your arms over your chest, or hold your hands behind your head.

(C) Exercise Performance. Allow your torso to incline backward until it is slightly below a 45-degree angle with the floor. Don't go too much lower than this position, however, because you could place dangerous stress on your lower back. You'll see bodybuilders bend backward until their torsos are below a position parallel to the floor, but they do so

Start.

Finish, showing the twisting variation.

for specific reasons other than toning their abdominal muscles. From the correct low position, slowly sit forward until your torso is almost perpendicular to the floor. Rock slowly back and forth between these two positions until you have done the appropriate number of repetitions.

(D) Movement Variations. For a slightly different effect on your abs, you can place a four-by-four-inch block of wood under the foot end of the Roman chair, which effectively makes this an incline sit-up movement. You can also twist your torso from side to side in order to involve the obliques and intercostal muscles more intensely. To add resistance to my Roman chair sit-ups, I often do the movement while holding across my shoulders a strap or rope attached to a floor pulley behind me. Or you can hold a light barbell plate on your chest or behind your head for extra muscle stimulation as you do the exercise. The added resistance will make it easier to feel the movement in your rectus abdominis muscles. Tune in

sharply on this sensation, concentrating on the abdominal contractions. With such intense concentration you'll even experience powerful muscle contractions with a relatively short range of motion.

(2) CRUNCHES

(A) Emphasis. Crunches give the rectus abdominis muscle wall, particularly the upper part, an opportunity for megaintense contractions *if* you concentrate intensely on your upper abs!

(B) Starting Position. Lie on your back on the floor and drape your lower legs over a flat exercise bench. Your thighs should be perpendicular to the floor in this position. Place your hands behind your head, over your abdomen, or across your chest during the movement.

Start.

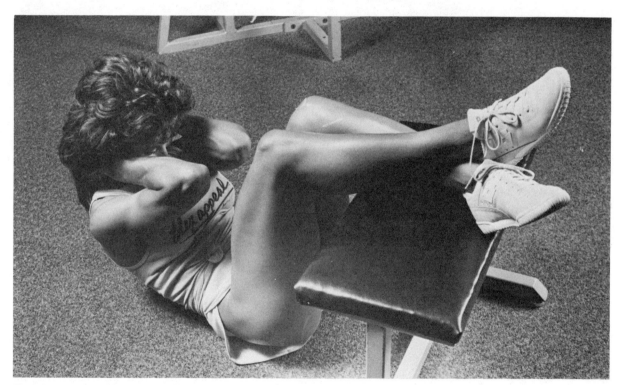

Finish.

(C) Exercise Performance. From this position you must simultaneously do four things: (1) Use lower abdominal strength to raise your hips from the floor (however, be sure that you don't raise your hips by flexing your buttocks and hamstrings); (2) raise your head and shoulders from the floor using upper abdominal strength; (3) force your shoulders toward your hips; and (4) forcefully blow out all of your air. When you do these four things correctly, you will feel a strong contraction in your frontal abdominal muscles. Hold this contracted position for a moment, relax, then repeat the movement.

(D) Movement Variations. Crunches can be done with your feet pressed against the wall so that your lower legs are parallel to the floor and your thighs are parallel to the wall during the movement, or you can do the exercise on a special bench made for crunches, such as the excellent one manufactured by the Universal Gym company. You can also perform crunches by twisting from side to side to accentuate the amount of stress placed on your intercostals and obliques.

Start.

Finish.

(3) V–SITS

(A) Emphasis. This is a very intense movement that stresses the entire frontal abdominal wall.

(B) Starting Position. Sit on the end of a flat exercise bench, incline your torso backward until it is at a 45-degree angle with the floor, and grasp the edges of the bench to maintain this torso position during the movement. Extend your legs down toward the floor, keeping your heels just clear of the floor. Bend your legs slightly and keep them bent during the entire set.

(C) Exercise Performance. Raise your legs upward as high as possible in this position, hold the top position for a moment, and repeat the exercise. To keep continuous tension on your abdominals, it's essential that you don't touch your feet to the floor at the end of each repetition when your heels are once more near the floor.

(D) Movement Variations. You can bend your legs a little more than I've recommended if you find this movement a bit too difficult for you to perform. You can add weight to this exercise by holding a light dumbbell between your feet.

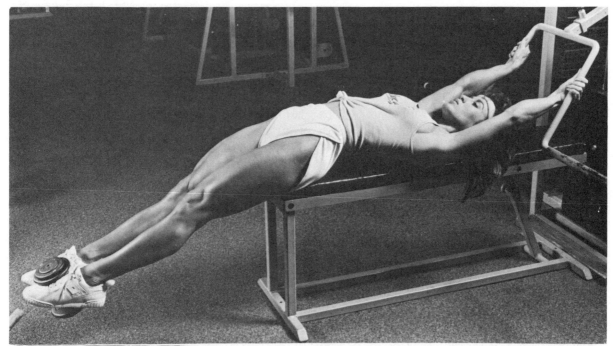

Start, using dumbbell for resistance.

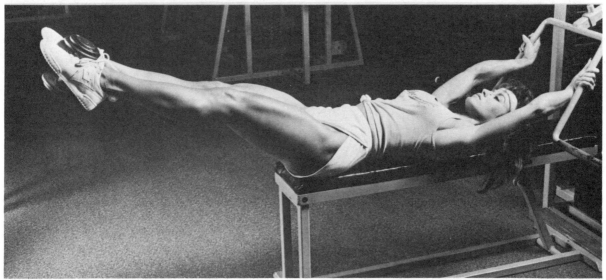

Finish.

(4) BENCH LEG RAISES

(A) Emphasis. Bench leg raises stress the frontal abdominals—particularly the lower part of the rectus abdominis group—over a greater range of motion (giving you a better stretch in the low position of the movement) than is possible in other abdominal movements.

(B) Starting Position. Position your hips at the end of a flat exercise bench, lie back on the bench, and grasp the edges of the bench either behind your head or at the sides of your hips to steady your torso in position during the movement. Bend your legs slightly to remove stress from your lower back and lift your feet from the floor. You can either press your legs together or cross your ankles as you perform the exercise.

(C) Exercise Performance. Slowly raise your feet in a semicircular arc from the starting point until they are directly above your hips. Lower your feet back along the same path to the starting point and repeat the movement for the suggested number of repetitions.

(D) Movement Variations. To keep tension on your abdominals, you can raise your legs up only until your thighs are at a 45-degree angle with the floor, then lower them back to the starting point. To add resistance to this movement, you can raise the head end of the bench by placing its legs on a four-by-four-inch block of wood, or you can wear ankle weights.

CHEST EXERCISES

(5) INCLINE BARBELL PRESSES

(A) Emphasis. Incline presses with a barbell, with two dumbbells, or on a pressing machine place primary stress on the upper pectorals, frontal deltoids, and triceps. Secondary stress is on the lower pecs, medial deltoids, and the latissimus dorsi muscles.

(B) Starting Position. Place a weighted barbell on the rack attached to the head end of an incline bench.

Start.

Finish.

Lie back on the bench and sit on the seat attached to the bench (if there is such a seat on your bench; if not, there will be a sturdy foot platform on which you can stand as you recline on the bench). Grip the barbell with your hands set slightly wider than shoulder width, your palms toward your feet. Straighten your arms and raise the barbell off the rack to a position directly above your shoulder joints. (From the side your arms will appear to be perpendicular to the floor when you have assumed the correct starting position.)

(C) Exercise Performance. Keeping your elbows held back and away from your torso, slowly bend your arms and lower the barbell directly downward until it touches your upper chest at the base of your neck. Without hesitating or bouncing the bar off your chest, immediately press it slowly back to straight arms' length. Repeat the movement for the suggested number of repetitions.

(D) Movement Variations. You can take a somewhat wider or more narrow grip on the bar when performing incline presses. You can also do the movement on benches set at a variety of angles, ranging from about 30 degrees to approximately 45 degrees. Each bench angle change stresses your upper pectorals a bit differently.

(6) DECLINE BARBELL PRESSES

(A) Emphasis. Decline presses with a barbell, with two dumbbells, or on a pressing machine directly stress the lower and outer pectorals, anterior deltoids, and triceps. Strong secondary stress is placed on the upper and inner sections of the pectorals, and minor secondary stress is put on the medial deltoids and latissimus dorsi muscles.

(B) Starting Position. Place a moderately weighted barbell on the rack attached to the head end of a de-cline bench. Lie back on the bench, being careful to first hook your toes beneath the restraint bar at the foot end of the bench to avoid sliding off the bench during the exercise. Take the same grip on the bar as for incline presses and straighten your arms to lift the bar from the rack to a position directly over your shoulder joints.

(C) Exercise Performance. Keeping your elbows back and away from your torso, bend your arms and slowly lower the barbell down to touch your upper chest. Since your neck and face are quite vulnerable

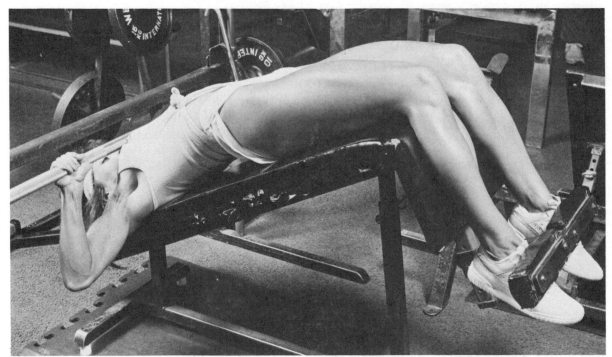

Start.

Finish.

in this position, it's essential that you have a training partner standing at the head end of the bench to spot you in the event you lose control of the bar. Slowly press the barbell back to straight arms' length and repeat the movement.

(D) Movement Variations. As with incline presses, you can vary the width of your grip on the barbell. Decline presses are normally performed on a bench set at approximately a 30-degree angle, but you can do them at any angle between 45 and 15 degrees.

Start.

Finish.

(7) CABLE FLYES

(A) Emphasis. Cable flyes can be performed on a flat, incline, or decline bench so all sections of your pectorals can be stressed by the movement. You will discover that you can place a more continuous form of resistance on your working pectorals when you do flyes with cables than when you perform the movement holding two dumbbells in your hands.

(B) Starting Position. Attach loop handles to two floor pulleys and place your selected exercise bench (flat, incline, or decline) directly between the pulleys so that your shoulders will be even with the pulleys when you are lying on the bench. Grasp the handles, lie down, bend your arms, and keep them bent throughout the movement. Allow the weights on the cables to pull your hands to as low a position below the level of your chest as possible. Be sure to feel a good stretch in your chest muscles at this bottom position of the movement before you complete the exercise and achieve a spectacularly intense peak contraction in your pecs. Incidently you should always reach for this "prestretched" position in all exercises in which it can be achieved.

(C) Exercise Performance. Slowly move your hands upward and together in semicircular arcs until they

touch each other directly above the middle of your chest. For an increased range of motion, which I usually prefer, you can actually cross your hands at the completion of the movement. Return to the starting point to stretch your pectoral muscles, then repeat the movement for the required number of repetitions.

(D) Movement Variations. This movement is usually performed with two floor pulleys, but you can use pulleys set as high as two or three feet from the floor. You can also shift the position of the bench so that your shoulders are either ahead of or behind a position directly between the pulleys as you perform the movement.

BACK EXERCISES

(8) BARBELL BENT ROWS

(A) Emphasis. The barbell bent row is one of the most basic of all upper-body movements in that it

stresses a wide spectrum of muscle groups. It strongly stresses the latissimus dorsi, trapezius, erector spinae, biceps, and brachialis muscles. Secondary stress is placed on the posterior deltoids and the gripping muscles of the forearms.

(B) Starting Position. Stand up to a moderately weighted barbell lying on the floor and bend over to take a shoulder-width grip on the barbell, your palms toward your legs. Keeping your legs slightly bent throughout the movement, straighten your arms and raise your torso up to a position parallel to the floor. In this position, with your arms completely straight at the start of each movement, the barbell plates should be clear of the floor.

(C) Exercise Performance. Keeping your elbows in close to your torso during the movement, slowly pull the barbell directly upward until it touches your torso where you upper abdominals attach to your lower rib cage. Be sure to arch your back at the top point of the movement. Hold this peak contracted position for a second or two, feeling the intense contractions in your upper back muscles. Slowly lower the barbell

Start.   *Finish.*

back to the starting position and repeat the movement. Be absolutely sure that you fully straighten your arms and stretch your latissimus dorsi and other back muscles before you begin your next repetition, and at the same time keep your back arched and your back muscles tensed.

(D) Movement Variations. If you are using substantial poundage on the barbell, the diameter of the plates may be such that you can't comfortably keep the barbell off the floor in the bottom position of the exercise. This problem can be solved by standing on either a thick block of wood or a flat exercise bench as you do the movement. You can also vary the width of your grip on the bar from a position in which your hands are set as far apart as the length of the barbell handle will allow to one in which your hands touch each other in the middle of the barbell bar.

(9) T–BAR ROWS

(A) Emphasis. As with barbell bent rows, T-bar rows place primary stress on the lats, erectors, biceps, and brachialis muscles. Secondary stress is on the traps, the posterior delts, and the gripping muscles of the forearms.

(B) Starting Position. Stand on the platform provided with the T-bar apparatus, bend your legs slightly, and keep them bent during the set. Bend over at the waist and grasp the handles attached to the lever arm of the machine. I then bring my torso up to a 45-degree angle in relation to the floor and maintain that position during the movement. Alternatively you can hold your torso parallel to the floor. In either case, fully straighten your arms and stretch your back muscles in this position exactly as for barbell bent rows.

(C) Exercise Performance. Without allowing your torso to move excessively up and down, slowly bend your arms as fully as possible, pulling the handles upward until the weights or machine bar touch your chest. Return to the starting point and repeat the movement.

(D) Movement Variations. There are several different handles that can be used in conjunction with a T-bar apparatus, and each stresses your upper back

Start.

Finish.

muscles a bit differently. There is also a variation of the T-bar machine that uses a cable instead of being plate-loaded. This version of the T-bar rowing machine allows you a longer range of motion.

(10) ONE–ARM DUMBBELL BENT ROWS

(A) Emphasis. One arm rows allow you to stress your lats, traps, posterior deltoids, biceps, brachialis, and forearm muscles in greater isolation than most other bent rowing movements allow.

(D) Movement Variations. This exercise is often performed with both feet on the floor. In this case, when using your left hand to pull the dumbbell upward, your right hand will rest on the bench to support your torso parallel to the floor; your right leg will be bent, with your right foot placed a bit forward; and your left leg will be relatively straight, with your left foot placed to the rear. Got it? Reverse the leg and arm positions when you pull the dumbbell with your right hand.

Start.

Finish.

(B) Starting Position. Stand with your right side toward a flat exercise bench and place your right knee and right hand on the bench. Your left foot should remain on the floor during the movement to help balance your body for the exercise. Grasp a moderately weighted dumbbell in your left hand, fully straighten your left arm, and rotate your left shoulder a bit toward the floor to stretch fully the upper back muscles on the left side of your body.

(C) Exercise Performance. Keeping your elbow in close to your side, slowly bend your arm and pull the dumbbell directly upward to touch the side of your torso near your hip. Lower the weight back to the starting point and repeat the movement. Be sure to do the same number of sets and reps with each arm.

Start.

Finish.

(11) FRONT LAT PULL–DOWNS

(A) Emphasis. All lat pull-down movements strongly stress the latissimus dorsi, biceps, and brachialis muscles. Secondary stress is on the trapezius and forearm muscles. While lat pull-downs behind the neck stress primarily the upper lats, front lat pull-downs tend to stress the lower insertions of the latissimus dorsi muscles more intensely.

(B) Starting Position. Grip the bar with your hands set a bit wider than your shoulders on each side and your palms facing forward on the lat bar. Straighten your arms fully, sit down on the seat provided on the lat machine, and wedge your knees under the restraining bar to keep your body from moving during the exercise. If there is no seat and/or restraining bar, you should sit or kneel on the floor directly beneath the pulley and have a training partner push down on

your shoulders to keep your torso from moving upward as you pull the bar down to your chest.

(C) Exercise Performance. Keeping your elbows back as far as possible, slowly pull the bar down to touch your upper chest at the base of your neck. Be sure to arch your back at the bottom position of the movement. Allow the weight to pull your arms back to the starting point and repeat the movement for the required number of repetitions.

(D) Movement Variations. You can use both wide and narrow grips, plus a reversed grip, in this exercise. You can also use a parallel-grip handle that sets your hands at shoulder width, or a parallel-grip handle that gives you a very narrow grip. You might also experiment with pulling your first repetition down in front of your neck, the next down behind your neck, the next one in front of your neck, and so on, alternating for your entire set.

SHOULDER EXERCISES

(12) MILITARY PRESSES

(A) Emphasis. Military presses (also called standing presses) directly stress the anterior deltoids and triceps. Secondary stress in the movement is placed on the medial deltoids, trapezius, and upper pectoral muscles.

(B) Starting Position. Stand up to a barbell that is lying on the floor with your feet set about shoulder width apart and your shins touching the bar. Bend over and grip the bar a bit wider than your shoulders on each side, your palms toward your legs. Dip your hips, straighten your back, and pull the barbell up to your shoulders by first straightening your legs, then your back, and finally rotating your elbows under the bar to secure it in position at your shoulders. Incidentally, this movement is called a "clean."

(C) Exercise Performance. Keeping your elbows directly beneath the bar, slowly press the barbell directly upward to straight arms' length above your head. Slowly lower the bar back to your shoulders in front of your neck and repeat the movement for the suggested number of repetitions.

(D) Movement Variations. You can vary the width of your grip on the bar for different angles of stress on your shoulder muscles. You can also do this movement on a Smith machine, an apparatus in which the bar is attached to runners up which it slides during the exercise, which allows you to lower the bar down to your shoulders behind your neck with relative security. You can also do overhead presses on a Universal Gym or any of several other similar machines.

Midpoint.

Finish.

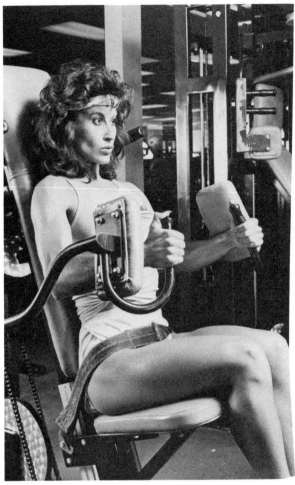

Start.

Finish.

(13) NAUTILUS SIDE LATERALS

(A) Emphasis. Side laterals performed on a Nautilus double-shoulder machine effectively isolate resistance on the medial and anterior heads of the deltoids, with minimal involvement of other upper body muscle groups.

(B) Starting Position. Adjust the height of the machine seat so that your shoulder joints are at the same level as the rotation points of the cams when you sit. Sit down on the seat, fasten the lap belt across your hips, and cross your legs beneath the seat. Place the backs of your wrists against the movement pads of the machine and lightly grasp the handles attached to the pads.

(C) Exercise Performance. Keeping your elbows above the level of your hands throughout the movement, contract your deltoid muscles to move your hands and the pads in semicircular arcs out to the sides and upward to as high a position as possible. Slowly lower your hands back to their starting points and repeat the movement for the suggested number of repetitions.

(D) Movement Variations. This machine can effectively be used one arm at a time. Some bodybuilders like to do this movement standing and facing the machine; this movement isn't quite as effective as it is when done seated, as illustrated, but it does offer you another version of the exercise to add variety to your shoulder training programs, especially in contrast to the strictly controlled arcs you must follow when doing the exercise seated.

Start.

Finish.

(14) NAUTILUS PRESSES

(A) Emphasis. All overhead pressing movements, including the one performed on a Nautilus double-shoulder machine, place strong stress on the anterior deltoids and triceps. Secondary stress is on the medial delts, upper pectorals, and upper back muscles.

(B) Starting Position. Adjust the machine seat to the same height as for Nautilus side laterals, sit on the seat, fasten the lap belt, and cross your ankles below the seat. Grasp the pressing handles of the machine near your shoulders with your palms facing inward. This is the easiest hand position for inexperienced women bodybuilders to master. However, I prefer to do this movement with my palms facing away from each other, a hand position that you should try after you've used the basic grip for a few weeks. In either case, rotate your elbows to a position directly beneath your hands.

(C) Exercise Performance. Slowly straighten your arms to push upward against the machine handles. Once you reach the locked-out position at the top of the movement, slowly lower back to the starting point. Repeat the movement.

(D) Movement Variations. You can do Nautilus presses one arm at a time. Or you can use a technique called negative emphasis by pushing the handles upward with both arms and lowering it one arm at a time, alternating arms with each repetition.

(15) DUMBBELL BENT LATERALS

(A) Emphasis. All bent lateral movements place primary stress on the rear delts and upper back muscles. Minor secondary stress is placed on the medial deltoids.

(B) Starting Position. Grasp two light dumbbells in your hands, place your feet a comfortable distance apart, and bend over at the waist until your torso is parallel to the floor. Hang your arms directly downward from your shoulders with your palms facing inward toward each other. Bend your arms slightly and maintain this rounded-arms position during the movement.

(C) Exercise Performance. Being sure to keep the front ends of the dumbbells tilted slightly below the level of the back ends of the weights, slowly raise the dumbbells directly out to the sides and slightly forward until they are just above the level of your shoulders. Your elbows must travel upward at least a couple of inches forward of your shoulder joints. Slowly lower the weights back to the starting point and repeat the movement for the required number of repetitions.

(D) Movement Variations. You can do dumbbell bent laterals one arm at a time by doing the movement with a floor pulley instead of a dumbbell, a truly great variation of the basic movement. This exercise is also frequently performed while seated at the end of a flat exercise bench and bent forward so that the torso is parallel to the floor.

Start.

Finish.

Start.   Finish.

ARM EXERCISES

(16) PULLEY PREACHER CURLS

(A) Emphasis. All variations of preacher curls strongly stress the biceps muscles, particularly the lower part of the biceps where it connects with the forearm near the elbow. Preacher curls performed with a pulley place a more continuous form of resistance on the biceps than the same movement done with a barbell or two dumbbells. Secondary emphasis in pulley preacher curls is placed on the brachialis muscles and powerful flexor muscles on the inner sides of the forearms.

(B) Starting Position. Place a preacher bench about three feet back from a floor pulley. Attach a bar handle to the floor pulley. With a shoulder-width under-grip on the bar handle, lean over the preacher bench so the top part of it is wedged under your armpits and your upper arms run down the angled surface of the bench parallel to each other. Fully straighten your arms.

(C) Exercise Performance. Keeping your wrists straight, slowly bend your arms completely. Return to the starting point and repeat the movement.

(D) Movement Variations. You can do cable preacher curls with a wider or narrower grip. And by attaching a loop handle to the cable, you can do the movement with one arm at a time.

(17) STANDING DUMBBELL CONCENTRATION CURLS

(A) Emphasis. This movement is excellent for accentuating the peak on your biceps.

(B) Starting Position. Grasp a light dumbbell in your left hand and rest your right hand on a flat exercise bench or a dumbbell rack to support your torso in a position parallel to the floor during the movement. Hang your left arm directly downward from your shoulder and rotate your hand so that your palm is up during the movement.

(C) Exercise Performance. Keeping your upper arm motionless, slowly bend your arm and curl the dumbbell up to your shoulder. Hold the contracted position for a moment, strongly supinating your hand, then lower back to the starting point. Repeat the movement for the desired number of repetitions. Be sure to do the same number of sets and repetitions with each arm.

(D) Movement Variations. You can perform standing concentration curls without a bench or rack for support by assuming a crouching position and resting your free hand on your knee.

Start.

Finish.

Start.

Finish.

(18) HIGH PULLEY LEANING TRICEPS EXTENSIONS

(A) Emphasis. Pulley triceps extensions performed in this position stress the entire triceps mass, but particularly the large inner head of the muscle group.

(B) Starting Position. Attach a short bar handle (or the short angled handle often used for pulley pushdowns) to an overhead pulley. Take a narrow over-grip on the handle, face away from the pulley, and extend your arms over your head. Staggering your feet for greater stability during the movement, lean forward at the waist until your torso is approximately parallel to the floor during the exercise.

(C) Exercise Performance. Keeping your elbows motionless and in close to the sides of your head, slowly bend your arms until they are completely flexed. Extend your arms to a fully locked-out position, return to the starting point, and repeat the movement for the suggested number of reps.

(D) Movement Variations. By attaching a loop handle to the cable and cupping the elbow of your working hand with your free hand, you can do this movement with one arm at a time. Another common variation is performed while kneeling on the floor and placing your elbows and head on a flat exercise bench during the movement. Finally you can do both the standing and kneeling versions of this exercise with a rope handle, which gives you a parallel-hands grip.

(19) DUMBBELL TRICEPS EXTENSIONS

(A) Emphasis. All of the variations of dumbbell triceps extensions directly stress the entire triceps muscle group, particularly the inner and medial heads of the muscle mass.

(B) Starting Position. Grasp a moderately weighted dumbbell so that your palms rest against the inner plates at one end of the weight and your thumbs encircle the handle of the dumbbell to keep the weight from slipping from your hands. The dumbbell handle will be held vertically throughout the movement. Standing erect, extend your arms directly over your head.

(C) Exercise Performance. Keeping your upper arms motionless and your elbows pointed directly toward the ceiling, slowly bend your arms completely to lower the dumbbell in a semicircular arc to as low a position down your back as possible. Extend your arms to return the dumbbell to the starting position and repeat the movement for the desired number of repetitions.

(D) Movement Variations. You can do dumbbell triceps extensions while seated at the end of a flat exercise bench, which isolates your legs from the exercise. A second variation is performed one arm at a time while holding a light dumbbell in your exercising hand. In this case you can lower the dumbbell more across the midline of your body rather than directly to the rear. Finally you can do the movement with both arms at once while either standing or seated and while holding two light dumbbells in your hands.

Start, while seated.

Finish.

Start.

tion that provides you with the type of stress you desire on your thigh muscles: (1) outward, for a gratifying contraction in the outer thigh muscles and inner buttocks; (2) inward, for stimulation of the inner thigh and outer buttock muscles; or (3) straight ahead, for a dynamic overall effect. It's important that you keep your torso in an upright position throughout the movement. Tensing your abdominal and back muscles will help you to maintain an upright torso position, as will keeping your head up by picking a spot on the wall at your standing eye level and focusing on it as you do the movement.

(C) Exercise Performance. Slowly bend your legs and lower yourself into a fully squatting position. Be careful not to bounce in the bottom position of the movement; rather, straighten your legs with a strict, fluid motion and return your body to the starting position. Repeat the movement for an appropriate number of repetitions.

Finish.

THIGH AND HIP EXERCISES

(20) SQUATS

(A) Emphasis. Squats build power and add quality muscle mass to your thighs. Primary stress is placed on the quadriceps, buttocks, and lower back. Secondary stress is on the hamstrings, upper back, and abdominal muscles.

(B) Starting Position. Position a weighted barbell on a squat rack. Step under the bar and position it across the top part of your upper back. Avoid placing it above shoulder level (i.e., across your neck), where the weight can cut into your vertebrae, pull you forward, and strain your lower back. Use padding on the bar if you feel you need it. Next, lift the bar off the rack, step back one pace, and set your feet about shoulder width apart. You should point your toes in the direc-

(D) Movement Variations. If you find that you lack sufficient ankle flexibility to perform this movement flat-footed, you can elevate your heels and make it easier to do by standing with your heels on a two-by-four-inch board. Other variations of squats are mostly centered around how far down you go in the squatting movement; experiment with quarter, half, parallel (down until your thighs are only parallel with the floor), and full squats, and let your body be the judge of which is best for you. You should also experiment with foot-placement widths much wider than shoulder width, as well as with your inner thighs pressed together and your feet very close to each other.

(21) FRONT SQUATS

(A) Emphasis. This is merely a squat movement with the bar held in front of your neck across the front of your shoulders and upper chest. Front squats stress the same muscles as regular squats, although I feel the movement more intensely in the quadriceps muscles just above my knees.

Start.

(B) Starting Position. Step up to a barbell resting on a squat rack and position it across your upper chest and shoulders. Once the bar is positioned, you can either grasp it with your hands placed a bit wider than your shoulders, or you can cross your arms over the bar. If you find yourself having difficulty balancing the bar securely on your shoulders, you can solve the problem by merely holding your elbows at least as high as the level of your shoulders during the movement. Next, place your feet in the position you have chosen for this variation of squats.

(C) Exercise Performance. Keeping your torso erect during the movement, slowly bend your legs and lower your body into a full squatting position and then return to the starting position. Repeat the movement for the suggested number of repetitions.

(D) Movement Variations. It is more likely that you will need to stand with your heels elevated by a board or a pair of thick barbell plates when doing front squats than when performing the normal type of back squat. You can also do quarter, half, and parallel front squats.

Finish.

Start.

Finish.

(22) HACK SQUATS

(A) Emphasis. Hack squats place primary emphasis on the outer sweep of the thigh muscles and the quadriceps muscles just above your knees. Secondary stress is on the hamstrings and buttocks.

(B) Starting Position. I most frequently use the hack machine that has yokes that fit over the shoulders. This machine frees my hands to assist with those last grueling reps, when I can push down on my knees to force out an extra rep or two. My feet are placed a bit closer than shoulder width on the angled foot platform, and my toes are pointed outward a bit. I never fully straighten my legs at the top of the movement, as this practice gives me continuous tension on my quads.

(C) Exercise Performance. From the starting point I fully bend my legs and then slowly straighten them to within about six inches of the fully straight position. Then I immediately start back down into the full squatting position. You should be sure to perform each repetition of hack squats in a slow and deliberate fashion in order to place maximum stress on your quads.

(D) Movement Variations. There is a second type of hack machine that consists of a sliding back platform with handles at each side of the bottom of the platform. With this machine you simply rest your back against the padded surface of the platform, grasp the handles with your arms straight, place your feet on the angled foot platform, and work against the resistance provided with repeated squatting motions. Regardless of the machine used for hack squats, you can vary the width of your foot placement and the angle of your feet on the platform to alter the area and degree of muscular contraction in your quadriceps.

(23) CABLE FORWARD LEG KICKS

(A) Emphasis. This is the fourth type of hip/thigh cable movement that I didn't give you to perform in Chapter 3. Forward leg kicks stress the quadriceps muscles and the flexor muscles of your hip girdle. Forward leg kicks give your thighs a finished, highly defined look for display onstage at a competition. This movement is also an excellent way to isolate your quadriceps muscles when you don't have a leg extension machine available.

(B) Starting Position. Attach a padded cuff to a floor pulley cable and fasten the cuff around the ankle of your right foot. Facing away from the machine, grasp a sturdy upright to steady your body in position as you perform the movement.

(C) Exercise Performance. Keeping your right leg straight, you can move it from a position behind the midline of your body to a position forward and upward as high as possible. Lower back to the starting point and repeat the movement for the required number of repetitions. Be sure to do an equal number of sets and repetitions with each leg.

(D) Movement Variations. You can do this exercise with your leg bent at a variety of angles. Or you can start the movement with your leg bent and finish it with you leg straight, as if you were kicking a soccer ball.

Start.

Finish.

(24) LUNGES

(A) Emphasis. This is an excellent movement for stressing all of the muscles of your thighs, hips, and buttocks. The length of your lunge—either a long or short lunge movement—will determine a shift in the intensity of contraction in your thighs and buttocks, the long lunge being more for the butt and the short lunge being more for thigh stimulation. Make this movement a weekly part of your training program and you'll end up loving it!

(B) Starting Position. Place a light barbell across your shoulders behind your neck, balancing it in position by grasping the barbell bar out near the plates. Set your feet about shoulder width apart and point your feet directly forward throughout the movement.

(C) Exercise Performance. From this starting position, step forward two and a half to three feet with your left foot, making sure that the foot is placed on the floor with your toes comfortably pointed ahead. For reference, this is the long lunge position. As you step forward, keep your right leg only slightly bent;

Start.   *Finish.*

then, when your left foot touches the floor, bend your left leg as fully as possible. In the lunging position your right knee should be 4 or 5 inches from the floor and your left knee should be a few inches ahead of your left ankle. Your torso should be inclined slightly forward with your back arched. In this position you will feel stress in your left quads and right buttock muscles. Push off with your left leg and return to the starting position of the movement. Repeat it with your right foot forward and continue alternating forward legs until you have done the suggested number of reps with each leg.

(D) Movement Variations. You may also want to do a shorter version of the lunge in which you step only about 2 feet forward and bend both of your legs much more than in the long lunge. In my sets, I sometimes alternate a long lunge with a short lunge. My first set of lunges is usually done in the conventional manner, alternating feet with every rep; however, in succeeding sets, I'll often do as many as 5 reps with each leg before switching to the other, which makes the movement more interesting and of higher intensity. You can also perform lunges either freehand or while holding two dumbbells down at your sides to add resistance to the movement. Many bodybuilders do the movement stepping up onto a thick block of wood with their front foot.

Start.

Finish.

CALF EXERCISES

(25) SEATED CALF RAISES

(A) Emphasis. Doing calf raises with your legs bent, as you do when working on a seated calf machine, you can directly stress the broad, flat soleus muscles that lie beneath the gastrocnemius muscles, since the soleus muscles can be fully contracted only when your legs are bent. Building up your soleus muscles gives width and flare to your calves. Seated calf raises place somewhat lesser stress on the gastrocnemius muscles.

(B) Starting Position. Sit on the seat of the calf machine and place your toes and the balls of your feet on the toe bar attached to the machine. Adjust the pads of the machine to an appropriate height by pull-

ing out and replacing the pin in the column of metal leading from the machine lever arm up to the pads. Pull the pads over your knees, push up against the pads by extending your feet, and move the machine stop bar forward to release the weight for your use. Relax your calf muscles to allow your heels to sag as far below the level of your toes as possible.

(C) Exercise Performance. From the starting position just described, rise up as high on your toes as you can, then sink back down to the starting position and repeat the movement. At first you can do this movement with your feet pointed directly forward, but with experience you should begin to use a foot rotation technique that I have developed. The ankle isn't a hinge joint that allows movement of the foot solely on one plane (up and down). Rather, it's a ball-and-socket joint that allows *rotational* movement. I noticed this several years ago and began rotating my feet— moving them from inward to outward foot positions and working from the inside to the outside soles of the balls of my feet—during each repetition. Once I began using this crucial training secret, my calves literally exploded with new growth! Try it. I know you'll get the same great results.

(D) Movement Variations. Experiment with foot placement widths on the toe bar to experience different degrees of muscle contraction in different areas of your calves. If you don't have a seated calf machine available, you can simply wrap a towel around the middle of a barbell to pad it and rest it on your knees for a similar movement. With your toes and the balls of your feet on a calf block and your butt on a flat exercise bench, this movement is just as good as one performed on a seated calf machine.

(26) ONE–LEGGED CALF RAISES

(A) Emphasis. This is a very effective exercise for the gastrocnemius muscles, and it requires a minimum of equipment—only a dumbbell and a block of wood or a stair tread.

(B) Starting Position. Stand with the toes and ball of your right foot on a calf block (or you can stand on a stair tread). Hold a light dumbbell in your right hand and use your left hand to balance your body in position during the movement. Bend your left leg to keep it out of the movement. Relax your right calf muscles and allow your right heel to sink as far below the level of your toes as possible.

Start.

(C) Exercise Performance. Slowly extend your right foot and rise up as high as you can on your toes. Sink back to the starting point and repeat the movement for the required number of repetitions.

(D) Movement Variations. You can also do this movement freehand with no weight as a means of pumping up your calves. Try doing a superset of one-legged calf raises in which you first do 25 reps with each leg and then 20 reps with each leg, pausing only long enough between sets to switch feet. This exercise can also be performed on a standing calf machine; you achieve negative emphasis by going up on both legs and then lowering back to the starting point on one leg, resisting the weight as powerfully as possible. Be sure to alternate legs for the negative part of the movement.

Finish.

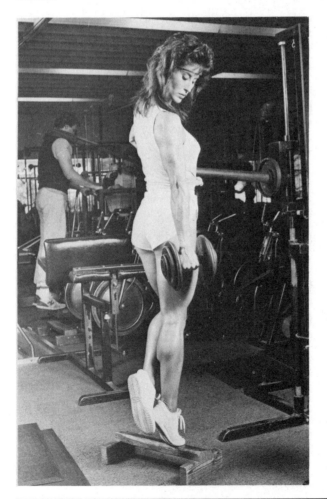

YOUR INTERMEDIATE ROUTINES

In this section I will give you three progressively more intense training programs that you can use to continue from the intensity level reached in Chapter 3 to the point where you can begin using the advanced routines in Chapter 7. It will take you four to six months to complete these three programs, but they will greatly increase your physical fitness, muscular development, and strength.

The following intermediate-level training program can be followed three nonconsecutive days per week for the next four to six weeks:

Exercise	Sets	Reps
(1) Roman chair sit-ups	2–3	25–50
(2) Bench leg raises	2–3	20–30
(3) Crunches	2–3	20–30
(4) Lunges	2	10–15
(5) Leg curls	3	10–15
(6) Squats	3	10–15
(7) Barbell bent rows	3	8–12
(8) Front lat pull-downs	2	8–12
(9) Incline barbell presses	3	8–12
(10) Decline barbell presses	2	8–12
(11) Military presses	2	8–12
(12) Nautilus side laterals	2	8–12
(13) Dumbbell bent laterals	2	8–12
(14) Pulley preacher curls	2	8–12
(15) Standing dumbbell concentration curls	2	8–12
(16) High pulley leaning triceps extensions	2	8–12
(17) Dumbbell triceps extensions	2	8–12
(18) Seated calf raises	3	10–15
(19) One-legged calf raises	2	15–20

It's important to note that you can do the exercises in the foregoing routine—as well as in all succeeding training programs—in any order that you wish, with one key exception: You should never train your upper arm muscles (biceps and triceps) prior to torso work (chest, shoulders, and back). The reason for this lies in the fact that the arm muscles are much smaller and weaker than the torso groups. When you do a basic torso exercise that also involves the arms, your arms will give out before you stress your torso group to the max. Therefore, fatiguing your biceps or triceps prior to working your torso muscles simply aggravates an already bad situation. That's why you should always do your torso training prior to your arm workout. Otherwise, the order in which you do your exercises is of little consequence.

Moving up a step in training intensity, you can begin to use the four-day split routine discussed in Chapter 4. The following is a four-day split routine program that you can use for the next four to six weeks:

MONDAY AND THURSDAY

Exercise	Sets	Reps
(1) Bent-knee sit-ups	3	25–30
(2) Bench leg raises	3	25–30
(3) Decline barbell presses	3	8–12
(4) Incline flyes	2	8–12
(5) Pec deck flyes	2	8–12
(6) Nautilus overhead presses	2	8–12
(7) Nautilus side laterals	2	8–12
(8) Dumbbell bent laterals	2	8–12
(9) Seated pulley rows	3	8–12
(10) One-arm dumbbell bent rows	2	8–12
(11) Front lat pull-downs	2	8–12
(12) Barbell upright rows	3	8–12
(13) Calf presses	3	15–20
(14) Standing calf raises	2	10–15

TUESDAY AND FRIDAY

Exercise	Sets	Reps
(1) V-sits	3	20–25
(2) Crunches	3	20–25
(3) Seated twisting	3	50
(4) Hack squats	3	10–15
(5) Front squats	2	10–15
(6) Leg extensions	3	10–15
(7) Leg curls	3	10–15
(8) Alternate dumbbell curls	3	8–12
(9) Pulley preacher curls	2	8–12
(10) Pulley push-downs	3	8–12
(11) One-arm dumbbell triceps extensions	2	8–12
(12) Seated calf raises	3–4	10–15

This final four-day split routine can be performed for four to six additional weeks, bringing you up to the point where you can legitimately consider yourself an advanced bodybuilder:

MONDAY AND THURSDAY

Exercise	Sets	Reps
(1) Bench leg raises	3	20–30
(2) Knee-ups	3	30–50
(3) Leg presses	3	10–15
(4) Lunges	3	10–15
(5) Leg extensions	3	10–15
(6) Leg curls	3	10–15
(7) Pulley leg/hip movements (four ways)	1–2	10–15
(8) Barbell upright rows	3	8–12
(9) T-bar rows	3	8–12
(10) Lat pull-downs behind neck	3	8–12
(11) Front lat pull-downs	2	8–12
(12) Seated pulley rows	2	8–12
(13) Seated calf raises	3	10–15
(14) Standing calf raises	3	10–15

TUESDAY AND FRIDAY

Exercise	Sets	Reps
(1) Roman chair sit-up	3	20–30
(2) Crunches	3	20–30
(3) Seated twisting	3	50
(4) Incline barbell presses	3	8–12
(5) Pec deck flyes	3	8–12
(6) Flat-bench cable flyes	2	8–12
(7) Alternate dumbbell presses	3	8–12
(8) Dumbbell side laterals	2	8–12
(9) Dumbbell bent laterals	3	8–12
(10) Alternate dumbbell curls	3	8–12
(11) Pulley preacher curls	2	8–12
(12) Pulley push-downs	3	8–12
(13) High pulley leaning triceps extensions	3	8–12
(14) One-legged calf raises	3	15–20
(15) Calf presses	3	15–20

LOOKING AHEAD

Actually, by the time you have completed the routines in this chapter, you will feel comfortable with the bodybuilding process and will have earned the right to consider yourself a legitimate bodybuilder. You will feel very confident in any gym situation because you have a firm knowledge of how to get what *you* want out of the gym rather than being a victim of the gym and the equipment it has available. Needless to say, this is a tremendous personal victory, because you have moved up from victim to self-determining athlete.

In the next chapter we will launch ourselves into advanced bodybuilder training. Are you ready to make the giant step up to being an advanced bodybuilder? Let's do it!

CHAPTER 6

advanced training techniques

With four to six months of steady training behind you, you're now an advanced bodybuilder seeking to further develop and refine your physique. In this chapter, I will discuss how to develop the right "feel" for an exercise, training instinct, muscle confusion workouts, aerobic weight training and bodybuilding practices, a formula for maximum training intensity, layoffs from training, stress management, flexibility training, augmenting personal energy levels, five-day and six-day split routines, six advanced-level training intensification techniques, and how a bodybuilding competition is conducted.

HOW IT SHOULD FEEL

It's important to develop the right feel for an exercise; without it you won't get as much out of your workouts. I firmly believe that it's much more important for a serious bodybuilder to feel a movement affect-

ing her working muscles than it is for her to use incredibly heavy weights.

Your first impressions of how a working muscle should feel will be guided by an anatomy chart and the description of which muscle(s) each exercise should be hitting. When you do barbell curls, for example, you can concentrate on your biceps and feel them begin to burn toward the end of each set. This burning sensation in a working muscle is caused by a rapid buildup of fatigue toxins. It's the first sensation you'll probably notice in a working muscle group.

A little later you will begin to sense your working muscles powerfully contracting and then extending under the load you place on them. With time these sensations will become more powerful, until you reach the point where you can instantly feel the stresses of any new exercise on a working muscle group. This is an important skill because it later allows you to work with subtle variations on each basic exercise you perform to stress your muscles in new and productive ways.

I will discuss this more fully in Chapter 9, but you should begin to experiment with different body positions as you perform each movement, noting how it affects your muscles differently from your usual method of performance.

TRAINING INSTINCT

Okay, here it is—the biggest secret of bodybuilding success! The secret is *you*! *You* deciding. *You* doing. *You* feeling. *You* experiencing and experimenting. *You*. This exercise form of bodybuilding is probably the most individualized activity you'll ever undertake. I truly wish I could tell you to do *X* number of sets and *Y* number of reps with *Z* weight and have it work perfectly for you. Unfortunately it doesn't work that way and I refuse to mislead you and fill your brain with empty hopes and promises. Here is the realization: We are all engineered (so to speak) the same way; however, our *interpretation* of every aspect of ourselves, be it physically, emotionally, or attitudinally, is precisely what defines us as unique. This is what separates us from the rest of the world. The best I can do is to give you my own formulas and guidelines and how I applied them.

Although there are many general training and nutrition principles that apply to every bodybuilder, each exercise, each training principle, each routine, and each dietary practice will have a slightly different effect on every individual. Therefore, I can tell you *approximately* what to expect from your training and diet, but only you can determine *precisely* what works for your own body. The longer you train and observe your body, the more precisely you can make this determination. Fortunately there is an effective method for doing this.

Training instinct is the result of monitoring the biofeedback signals that your body gives you. Each piece of biofeedback gradually leads to a more refined training instinct. What does posttraining muscle soreness tell you? Or a visible gain or loss in body fat? An increase of 10 pounds in your incline press poundage? Low or high energy levels? Lack of enthusiasm for training? Increased appetite? The force of a muscle contraction? A good pump in the muscle?

Within a few months your training instinct will be so good that you will actually be able to tell by the *feel* of a muscle group during or immediately after a set or two how good the exercise or technique was.

There is, however, one piece of biofeedback that I have found to be relatively useless. So many people seek a burning sensation in their muscles during a set; they consider it a sign that they have trained a muscle optimally. Actually this is not a good indicator of whether or not an exercise or set has been valuable. The actual *force and quality of contraction* in a working muscle *per rep* is a much better indicator.

MUSCLE CONFUSION WORKOUTS

When I discussed when to change training programs in Chapter 4, I mentioned that your body and mind can quickly become used to a particular training program, which results in a progress plateau. The solution to this problem is to change periodically from the routine you're using to a new one.

Some bodybuilders grow used to a new routine so quickly that they must use a new training program every workout day. They essentially follow a "nonroutine routine" to get results continually in their training. This technique is called *muscle confusion training*.

Perhaps muscle confusion will work for you; it's certainly something that you should include in your bodybuilding experiments. You might do the same exercises from one day to the next, but you can always think up new angles at which to do each movement. For example, you can do incline presses with a barbell, two dumbbells, or on a variety of exercise machines. You can also perform incline presses at a variety of angles, each of which stresses the upper pectorals and frontal deltoids a bit differently.

You should also change the number of reps and sets you perform for each movement, the amount of weight you use in each exercise, the length of rest intervals between sets, and the training principles you use each workout. Combine these factors with the wide variety of exercises available to you, and you can come up with an infinite variety of workouts per muscle group to occupy your body and mind in your super bodybuilding workouts.

I use muscle confusion extensively in my own workouts, and I do so for two reasons. First, it allows me to keep my level of progress and results quite high. Second, I am constantly learning more and more about bodybuilding and how it affects the human body by experimenting with new exercises, routines, and techniques. Both of these factors help me to help both myself and you to get the best of what we want out of bodybuilding.

AEROBIC WEIGHT WORKOUTS

One of the main criticisms of weight training over the years has been the assertion that the activity does not provide aerobic (heart, lung, and circulatory system) fitness. That is a *wrong* accusation. Weight training *does* provide aerobic conditioning, and its aerobic effect can be greatly increased by using the three techniques outlined in this section.

The best aerobic weight-training method is called *circuit training.* It involves setting up around a gym twelve to fifteen "stations," each featuring an exercise for a different part of your body (of course, the more stations provided, the greater the chance of having more than one exercise ·for each muscle group). You then move in a circuit from one exercise station to the next with very short rest intervals between stations. To increase the intensity of circuit training, you should both add weight to each movement from time to time and reduce the length of rest intervals between stations.

A sample circuit training program is depicted in Figure 6-1 on page 116. You can begin by going through this circuit one or two times and work up to four or five full trips around the circuit with as little rest as possible between stations. You can do 10 to 15 reps of each exercise. Work out three nonconsecutive days per week. The key here is minimal rest and keeping your heart rate elevated to 65 to 80 percent of maximum.

The second form of aerobic weight workouts is called *peripheral heart action (PHA) training.* It consists of performing short circuits of four to six movements with minimal rest between exercises. Four to six such short circuits can be performed of each movement three times each week, with 10 to 15 reps each movement.

The PHA system takes advantage of the peripheral heart-action phenomenon. In essence your heart is not strong enough to pump blood throughout your body when you are standing erect. As a result, your heart relies on more than six hundred peripheral "hearts," your skeletal muscles, which squeeze blood past one-way valves in your arterial system each time they contract. This peripheral heart action system both assists your body in blood circulation and helps to combat cardiorespiratory and local muscular fatigue. This in turn allows you to train almost nonstop with minimal fatigue, thereby increasing your level of aerobic fitness.

A sample PHA training program is presented in Table 6-1 on page 116. It will take you several workouts to break into this type of training system, so begin with only one trip through each circuit the first workout. Gradually increase training intensity by doing more and more circuits until you are going through each short circuit four or five times before moving on to the next one. Rest as little as possible between stations of your mini-circuits.

The final form of aerobic weight training involves using a normal workout program and progressively decreasing the length of rest interval between sets. This method, called *quality training,* is fully discussed near the end of this chapter.

MAXIMUM TRAINING INTENSITY

The highest-intensity bodybuilding training involves performing as much work as possible in a short period of time. The more work you can do in a set length of time, the greater the intensity of your workout.

In order to increase the intensity of a workout to the max, you must combine training to failure, forced reps, negative reps, and pre-exhaustion supersets in the same body part. A very intense set is first taken to failure at 6 to 8 repetitions. It is continued with 3 or 4 forced reps until you can no longer push hard against the weight. And it is concluded with 2 to 4 pure negative reps.

If you perform this type of extended, high-intensity set, you will feel a great deal of pain in your working muscles. You will also be pushing your muscles to work harder than they have ever worked before, thereby forcing them to increase hypertrophically at an unprecedented rate of speed. You can also save time training in this manner because one extended, high-intensity set is worth six to eight sets performed in the normal fashion.

With your large torso muscles and quadriceps, you

Figure 6-1: Sample Circuit Training Program

```
        Leg presses                    Incline presses

Start/finish        Sit-ups                        Toe presses

        Side laterals                  Barbell curls

Pulley rows                                         Leg curls

        Standing calf raises           Pulley push-downs

Reverse wrist curls                                 Lat pull-downs

        Military presses               Wrist curls

                    Leg extensions
```

Table 6-1: Sample PHA Training Program

Series I

(1) Squats
(2) Sit-ups
(3) Seated pulley rows
(4) Incline presses
(5) Barbell curls
(6) Side lateral raises

Series II

(1) Bent lateral raises
(2) Standing calf raises
(3) Barbell wrist curls
(4) Barbell shrugs
(5) Leg curls
(6) Hyperextensions

Series III

(1) Pulley push-downs
(2) Military presses
(3) Seated calf raises
(4) Barbell reverse wrist curls
(5) Front dumbbell raises
(6) Leg presses

Series IV

(1) Leg raises
(2) Lat pull-downs
(3) Cable crossovers
(4) Incline dumbbell curls
(5) Alternate dumbbell presses
(6) Parallel bar dips

Series V

(1) Knee-ups
(2) Leg extensions
(3) Seated twisting
(4) Stiff-legged deadlifts
(5) Decline presses
(6) Reverse curls

Series VI

(1) Dumbbell wrist curls
(2) Calf presses
(3) Cable side laterals
(4) Lying triceps extensions
(5) Crunches
(6) Upright rowing

should also use pre-exhaustion supersets, pushing each exercise with forced reps and negatives. For example, you'll never push your pectorals harder than when you do incline flyes to failure with forced reps and negatives, followed immediately—with zero rest time in between—by incline presses to failure with forced reps and negatives. It's torture, but it works!

STRESS MANAGEMENT

We are all bombarded by stress. Yes, stress is one of the leading causes of heart disease and mental illness. It also holds many people back from achieving the ultimate degree of success in their bodybuilding endeavors.

The late Dr. Hans Selye, an Austrian-born physician who did his research while living in Canada, was the leading authority on stress. He identified two types of stress—a negative type that he called *distress* and a positive type that he called *eustress*. Both evoked the same physiological responses (e.g., an accelerated pulse rate), but distress was harmful to the human organism while eustress was beneficial. The trick, Dr. Selye told us, was to minimize distress in our lives while maximizing eustress.

Progressive bodybuilding training is a eustressful activity, and it can do a great deal to reduce the negative stresses in your life. This is one big reason why I recommend progressive resistance training to all women, particularly those who are under a great deal of stress.

It's possible that excessive levels of stress won't be completely absorbed by your training, but it will definitely help; it *always* does. If excessive stess is slowing your progress, you must take steps to minimize this distress in your life or deal with it constructively.

Stress is definitely a fact of life and there are countless ways to cope with it; some are dead-end streets, and others may prove to be helpful. But whatever you do, don't eat anything while you're trying to decide. This rule always works: Make yourself a cup of delicious hot herbal tea and evaluate your particular dilemma. Now, for something a little more profound: Accept the fact that attitudes are more important than circumstances. Any problem confronting you, no matter how hopeless it may seem, is not nearly as im-portant as your attitude toward it. Circumstances give you neither defeat nor victory; they just give you the opportunity to reveal what your thoughts and convictions really are and what you intend to do about the whole stressful mess! Chapter 11 gives great insight into how I deal with this subject.

FLEXIBILITY TRAINING

The greater the range of motion over which you work a muscle, the better your ultimate physical development. By adding stretching to your bodybuilding philosophy, you can greatly improve your muscular development.

There are stretching exercises for every part of your body explained and illustrated in Chapter 10. Keep in mind that you must consider stretching to be a gentle art rather than a forceful activity. You will actually retard your progress toward more flexible joints and muscles by forcing yourself to stretch to the point of pain in your stretched muscles.

Approach each stretched position slowly, because ballistic stretching movements will actually prevent you from reaching a fully stretched position. Slowly approach the point where you begin to feel pain in the muscles being stretched, then back off a few degrees until you are almost out of the pain zone. Hold this stretched position in a relaxed attitude for thirty to sixty seconds.

You will get the most out of your stretching program if you perform it every day. Stretching makes an excellent warm-up, so I suggest that you do it before your weight-training and aerobic workouts. However, stretching practiced after the entire workout is best for developing flexibility, since your muscles, tendons, and joints are as warm as they'll ever be. Therefore, warm up your muscles and joints, both before and after working out, to help prevent training injuries.

INCREASING PERSONAL ENERGY LEVELS

If you initially suffered from low energy levels, you have discovered that regular bodybuilding training greatly increases the energy you have available for everyday use. There are also three food supplements that you can take to increase your energy production further.

Dessicated liver tablets are made from whole liver that was defatted and then dried at a low heat until all of the water was removed. Scientists have discovered that dessicated liver increases endurance. They took three groups of lab rats and fed them different diets. The first group was fed a normal lab rat diet; the second group was fed that diet plus synthetic vitamins; and the third group was fed the normal diet plus all of the dessicated liver they wanted. After six weeks each group was placed in a drum of water from which they could not escape. They had to keep swimming or drown, a pure test of physical endurance.

The results? The first group of rats swam an average of thirty minutes before drowning. The second group swam only a few minutes longer. But the third group swam an average of 75 percent longer than the other two groups, and two rats were still swimming vigorously at the end of two hours, when the scientists terminated their experiment! While humans don't react as dramatically to dessicated liver as the rats did, you will definitely notice an increase in your personal energy levels if you take ten to fifteen dessicated liver tablets each day during different periods of your training cycles.

Second, you should add vitamin E capsules to your diet, taking 400 IUs to 800 IUs per day. Vitamin E not only adds to your levels of personal energy, it also increases the health of your heart and circulatory system. Alternatively you can take raw wheat germ oil (available in bottles at health food stores) spooned on a salad.

Third, you can take an iron tablet each day. Iron is an essential component of the hemoglobin in your blood, and hemoglobin aids in oxygen transfer from your lungs through your blood to your working muscles. Since iron is lost during menstruation, many women are deficient in the mineral. Incidently, you should never take iron and vitamin E at the same meal, since they have the ability to cancel out each other's effects.

FIVE–DAY AND SIX–DAY SPLIT ROUTINES

One step up in training intensity from a four-day split routine is a five-day split, which can be used in the off-season or prior to a competition, depending on how your body adapts to frequent training. With a five-day split routine you must divide your body into equal parts as you would for a four-day split routine. Then you simply alternate halves every weekday, being sure to start each week with a different half from week before.

While it's best for most women bodybuilders to train four or five days a week in the off-season, you should work out more frequently during a precontest cycle. A six-day split routine is most frequently used, although you might need to follow a double-split routine for a few weeks if you have difficulty cutting up. The more frequently you train each day, the higher your rate of metabolism and the more body fat you'll burn.

There are two types of six-day split routines. In the least intense of these splits, you will train each major muscle group twice a week. Here is an example of how you can divide up your muscle groups for such a six-day split routine:

Monday and Thursday

Abdominals
Chest
Biceps
Triceps

Tuesday and Friday

Back
Shoulders
Calves
Forearms

Wednesday and Saturday

Abdominals
Thighs
Buttocks

A more intense form of six-day split routine involves working each major muscle group three days a week. Here is an example of this type of six-day split routine:

Monday, Wednesday, and Friday

Abdominals
Chest
Shoulders
Back
Calves

Tuesday, Thursday, and Saturday

Abdominals
Thighs
Biceps
Triceps
Forearms

There are several forms of double-split routines. In the least intense of these programs, you can train your major muscle groups early in the day, and train your calves, forearms, and abdominals in the evening. Since this is the least intense form of double-split routine, it's the one you should try first.

A more intense form of double-split involves performing two workouts a day three days a week and only one workout the other three training days. Here is an example of this type of double-split routine:

Monday, Wednesday, and Friday (A.M.)

Abdominals
Chest
Shoulders

Monday, Wednesday, and Friday (P.M.)

Calves
Back
Biceps

Tuesday, Thursday, and Saturday (A.M.) or (P.M.)

Abdominals
Thighs
Triceps
Forearms

In the most intense form of double-split routine you will actually work out twice a day six days a week. Here is an example of a full double-split routine:

Monday, Wednesday, Friday (A.M.)

Abdominals
Chest
Calves

Monday, Wednesday, and Friday (P.M.)

Shoulders
Triceps
Forearms

Tuesday, Thursday, and Saturday (A.M.)

Abdominals
Thighs
Lower back

Tuesday, Thursday, and Saturday (P.M.)

Upper back
Biceps
Forearms

The type of six-day split or double-split routine you use will depend on what your training instinct and experimentation tell you. It will probably take several peaking attempts, some of them dry runs that don't actually conclude with a competition. Once you have a good peaking philosophy together, however, you'll have little trouble getting into great shape for each of your contests.

ADVANCED TRAINING INTENSIFICATION TECHNIQUES

I will discuss six advanced-level training intensification techniques in this section: trisets and giant sets, peak contraction, continuous tension, staggered sets, rest-pause training, and quality training. You should experiment with these six techniques and use your training instinct to determine which should be included in your overall peaking strategy.

Trisets and Giant Sets

Trisets—groups of three exercises with no rest between movements—are a significant step up from supersets on the ladder of training intensity. Trisets are best used for muscle groups that have three or more aspects, such as the deltoids with anterior, medial, and posterior heads. Here is a sample triset for your back:

(1) Barbell shrugs (trapezius)
(2) Seated pulley rowing (latissimus dorsi)
(3) Hyperextensions (erector spinae)

Giant sets are groupings of four to six movements performed with no rest between exercises. Contrast this giant set for your back with the triset just presented:

(1) Dumbbell shrugs (trapezius)
(2) Seated pulley rowing (latissimus dorsi—thickness)
(3) Stiff-legged deadlifts (erector spinae)
(4) Lat machine pull-downs (latissimus dorsi—width)

Six-exercise giant sets are usually done for two antagonistic muscle groups. Here is such a giant set for the chest and back:

(1) Incline presses
(2) Seated pulley rowing
(3) Decline presses
(4) Lat machine pull-downs
(5) Incline flyes
(6) Stiff-arm lat machine pull-downs

I personally don't use many trisets in my workouts and have always found giant sets to be too exhausting for me. Still, either or both of these techniques may work well for you, so you should try them out.

Peak Contraction

Muscles are made up of thousands of bundles of individual muscle fibers. Each fiber is a chain of muscle cells attached end to end. When a load is placed on a muscle, each cell either contracts completely to shorten its muscle fiber or it doesn't contract at all. There are no halfway contractions. This is what exercise physiologists call the "all-or-nothing" principle of muscle contraction.

You will receive the greatest benefit from an exercise when you place a heavy load on a working muscle when it has a maximum number of cells "fired," or contracted. This position is the one in which the muscle has been maximally shortened, as is the case with your biceps when your arm is fully bent. Peak contraction training simply means that a muscle has a full load on it in this completely contracted position.

As you're probably aware, in many bodybuilding exercises there is little or no stress on the working muscles in the fully contracted positions. The standing barbell curl is a good example of such a movement. When the barbell has been curled to your shoulders and your biceps are fully contracted, the weight is actually supported by your deltoids, not your biceps. No weight is on the biceps at the finish position of a barbell curl.

With rotary machine movements, such as those performed on Nautilus apparatus, you will always have a full load on a completely contracted muscle group. There are also many free-weight exercises that allow a peak contraction effect. These movements include all calf exercises, hanging leg raises, hyperextensions, leg extensions, leg curls, chins, pull-downs, all rowing movements, side laterals, front laterals, bent laterals, cable crossovers, dumbbell kickbacks, and barbell concentration curls.

I've found that during my precontest cycle I need to do plenty of peak contraction exercises—incorporating a burn in the peak contracted position—to bring out maximum muscle detail. Combined with continuous tension reps, peak contraction exercises will bring out optimal muscularity once your percentage of body fat is down to the acceptable competition level.

Continuous Tension

One of the biggest mistakes a bodybuilder can make is to allow momentum to rob the working muscles of much of the stress they should be receiving in an exercise. For example, curling a barbell too fast forces the biceps to work hard to get the weight moving initially, but there's not much stress on the muscles after that. At the top of the barbell curl, the bar is moving so quickly that momentum effectively makes it feel much lighter than its actual weight.

You can solve this problem by curling the barbell relatively slowly, thus eliminating momentum from the movement. In fact, all bodybuilding exercises should be done in this manner.

During my precontest cycle I move the weights slowly, but I also build as much tension as possible into each movement by tensing both the working muscles and the antagonistic muscles. Therefore, when I'm doing seated dumbbell concentration curls, my triceps are contracted almost as much as my biceps, causing my biceps to be under continuous tension as they slowly contract and extend.

Due to the nature of muscle contractions experienced in this training technique, it is called *continuous tension* training. You can perform continuous tension reps in almost any exercise, and continuous tension is even more effective for etching details into a muscle group when it is combined with peak contraction reps.

You can legitimately perform continuous tension exercises during an off-season training cycle, but I feel that they are best used to enhance muscularity during a peaking phase. Combined with peak contraction reps, isotension contraction (which is discussed in Chapter 9), quality training, aerobic exercises, and a tight precontest diet, continuous tension reps will give you the ultimate degree of contest muscularity. This is how I've done it, and it hasn't let me down yet!

Many bodybuilders use the staggered-sets technique. In this system you "interset" a set of abdominal work after every three or four sets that you do for a major muscle group.

If, for example, you are training your back, you might do three sets of seated pulley rows, a set of abdominal work, three sets of lat machine pull-downs, a set of abdominal work, three sets of one-arm dumbbell bent rows, a set of abdominal work, and so forth until you have done all of your abdominal training.

Staggered sets are best utilized when you have at least ten sets of abdominal and sometimes calf work to complete. It would normally be quite boring to do that many sets of ab work, but intersetting it between sets of training for a major muscle group, you will find it possible to do ten to fifteen sets of normally boring training without even noticing that you've completed it. It's also a great way to save time during a workout.

Rest-Pause Training

No one questions the fact that you must use heavy weights in your workouts in order to add the greatest possible muscle mass to your physique. Unfortunately a rapid buildup of fatigue by-products and a failure in the strength of your muscles prevent you from doing more than 2 or 3 reps with a truly heavy weight. Obviously, if you could perform 10 repetitions with that heavy weight, you could greatly benefit from doing the exercise.

With the rest-pause training techniques, you can effectively perform 8 to 10 reps with a very heavy weight. With rest-pause training, you will warm up thoroughly and then load a very heavy weight on the bar for two or three limit reps. After these reps you take a ten-to-fifteen-second rest-pause, again take up the bar, and force out a couple more reps. Another rest-pause is followed by 2 more reps, a third rest-pause, and a final 1 or 2 reps. Somewhere along the line, you may need to reduce the weight by about 10 percent, but by using rest-pause work like this, you will have performed 8 to 10 reps with maximum weight.

Rest-pause works because your fatigued muscles can recover quite quickly between sets. After only about fifteen seconds you will have reached approximately 75 percent of full recovery. Therefore, when you take up the weight after a rest-pause, your muscles are nearly recovered from the previous 3 reps and can really push on the bar. And because you rest so little between "sets" in a rest-pause workout, you're essentially performing one extended set with the heavy weight, which forces your muscles to grow in mass and strength exceedingly quickly.

If you work out in a public gym, you've probably seen bodybuilders who instinctively use rest-pause training. When they do a set of heavy squats, toward the end of the set they rest briefly between reps of the movement. That allows them to recover between reps, since standing with legs straight is a resting position for them.

Rest-pause training is intense work, so it can't be used on more than one basic exercise per muscle group, nor more frequently than once every two or three weeks. Performed more than this, rest-pause work will lead to an overtrained state.

Photos by Michael Neveux

Quality Training

Quality training is another precontest workout technique that adds to training intensity and helps to increase overall muscularity. It involves gradually reducing the rest intervals between sets. Some bodybuilders rest so little between sets when doing this type of training that they almost appear to be working out nonstop.

While there *is* a place for quality training in your precontest preparation philosophy, I don't believe in cutting rest intervals down to ten to fifteen seconds. With such short rest intervals between sets, you simply can't handle heavy enough weights in your workouts to retain a maximum degree of muscle mass when training and dieting for a major competition.

I reduce my rest intervals between sets from an average of sixty seconds to about forty-five seconds during a precontest cycle. I used the word *average* intentionally, because I may rest five seconds between exercises in a superset and eighty-five seconds between supersets, which averages out to a forty-five-second interval between sets.

There are some bodybuilders who I believe would benefit from reducing rest intervals more drastically—say, down to twenty to thirty seconds between sets. If you tend to have greater-than-average muscle mass and experience difficulty getting acceptably cut up for a competition, you fall into this group of bodybuilders.

It's really tough for some women to achieve contest level muscularity. The answer to this problem is short-

interval quality training, a double-split routine, *plenty* of aerobic exercise, and a strict low-fat, low-calorie diet. Combined with all of the other precontest-training intensity techniques previously discussed, such a plan would put cuts on a walrus!

BODYBUILDING COMPETITION

Bodybuilding competition is conducted in both amateur and professional divisions for men, women, and mixed pairs. In the United States, women's amateur bodybuilding competitions are sanctioned by the American Federation of Women Bodybuilders (AFWB), while in Canada it is administered by the Canadian Amateur Federation of Bodybuilders (CAFB). Internationally the sport is governed by the International Federation of Bodybuilders (IFBB), which has more than 115 countries affiliated with it. The IFBB administers professional competitions both in the United States and internationally.

You should attend as many competitions as possible in order to learn everything you can about how a competition is conducted. Upcoming shows are listed in the coming-events columns of most bodybuilding magazines, as well as via posters on bulletins boards at gyms in the areas where shows are to be held. As soon as you notice the announcement of an upcoming show, you should send away for tickets for both the evening presentation and the morning or afternoon

prejudging, at which all of the real action at a show takes place. Sending off early for tickets will ensure that you get the best seats possible.

Judging is conducted in three rounds of posing, each of which tests a different physical quality. The first round consists of five compulsory poses—front double biceps, left side chest, back double biceps, right side triceps, and front abdominal-and-thigh poses—which reveal a bodybuilder's overall physical development, particularly her muscularity, under equal circumstances. In round two each bodybuilder stands semirelaxed with her arms down at her sides and with her front, back, and both sides toward the judges, a round that reveals general body symmetry. In the third round each bodybuilder presents her free-posing routine to music to display her body under the most favorable circumstances.

In rounds one and two, each competitor comes out to do the required poses by herself, then later in small groups so that the judges can compare her with other women near her level of development. Finally each of seven judges awards placings for every contestant in each round. To prevent favoritism from entering the picture, the high and low placings are eliminated and the remaining five places are totaled. The lowest score in each round is the best, but the scores from all three rounds of posing are totaled to result in a final placing.

While competitors are compared in the first two rounds, every contestant poses alone in round three. You will find the free-posing round quite beautiful to view, as each bodybuilder uses all of her dance and gymnastics ability to choreograph an original eye-catching routine. Watch particularly for the unique transitions that each bodybuilder places between her poses, since they make up the true art of bodybuilding posing.

After three full rounds of posing, the top five contestants enter an exciting posedown in which a final few crucial points are awarded. This posedown can get pretty frantic as the women rapidly hit their best poses, sometimes switching position in the lineup to confront an individual competitor. Normally the first three rounds of judging are held at the prejudging and only the posedown is judged at the evening show.

There are some surprising things that take place at a prejudging or evening show, so attending and carefully observing a number of shows prior to actually entering one will totally familiarize you with how you should present yourself onstage during a show. I don't think it's possible today for a woman to enter a high-level bodybuilding competition and win it her first time out. Experience pays big dividends in bodybuilding competition.

Once you decide to enter bodybuilding competi-tions, it's vital that you make your debut at the local level. It's a shame to see an outclassed novice enter-ing a state or regional show when she should have started with a local event. Then, once you have won a local title, you can set your sights on the next highest level. Step by step you can climb your way slowly up the ladder of success until you are at the highest level of the sport, Miss Olympia.

LOOKING AHEAD

In Chapter 7 you will learn the final eighteen move-ments that make up the collection of exercises in this book. You will also receive two final suggested rou-tines that will bring you to a high level of physical con-dition, ready to buckle down to serious competition training.

CHAPTER 7

advanced exercises and routines

With the final eighteen exercises and their variations, which are described and illustrated in this chapter, you will have a complete pool of nearly seventy basic movements and enough variations to give you nearly two hundred total bodybuilding exercises to employ in your workouts. However, don't let this be the end of your "exercise-collecting," for there are many more movements that you can learn from observing others training in public gyms, reading weight-training and bodybuilding magazines and books, and attending training seminars conducted by champion bodybuilders.

Each time you encounter and master a new weight-training exercise, you should give it a four-to-six-week trial in your workouts. Then, if it proves fruitful, you can periodically include it in your training programs. Every bodybuilding movement has at least some value if you look for it. At the very least you can use the wide variety of exercises that you now know to keep a high level of interest in your training.

ABDOMINAL EXERCISES

(1) HANGING LEG RAISES

(A) Emphasis. This is a very intense frontal abdominal exercise. It particularly stresses the lower sections of the rectus abdominis muscle wall.

(B) Starting Position. Jump up and take a shoulder-width grip on a chinning bar. Allow your body to hang straight down from the bar for a moment, then bend your legs slightly and keep them bent during your set to minimize stress on your lower back.

(C) Exercise Performance. Slowly raise your feet in a semicircular arc upward until they are level with your hips or slightly higher. Lower your feet back to the starting point and repeat the movement for the desired number of reps. If you experience a problem with your body swinging back and forth as you do this exercise (a common problem), have your training partner hold your hips as you perform the movement.

Start.

Finish.

Twisting frog kick variation.

(D) Movement Variations. A less intense form of this exercise, called frog kicks, can be performed if you lack sufficient strength to do full hanging leg raises. In this movement you start in the same position but merely pull your knees up to your chest while simultaneously bending your legs. With both frog kicks and normal hanging leg raises, you can intensify the stress on your intercostals by twisting slightly to one side or the other as you do the movement. Try doing this exercise without bringing your legs all the way down to starting position for an *added* effect.

(2) GRAVITY BOOT FRONT/SIDE SIT–UPS

(A) Emphasis. Depending on how you perform the sit-up movement in this exercise, you can stress virtually all of the muscles at the sides and front of your abdomen.

(B) Starting Position. Put on a pair of gravity boots, jump up to hang from a chinning bar, curl your body upward to hook your feet on to the chinning bar, then hang straight down from the bar. You can either cross your arms on your chest as you perform the movement, or hold your arms straight above your head.

(C) Exercise Performance. In the most basic movement you will flex your torso forward at the waist as completely as possible. At first this will seem much like a crunch movement, but with time you'll be able to do a complete sit-up movement, flexing your torso up to touch your thighs.

(D) Movement Variations. You can also curl your torso directly to the sides, going back and forth from side to side rather than curling your torso directly forward. You can also hold a light dumbbell or a loose barbell

Start.

Finish.

plate on your chest to add resistance to the movement. Incidentally, you will discover that hanging from your feet like this, twisting easily at the waist from side to side, will align your back vertebrae at the conclusion of a workout and minimize any lower back problems that you may be experiencing.

CHEST EXERCISES

(3) CABLE CROSSOVERS

(A) Emphasis. Cable crossovers are a shaping and defining exercise for the pectoral muscles. The movement carves deep grooves of muscular striations across the pectorals and improves the sharp outline around the muscle group.

(B) Starting Position. Attach loop handles to two high pulleys. Stand between the pulleys and grasp the handles with your palms facing toward the floor and your arms extending upward at approximately 45-degree angles with the foor. If standing, use a staggered-feet stance, but whether standing or kneeling, arch your back.

(C) Exercise Performance. Slowly pull your hands downward and inward in semicircular arcs until they touch each other—or, better yet, until your wrists cross each other—a few inches in front of your hips. Make an effort really to push your chest into the movement—make it count! At the conclusion of the movement, hold your position for a moment, tensing your pectorals and deltoids as tightly as possible. Return your hands along the same arcs to the starting point of the movement, and repeat it for the suggested number of repetitions.

(D) Movement Variations. The more you bend over at the waist as you perform cable crossovers, the higher up on your pectorals you will feel the movement. When doing normal crossovers you will feel the exercise more in your lower pecs, but by bending over at the waist until your torso is parallel with the floor, you can feel the movement in your upper pecs. You can also profitably perform cable crossovers one arm at a time, holding your free hand on your hip. One-armed movements more intensely stress the working muscles—in this case the pectorals—because your mental focus need not be split between the two arms; it can be focused on your one working muscle group.

Start.

Finish.

(4) CROSS–BENCH DUMBBELL PULLOVERS

(A) Emphasis. All pullover movements stress both the pectorals and latissimus dorsi muscles. When performed with an exaggerated range of motion and relatively light weights, pullovers stretch the rib cage and enlarge the chest cavity.

Start.

(B) Starting Position. Place a dumbbell of moderate weight on its end on a flat exercise bench. Lie back on the bench with only your upper back in contact with the bench; your feet should be placed about shoulder width apart near the bench to balance your body in position during the movement. Grasp the dumbbell in the same manner as for dumbbell triceps extensions (i.e., with your palms against the inner plates on one end of the dumbbell) and bring it to straight arms' length directly above your chest.

(C) Exercise Performance. With your arms slightly bent, slowly lower the dumbbell in a semicircular arc from the starting point to a position as far behind your head as comfortably possible. Slowly return the weight to the starting point and repeat the movement for the required number of repetitions. You will find that you can achieve a higher quality of movement if you lower your hips as you lower the dumbbell behind your head.

(D) Movement Variations. You can perform a similar pullover movement with a barbell while lying lengthwise on a flat exercise bench and holding your arms straight; this is called a barbell stiff-arm pullover. Or you can do the same movement with your arms bent (called a bent-arm pullover) with a substantially heavier poundage.

Finish.

BACK EXERCISES

(5) STRAIGHT–ARM LAT PULL–DOWNS

(A) Emphasis. This movement is very similar in effect to the pullovers just discussed. Primary stress is placed on the latissimus dorsi muscles—particularly the lower section of the muscle group—and the pectorals. You will also find straight-arm lat pull-downs to be an excellent movement for developing the hard-to-reach serratus muscles.

(B) Starting Position. Stand about two feet back from an overhead pulley with a lat bar attached to it and take a narrow over-grip on the bar (there should be no more than four to six inches of space between your index fingers). Stiffen your arms and hold them straight throughout the movement. At the start of the exercise, your torso should be arched and inclined forward at about a 45-degree angle with the floor, and your arms should be held in a straight line with your torso.

(C) Exercise Performance. Maintaining this body position, use lat strength to move the bar slowly in a semicircle from the starting position to a finishing point touching your upper thighs. Return the bar back along the same arc to the starting point, and repeat the movement for the suggested number of repetitions.

(D) Movement Variations. Many gyms have a special handle formed from two loops of nylon webbing that can be used for this movement; simply push your hands through the loops and do the exercise. You can also do this movement with your arms bent at varying angles.

Start.

Finish.

Start.

Finish.

(6) CLOSE–GRIP LAT PULL–DOWNS

(A) Emphasis. This movement primarily stresses the lats and biceps, with secondary stress placed on the posterior deltoids and the gripping muscles of the forearms. Generally speaking, you will stress your lats over a longer range of motion when you perform a pull-down movement with a narrow grip than when you do it with a wider grip on lat bar.

(B) Starting Position. Attach the handle that you use to achieve a narrow parallel grip for seated pulley rows to the end of an overhead pulley. Grasp this handle with your palms toward each other, sit on the seat provided on the lat machine, wedge your knees be-

neath the restraining bar, and completely straighten your arms.

(C) Exercise Performance. With your back arched, slowly pull the handle down until it touches low on your chest in front of your neck. Return the handle to the starting point and repeat the movement.

(D) Movement Variations. You can also do this exercise with a straight bar handle, using either an over-grip or an undergrip on the bar (the under-grip puts your biceps in the most powerful pulling position, incidentally). Regardless of the handle used, you can experiment with different degrees of backward incline to your body.

Start.

Finish.

(7) GRAVITY–BOOT INVERTED BARBELL ROWING

(A) Emphasis. Gravity-boot inverted barbell rowing is analogous to lat machine pull-downs or chins, but stresses your lats and biceps somewhat differently. Secondary stress is placed on the posterior deltoids and the gripping muscles of the forearms.

(B) Starting Position. Fasten a pair of gravity boots to your ankles, jump up to grasp a chinning bar, hoist yourself up to hook the boots to the bar, then hang directly down from the bar from your ankles. From this position you must have a training partner hand you a moderately heavy barbell in such a way that you can take a shoulder-width over-grip on the bar. Fully straighten your arms.

(C) Exercise Performance. With your back arched, slowly pull the barbell upward to touch the middle of your chest. As you pull on the bar, try to think about pulling your elbows back and up at the same time. Lower the weight back to the starting point of the exercise and repeat the movement for the required number of repetitions.

(D) Movement Variations. You can vary the width of your grip on the barbell that you use for gravity-boot inverted barbell rowing. You can also use dumbbells for this movement.

(8) STIFF–LEGGED DEADLIFTS

(A) Emphasis. This is an excellent movement for developing the powerful erector spinae muscles of your lower back. You will also find that stiff-legged deadlifts strongly stress the biceps femoris muscles (hamstrings) at the backs of your thighs. Secondary stress is placed on the upper back muscles and the gripping muscles of the forearms.

(B) Starting Position. To achieve the fullest possible range of motion in this movement, you should perform it while standing on either a flat exercise bench or a thick block of wood. Take a shoulder-width overgrip on a moderately weighted barbell and stand erect on the bench or block of wood. Straighten your legs and arms, and keep both sets of limbs stiffened throughout the movement.

(C) Exercise Performance. Slowly bend at the waist and lower the barbell downward until it touches your toes, then slowly recover to the starting position by standing erect. It's important that this movement be done in a slow and fluid manner, since the lower back is in a mechanically weak position when doing stiff-legged deadlifts. Repeat the movement for the suggested number of reps.

(D) Movement Variations. For an interesting variation, try performing your stiff-legged deadlifts while holding a pair of relatively heavy dumbbells. You'll find that you can do the dumbbell variation of the movement without standing on an elevated surface. When you do stiff-legged deadlifts with a barbell, the plates on the bar are usually of such large diameter that they touch the floor and terminate the movement short of its potential unless you stand on an elevated surface.

Start.

Finish.

Start.

Finish.

SHOULDER EXERCISES

(9) PULLEY SIDE LATERALS

(A) Emphasis. This movement isolates stress on the medial and anterior heads of the deltoids, with minimum assistance from the remainder of the body.

(B) Starting Position. Attach a loop handle to a floor pulley. Grasp the handle in your left hand with your right side toward the pulley and your right foot about two feet away from the pulley (the cable should run diagonally across your body). Bend your left arm and hold it rounded like that throughout the movement. Allow the weight on the cable to pull your left hand (palm down) across the midline of your body.

(C) Exercise Performance. Keeping your left hand ahead of your body and your palm toward the floor during the movement, slowly raise your hand in a semicircular arch out to the side and upward until it reaches shoulder level. It is important that your index finger is lower than the level of your little finger at the top point of the movement. Lower your hand slowly back to the starting point and repeat the movement for the suggested number of repetitions. Be sure not to straighten your arm fully when you reach the finish position, to keep your triceps out of the movement.

(D) Movement Variations. You can perform this movement with both arms simultaneously if you cross the cables in front of your body during the exercise. When performed one arm at a time, you can also run the cable diagonally in back of your body during the movement.

(10) PULLEY BENT LATERALS

(A) Emphasis. Bent lateral movements place primary stress on the posterior heads of your deltoids and your upper back muscles. Minor secondary stress is on the medial delts and upper triceps.

(B) Starting Position. Stand between two floor pulleys that have loop handles attached to the ends of the cables. Reach to your left across your body with your right hand and grasp the handle attached to the cable on that side of your body. Then reach across your body with your left hand to grasp the other cable. Bend forward at the waist until your torso is parallel to the floor, and be sure that your arms are crossed at the beginning of the movement. (At the top of the exercise the cables will cross each other.)

(C) Exercise Performance. Slowly move your hands in semicircular arcs out to the sides and upward until they are above the level of your shoulders. You will find that you experience a more direct stress in your posterior deltoids if you keep your arms slightly bent

Start.

Finish.

during the movement. Lower your hands back to the starting position and continue the movement.

(D) Movement Variations. I most frequently do this exercise with one arm at a time, with the cable passing beneath my torso as I raise my working arm out to the side. You can either rest your free hand on your knee or the floor to brace your body in position during the movement. In the same manner you can also do dumbbell bent laterals one arm at a time, but I like these better.

(11) MACHINE REAR DELT MOVEMENT

(A) Emphasis. As with bent lateral movements, this exercise directly stresses the posterior deltoids and upper back muscles. Secondary stress is placed on the medial deltoids and the upper triceps.

(B) Starting Position. This movement is performed while sitting backward in a pec deck machine. Sit down on the seat with your chest pressed against the backrest of the machine. Extend your arms directly forward and rest your elbows against the movable pads of the apparatus.

Start.

Finish.

(C) Exercise Performance. Without changing the position of your torso or your elbow placement on the pads, use rear deltoid strength to move the pads as far to your rear as possible. Hold this peak contracted position for a moment before returning the pads to the starting point. Repeat the movement for an appropriate number of reps.

(D) Movement Variations. You can do this movement on a Nautilus torso-rowing machine. On either machine the exercise can be performed with one arm at a time. I know it's difficult to do the movement without a partner if you really want to get the most out of it while doing it with both arms; I grasp a Nautilus pad (around four by six inches) with my fingertips and spot myself by exerting pressure on the pad as I complete the movement; this also helps to provide a greater range of movement.

(12) STANDING ONE–ARM PULLEY CURLS

(A) Emphasis. Pulley curls are good for shaping the biceps, particularly in terms of enhancing whatever natural biceps peak you may have.

(B) Starting Position. Attach a loop handle to a floor pulley and grasp it with your left hand. Stand erect with your left arm running down the side of your body, your palm facing forward. You can rest your right hand on your hip during the movement. Press your left upper arm against your side and keep it motionless throughout the set.

(C) Exercise Performance. Slowly curl your left hand up to your shoulder, building as much tension into your working biceps as possible over the movement's full range of motion. Hold the peak contracted position for a moment before returning your hand slowly to the starting position. Continue with the exercise until you have performed the desired number of repetitions.

(D) Movement Variations. This exercise can also be done in a crouching position, as if you are doing standing concentration curls, except that you hold a pulley handle rather than a dumbbell to provide resistance to your biceps. You can even do a pulley reverse curl with one arm at a time in a standing position.

Start.

Finish.

Start.

(13) ONE–ARM PULLEY KICKBACKS

(A) Emphasis. All kickback movements stress the entire triceps muscle group, but particularly the outer head of the triceps.

(B) Starting Position. Attach a loop handle to a pulley set at about shoulder level. Grasp the pulley handle with your right hand, stand about three feet back from the pulley, and bend over at the waist until your torso is below a 45-degree angle with the floor. Hold your right upper arm tightly against the side of your torso and fully straighten your arm.

Finish.

(C) Exercise Performance. Without moving any part of your body except your forearm, fully bend your right arm. Use triceps strength to return your hand slowly to the starting position, and repeat the movement. Be sure to do the same number of sets and repetitions with each arm.

(D) Movement Variations. You can do this exercise with a floor pulley while holding your torso parallel to the floor. You can also perform a dumbbell kickback in the same position, holding your working upper arm tightly against the side of your torso as you bend and then extend your working arm. In the finish position, lift your arm one to two times for a different peak contraction.

(14) BARBELL WRIST CURLS

(A) Emphasis. When performed with the palms upward, wrist curls stress the large flexor muscles on the inner sides of your forearms. Performed with the palms toward the floor, wrist curls place stress on the extensor muscles on the outer sides of the forearms.

(B) Starting Position. Take a shoulder-width undergrip on a barbell and sit at the end of a flat exercise bench. Place your feet about shoulder width apart and rest your forearms on your thighs so that your wrists and hands extend beyond your knees and are hanging in space.

(C) Exercise Performance. From a position with your wrists extended and your hands hanging as low as possible, slowly flex your wrists and curl the barbell upward in a small semicircular arc to as high a position as possible. Lower the barbell back to the starting point and repeat the movement for the appropriate number of repetitions.

(D) Movement Variations. You can perform barbell reverse wrist curls in exactly the same manner as regular barbell wrist curls, except that your palms will be facing downward during the movement. You can do both types of barbell wrist curls, and particulary reverse wrist curls, in a supported position by resting your forearms across a flat exercise bench as you do the movement.

Dumbbell wrist curls are another variation on barbell wrist curls; as you've already guessed, you simply substitute two light dumbbells for the barbell and perform the exercise the same way, slowly flexing your wrists in small semicircular arcs to as high a position as possible, or reverse the movement by rotating your wrists with your palms toward the floor (dumbbell reverse wrist curls). Many bodybuilders do dumbbell wrist curls one arm at a time, supporting the forearm by resting it lengthwise on a flat exercise bench with the wrist and hand extending over the end of the bench. This is a particularly effective movement when done with the palm facing upward.

Start.

Finish.

Start.   *Finish.*

THIGH AND HIP EXERCISES

(15) FOURTH–POSITION LUNGES
("Bugs Bunny" Lunges)

(A) Emphasis. This interesting movement stresses the thigh muscles—particularly the inner thigh muscles, buttocks, and upper hamstrings—from a unique angle.

(B) Starting Position. Stand erect with your feet in a "Bugs Bunny" position (both feet pointed outward) with only about four to six inches of space between your heels.

(C) Exercise Performance. Slowly step about two and a half to three and a half feet directly in front of your other foot, keeping the same pointed-out foot position. The length of the stride depends on the specific muscles you want to affect. A long stride with a straight back left leg will stress and stretch the quads as you're tightening your buttock. The forward leg muscles—a tight contraction in the right buttock— and the "teardrop" quad—will be greatly affected as well as the entire inner thigh.

(D) Movement Variations. Vary the length of your stride from set to set. A different overall effect, shorten the stride and bend both legs. Also try several reps per leg before switching to the other leg.

(16) SISSY SQUATS

(A) Emphasis. Sissy squats intensely stretch and stress the quadriceps muscles, giving them a totally finished look. Sissy squats don't build muscle mass in the quads, but they do rip the frontal thighs to shreds.

(B) Starting Position. You can perform sissy squats anywhere in the gym where you have a sturdy upright to grasp with one hand to balance your body during the movement. However, you will find it easiest to perfrom sissy squats if you stand between the dipping bars in your gym, since you can use these bars to balance your body with both hands. Set your feet about shoulder width apart and grasp either the parallel bars themselves or the upright posts attached to the bars.

(C) Exercise Performance. You must do four things in concert to reach the correct stretched position in a sissy-squat rep: (1) rise up on your toes; (2) incline your torso backward until it is at approximately a 45-degree angle with the floor; (3) bend your legs to at least a right angle; and (4) thrust your knees as far in front of your ankles as possible. When you do this movement correctly, you will feel a very strong stretching sensation in your quads. Return to the starting position by reversing the procedure you used to reach the bottom point of the exercise. Continue the movement for the appropriate number of reps.

(D) Movement Variations. Many bodybuilders do partial reps of this movement, either from the bottom of the exercise up to the halfway point (the most difficult version by far), or from the halfway point to the top position. Or you can do "Twenty-one Sissy squats," in which you first do seven reps from the midpoint to the top of the movement, seven from the bottom position to the midpoint, and finally seven complete reps. This is really a thigh burner! You ought to try this exercise immediately after a set of leg extensions!

Start.

Finish.

(17) STANDING LEG CURLS

(A) Emphasis. Most gyms now feature a leg curl machine on which you can do leg curls in a standing position with one leg at a time to isolate resistance on your hamstring muscles. You will feel a stress in your leg biceps when doing standing leg curls that is much different from the type of stress you feel performing the same movement in the usual prone position.

(B) Starting Position. Stand with your left knee against the padded surface set at knee height and wedge your left heel against the roller pad on the right side of the standing leg curl machine. Grasp the uprights of the machine to steady your body in position during the movement.

(C) Exercise Performance. Slowly bend your left leg as completely as possible, holding the fully contracted position of the movement for a moment to intensify the peak contraction effect of the rep. Lower slowly back to the starting point and repeat the movement for the suggested number of repetitions.

(D) Movement Variations. I like to do partial movements of this exercise, from the halfway point of the exercise up to the fully contracted position. If you have access to both lying and standing leg curl machines, you should definitely use both types of apparatus in your leg biceps workouts, since they both stress the hamstrings from unique angles.

CALF EXERCISES

(18) DONKEY CALF RAISES

(A) Emphasis. To many this exercise has an amusing appearance, but it is nonetheless a very direct and intense movement for stressing the gastrocnemius muscles of your calves.

(B) Starting Position. Place the balls of your feet on a calf block and rest your forehead and arms on a high padded bench. (You can also lean over with your torso held parallel to the floor and rest your hands on a flat exercise bench to support your body in position during the movement.) Have a heavy training partner sit up astride your hips, almost like a cowboy riding

Start.

Finish.

a horse, to provide resistance against your calves. Sag your heels as far below the level of your toes as possible to stretch your calves at the start of the movement.

(C) Exercise Performance. Slowly rise up on your toes as high as possible, return to the starting point, and repeat the movement.

(D) Movement Variations. You can angle your feet in different directions as you do this movement or, better yet, rotate your foot positions during a movement in the manner I've previously described. If your partner is too lightweight, he or she can hold addi-

tional weight against your lower back as you do your set—or invite someone else to hop on!

ADVANCED TRAINING ROUTINES

In this final section of training programs I will give you four-day, five-day, and six-day split routines that you can try out in your bodybuilding workouts. You should also look in Chapter 9 to see one of my personal precontest training routines.

Four-Day Split Routine

MONDAY AND THURSDAY

	Exercise	Sets	Reps
(1)	Hanging leg raises	3	10–15
(2)	Gravity boot sit-ups	3	10–15
(3)	Gravity boot side sit-ups	3	10–15
(4)	Incline machine press	3	6–10
(5)	Flat-bench cable flyes	2	8–12
(6)	Cable crossovers	2	10–15
(7)	Seated pulley rowing	3	8–12
(8)	Pull-downs behind neck	3	8–12
(9)	Stiff-arm pull-downs	2	8–12
(10)	Barbell upright rows	3	8–12
(11)	Alternate dumbbell presses	3	6–10
(12)	Cable side laterals	2	8–12
(13)	Cable bent laterals	2	8–12
(14)	Donkey calf raises	3	15–20

TUESDAY AND FRIDAY

	Exercise	Sets	Reps
(1)	Roman chair sit-ups	3	25–30
(2)	Bench leg raises	3	25–50
(3)	Seated twisting	3	50
(4)	Standing leg curls	3	10–15
(5)	Hack-machine squats	3	10–15
(6)	Sissy squats	3	10–15
(7)	Lying leg curls	3	10–15
(8)	Fourth-position lunges ("Bugs Bunny" lunges)	3	10–15
(9)	Alternate dumbbell curls	3	8–12
(10)	One-arm pulley curls	3	8–12

Exercise		Sets	Reps
(11)	Triceps push-downs	3	8–12
(12)	Two-arm dumbbell triceps extensions	3	8–12
(13)	Barbell wrist curls	3	10–15
(14)	Barbell reverse wrist curls	3	10–15
(15)	Seated calf raises	3	10–15
(16)	One-legged calf raises	2	15–20

Five-Day Split Routine

DAY ONE

Exercise		Sets	Reps
(1)	Bent-knee sit-ups	3	20–30
(2)	Jackknives	3	15–20
(3)	Crunches	3	20–30
(4)	Incline dumbbell flyes	3	8–12
(5)	Machine decline presses	3	6–10
(6)	Cross-bench pullovers	3	8–12
(7)	One-arm cable crossovers	2	10–15
(8)	Leg extensions	3	10–15
(9)	Squats	3	10–15
(10)	Lunges	3	10–15
(11)	Standing leg curls	3	10–15
(12)	Lying leg curls	3	10–15
(13)	Dumbbell wrist curls	3	10–15
(14)	Dumbbell reverse wrist curls	3	10–15
(15)	Standing calf raises	3	10–15
(16)	Calf presses	3	15–20

DAY TWO

Exercise		Sets	Reps
(1)	Roman chair sit-ups	3	25–30
(2)	Hanging leg raises	3	10–15
(3)	Crunches	3	20–25
(4)	Close-grip lat pull-downs	3	8–12
(5)	One-arm dumbbell bent rows	3	8–12
(6)	Front lat pull-down	3	8–12
(7)	Barbell upright rows	3	8–12
(8)	Military presses	3	6–10
(9)	Dumbbell side laterals	3	8–12
(10)	Cable bent laterals	3	8–12
(11)	Pulley preacher curls	3	8–12
(12)	Standing dumbbell concentration curls	3	8–12
(13)	High-pulley leaning triceps extensions	3	8–12
(14)	Triceps dips between benches	3	8–12
(15)	Seated calf raises	3	10–15

MONDAY AND THURSDAY (Day One)

	Exercise	Sets	Reps
(1)	Hanging leg raises	3	10–15
(2)	Gravity boot sit-ups	3	10–15
(3)	Incline barbell presses	3	6–10
(4)	Decline machine presses	2	6–10
(5)	Flat-bench cable flyes	2	8–12
(6)	Cross-bench dumbbell pullovers	3	8–12
(7)	T-bar bent rows	3	8–12
(8)	Pull-downs behind neck	3	8–12
(9)	Seated pulley rowing	2	8–12
(10)	Gravity-boot inverted barbell rowing	2	10–15
(11)	Seated calf raises	3	10–15
(12)	One-legged calf raises	3	10–15

TUESDAY AND FRIDAY (Day Two)

	Exercise	Sets	Reps
(1)	Roman chair sit-ups	3	20–30
(2)	Bench leg raises	3	20–30
(3)	Crunches	3	20–30
(4)	Leg extensions	3	10–15
(5)	Hack-machine squats	3	10–15
(6)	Side lunges	3	10–15
(7)	Leg presses	3	10–15
(8)	Lying leg curls	3	10–15
(9)	Stiff-legged deadlifts	3	10–15
(10)	Dumbbell wrist curls	3	10–15
(11)	Barbell reverse wrist curls	3	10–15

WEDNESDAY AND SATURDAY (Day Three)

	Exercise	Sets	Reps
(1)	Knee-ups (as a warm-up)	3	30–50
(2)	Barbell upright rows	3	10–15
(3)	Military presses (as a warm-up)	1	15–20
(4)	Nautilus side laterals	3	8–12
(5)	Nautilus presses	3	6–10
(6)	Cable side laterals	2	8–12
(7)	Dumbbell seated bent laterals	3	8–12
(8)	Standing barbell curls	3	8–12

Exercise		Sets	Reps
(9)	Alternate dumbbell curls	3	8–12
(10)	Barbell reverse curls	3	8–12
(11)	Triceps push-downs	3	8–12
(12)	Dumbbell triceps extensions	3	8–12
(13)	Cable triceps kickbacks	2	8–12
(14)	Barbell wrist curls	3	10–15
(15)	Standing calf raises	3	15–20
(16)	Calf presses	3	15–20

Training with Four-Day Cycles

The foregoing six-day split routine can be adapted for use in the four-day training cycle that is so popular among champion bodybuilders these days. In this cycle you split your body into three parts (note the "Day One," "Day Two," and "Day Three" designations for each of the three segments of the routines), train each part on three successive days, rest the fourth day, then begin the cycle anew on the fifth training day. This routine allows a bit more recuperation time between workouts than a six-day split routine does, so it is often better for use in the off-season when attempting to build greater muscle mass.

This program often involves training on weekends, but it may fit your personality and unique physical needs better than the six-day split routine. You should give it a trial in the off-season and determine how well it works for you.

LOOKING AHEAD

In the next chapter I will discuss the topic of bodybuilding nutrition. Subjects covered include weight-gain dieting; fat-loss dieting; the vegetarian diet; the macrobiotic diet; the cytotoxic diet; when to eat; food supplementation; protein foods and protein requirements; red versus white meats; simple versus complex carbohydrates; my favorite bodybuilding recipes; and my typical off-season and precontest diets.

Photo by Luke Wynn

CHAPTER 8

bodybuilding nutrition

Food is an external stimulus to which your body invariably responds relatively quickly, and each type of food causes a different biochemical reaction in your body. If you constantly eat fatty, highly processed foods, your body will become soft, flabby, and shapeless. But if you eat fresh, wholesome, and natural bodybuilding foods, your body will be lean, strong, and healthy, the way it's supposed to look. Therefore, in terms of nutrition, the choice is yours: You can look like a jelly doughnut, or you can achieve a lean and physically attractive appearance. Seriously, there are some absolutes that we must accept at one point or another, and the direct effect that food has on our physical appearances is one of them. Sadly enough, or happily enough, the choice is yours. Read on.

LIFE–STYLE DIET

To some women a bodybuilding diet—particularly in the last few weeks before a major competition—can seem rather bland-tasting. At first it may seem difficult to eat exclusively for function as a bodybuilder, but it soon becomes an agreeable part of your lifestyle. I enjoy the taste of fresh, natural bodybuilding foods as much as the taste of chocolate ice cream, and I must confess that I happen to be a closet chocoholic.

You can feel the same as I do toward good bodybuilding foods if you simply accept the fact that you must eat them regularly—*and* avoid junk foods just as regularly—if you genuinely desire to become a champion bodybuilder. It will be easier to accept this burden if you use the visualization methods that I will discuss in Chapter 11.

You needn't become an automaton totally devoted to maintaining a strict bodybuilding diet 365 days a year, however. You really don't have to sacrifice that much food, rest, and comfort in getting ready for a competition *if* you go about it intelligently. The key for me is maintaining a 1,500-calorie-a-day diet for four to six weeks prior to a competition, the length of my peaking cycle, depending on the relative excellence of my off-season physique.

Additionally, I don't think that many women do as

much aerobic training each day as I do to burn off excess, definition-blurring fat in the off-season. It's vitally important that you stay within five pounds of your best precontest weight during an off-season cycle, so you *must* keep your off-season body weight to a minimum.

Close to a competition, I will drink wine virtually every evening. Wine is good for relaxation, and I really enjoy quality wines and champagne. Wine isn't very high in calories, so it's quite easy to drink a glass of champagne or Pinot Chardonnay and still consume less than 1,500 calories for the day. And white wine has a mildly beneficial diuretic effect on your body.

Like every bodybuilder on a diet, I have occasional cravings for certain foods, but I never abuse my body by eating junk food without a purpose. A craving is usually a good indication that my body requires the nutrients I crave, so I eat them. But I'm also sure the day after eating some sweets or other junk food to take a long, heavy workout to burn up the excess calories left in my bloodstream and liver.

As a practical example of why I might have a junk-food meal, a few days before writing this chapter I felt that I had to eat four scoops of chocolate ice cream. When I reviewed my training diary entries, I saw that I consumed very little dietary fat over the previous four days. My body was craving the fats in ice cream, so it was only natural for me to scarf it down.

Like training, bodybuilding nutrition is not an exact science. It does have a few scientifically proven general guidelines on how you should eat, but your unique body will react a little differently from my own or that of any other bodybuilder. Therefore you'll need to conduct a number of experiments over the next few months, meticulously record the results of each experiment in your training diary, then use your training instinct to develop a personal philosophy of bodybuilding nutrition.

This chapter includes discussions of the major nutrients that you must understand in order to become a champion. It also includes discussions of off-season diet, when to eat, the sodium balance, vegetarian diet, cytotoxic diet, food supplementation, red meat versus white meat, simple versus complex carbohydrates, and my exact personal diet. Finally, I have included in this chapter many of my favorite bodybuilding recipes.

You should use this chapter as a springboard for future readings about nutrition. There are many books available in health food stores, and all of the major bodybuilding magazines sold on newsstands regularly publish articles on nutrition. You'll discover a lot of conflicting advice in these publications, so compare each new bit of information with what you already know about nutrition and check the references to make sure that the authors are presenting documented evidence.

Remember, eat for function, because the texture of your flesh will probably resemble the texture of your food (remember the jelly doughnut?).

NUTRIENT CLASSIFICATIONS

There are seven basic classifications of foods that must be consumed by humans: protein, carbohydrates, fats, vitamins, minerals, fiber, and water. In order to maintain optimal health and hence to continue making good bodybuilding gains, you must consume adequate quantities of each of these seven classes of food.

For "normal" men and women, health can be maintained by eating one or more servings from each of four general food groups: milk and milk products; meat, fish, chicken, eggs, and other protein foods; fruits and vegetables; and grains and cereals. Active bodybuilders, however, must eat with greater care and precision in order to allow their bodies to add muscle mass at an acceptable rate.

Protein

Protein is an essential factor in any bodybuilder's diet, since all muscle tissue (to say nothing of other body tissues, organs, the blood, skin, hair, and such body secretions as hormones and enzymes) are made up of protein. The US Food and Drug Administration (FDA) recommends 1 gram of protein per kilogram (2.2 pounds) of body weight each day as an adult minimum daily requirement (AMDR). This amounts to approximately ½ gram of protein per pound of body weight.

There is evidence that physically active people require a greater daily protein intake. As a result, I believe that hard-training bodybuilders should consume approximately 1 gram of high-quality protein per pound of body weight each day. This is the amount of protein I personally try to consume each day, both in off-season and precontest cycles, and I have made very good bodybuilding gains on similar amounts of dietary protein intake, although it is difficult for me.

Don't make the mistake of eating excessive amounts of protein, however, because a chronically excessive protein intake is potentially damaging to your kidneys. Certainly there are a few unethical promoters in the health food industry, and they will tell you that you need between 200 and 250 grams of protein supplements per day. These salesmen are operating all over the world, so beware.

The quality of protein that you consume is important. The protein in human muscle tissue contains twenty-two different amino acids, eight of which cannot be manufactured in the body and must be consumed in the food you eat. These eight amino acids are termed essential amino acids. Foods from animal sources (e.g., meat, fish, chicken, milk, and eggs) contain good supplies of the eight essential amino acids, which makes them ideal bodybuilding protein foods.

With the exception of soybeans and sprouted seeds or grains, vegetable-source proteins lack sufficient quantities of one or more essential amino acids. And even soybeans and sprouts have relatively low levels of some essential amino acids.

Due to their poor amino acid balance, vegetable-source proteins are of lesser value to bodybuilders for building muscles unless they are consumed in combination with animal proteins that help to "complete" the amino acid balance of the vegetable protein by lending missing amino acids. The best combinations of animal and vegetable proteins are milk and rice, milk and corn, and milk and beans. Actually, any animal source of protein will complete any insufficient form when taken together.

There are a number of successful vegetarian bodybuilders, but these men and women consume milk and/or eggs with their vegetarian foods. I will discuss vegetarian bodybuilding a bit later in this chapter.

Carbohydrates

Carbohydrates are the natural sugars found in large quantities in fruits and vegetables. Because of a number of low-carbohydrate diets that became popular during the late 1960's and early 1970's, carbohydrates were undeservedly given a bad name. In reality they are a valuable part of the diet of any serious bodybuilder.

While your body can convert protein and fats into workout energy, its preferred source of energy is carbohydrates. The sugars in carbohydrates are easily broken down into glycogen, or blood sugar, which is then used to power your muscles through a heavy workout.

I consume plenty of carbohydrate foods throughout the year, regardless of whether I am in an off-season or precontest cycle. I probably consume more carbs than protein, but I vary the amount of fats I consume from cycle to cycle. When I am trying to cut up, I decrease only the amount of fats in my diet. Of course, I also increase the amount of aerobic training I perform each day.

Fats

Fats are a very concentrated source of energy. Each gram of fat yields approximately nine calories when metabolized in your body for energy. Compare this with the four calories yielded by a gram of either protein or carbohydrate, and you can see how concentrated a source of energy fats actually are. Consequently you can most easily reduce your intake of calories when on a diet by curtailing the amount of fat you consume.

Your body needs a certain amount of fat in order to function properly, particularly in terms of maintaining the health of your nervous system. You also need dietary fat to help utilize the fat-soluble vitamins: A, D, E, and K.

There are two types of dietary fats, unsaturated fats and saturated fats. Unsaturated fats, which are found in vegetable, seed, nut, and grain oils, are the more healthy type for a bodybuilder to consume. The lipotropic factors in such vegetable oils as safflower oil will even help you metabolize body fat for energy.

The saturated fats found in meat, milk products, egg yolks, and coconut are more harmful to your body. Many researchers have targeted saturated fats as a leading culprit in cardiovascular disease. This fact—coupled with the high caloric content of fatty meats—has led many bodybuilders to abandon eating red meats. While I eat red meat from time to time, the bulk of my protein comes from white meats, like chicken, turkey, and fish; nonfat milk products; and egg whites.

Fiber

Fiber is an undigestible form of carbohydrate found in fruits and vegetables. It is sometimes called roughage. Fiber is essential for proper digestion and the elimination of waste products through the bowel system. Scientific studies have indicated that societies in which dietary fiber intake is high suffer from far fewer diseases of the digestive tract than societies that consume less fiber.

You should include regular servings of high-fiber foods in your diet. The easiest way to do this is to consume bran cereal, bran muffins, raw vegetables, and such high-roughage fruits as pears. A new discovery I have recently made is psyllium seed husks. They have zero calories, are *great* for digestion, and add body to some of my favorite recipes, which I'll tell you about later.

Vitamins and Minerals

Vitamins and minerals are micronutrients found in all of the foods that you eat and particularly in fresh fruits, vegetables, nuts, seeds, and grains. The FDA insists that a balanced diet will provide you with all of the vitamins and minerals that you require each day for optimal health. However, with the highly processed nature of food today, it's unlikely that a physically active bodybuilder can acquire adequate vitamins and minerals from a normally "balanced" diet.

On the other hand, I don't feel that you need to go overboard in supplementing your diet with vitamins and minerals. I've known many aspiring bodybuilders who spent literally hundreds of dollars a month on vitamins and minerals (I used to be one of them!), a large share of which merely gave them the most expensive urine in the sport. Food supplements should be *supplements,* not replacements for wholesome food.

One or two multipacks of vitamins and minerals per day will be adequate nutritional supplementation for any active bodybuilder, except perhaps during a precontest cycle. It's always best to consume your supplemental vitamins and minerals *with* a meal, since they will be more efficiently assimilated when accompanied by natural food.

Incidently, if you do incur a nutritional deficiency, it will most likely be a mineral deficiency. In hard training, you will perspire freely and slough off minerals in your perspiration, particularly potassium, calcium, magnesium, and sodium. A deficiency in any of these minerals, especially potassium, will be reflected by a decrease in energy. If you feel weak and lacking in energy, simply supplement your diet with these minerals.

Water

Water makes up the largest share of your body, and you must drink sufficient quantities of pure water each day to maintain a healthy water balance within your body. If you are training hard and perspiring freely, you will need to drink even more water than is normal for sedentary individuals.

The amount of water you drink each day can vary according to your body mass and relative work output. Normally you should drink six to ten glasses of water daily. Merely drinking water when you feel thirsty, even if this occurs in the middle of a fast-paced workout, will not always ensure that you consume enough fluid. I have never considered myself a drinker—of water or anything else—and although I know in my head the importance of enough water in my system, the thought of forcing water down my throat makes me gag. Actually, the very act of attempting to force down my eighth glass of water to meet my daily quota *does* make me gag. The lesson I've learned is to pace myself: Upon rising in the morning I have my first shot of water—*before* my coffee or tea; after breakfast, same thing; before and after lunch—you guessed it; during and after my workout—right again. Before dinner and after dinner, H$_2$O for the last time. In fact, this was one of my 1984 resolutions, and I intend to keep it. The benefits are really remarkable: My digestion is like clockwork, which in turn keeps my system clean and pure. A great side benefit is a beautifully clear complexion too! I thought I was destined to have zits the rest of my life. Thank goodness I was wrong!

MUSCLE GAIN DIET

In order to gain muscle mass as quickly as possible, you must train with heavy weights and consume a diet rich in high-quality carbohydrate and protein foods. Unfortunately eating the traditional two or three meals a day will not provide your trained muscles with enough protein to allow them to grow in mass and strength at the fastest rate. It takes a special diet, as outlined in this section, to provide your body with the greatest possible amount of protein for muscle building, and carbs for muscle contractions.

Under normal circumstances your body can digest and make available for assimilation into muscle tissue only about 20 grams of protein each time you eat. The amount can vary slightly as a function of your body weight and relative digestive efficiency. Still, you are limited in the amount of protein your digestive system can process when you eat only two or three meals per day.

If you eat three meals per day, then your body will digest only about 60 grams of protein. But what if you eat five or six meals per day? That would allow your body to process nearly twice as much protein each day, which would then be available in the blood stream in greater amounts than normally possible for increasing muscle tissue.

The best way to follow such a dietary plan is to eat three small meals at your normal meal times, then consume two or three snacks between meals. Be sure that each of your meals and snacks contains approximately 20 grams of protein and no more, since eating too much food at each meal will actually reduce the amount of protein your body can process.

Here is a tasty and time-tested protein drink recipe that you can whip up in a minute in a blender:

8 ounces of raw milk (preferably nonfat)
1 tablespoon of egg-white protein powder
1 piece of soft fruit for flavoring
1 teaspoon of psyllium husk

My favorite fruits for protein drinks are fresh peaches, strawberries, and bananas.

And here is a sample daily menu for maximum protein digestion and absorption that you can try out and modify to suit your own needs:

Meal 1 (8:00 A.M.)—3 soft-boiled eggs (toss out 1 yolk), whole grain toast, glass of nonfat milk or fresh juice, multipack of vitamins and minerals
Meal 2 (11:00 A.M.)—protein drink
Meal 3 (1:00 P.M.)—tuna salad, piece of fruit, glass of milk

Meal 4 (4:00 P.M.)—protein drink
Meal 5 (7:00 P.M.)—broiled chicken, rice, herbal tea (with lemon or fructose sweetening), multipack of vitamins and minerals
Meal 6 (10:00 P.M.)—cold cuts or hard-boiled eggs.

You can experiment with the sixth meal in this program. If you discover that it's difficult to sleep when you eat this late in the evening—or late meals tend to add to existing body fat levels—feel free to drop the sixth meal from your program and substitute it with free-form L-amino acids.

To a degree it is also possible to increase the amount of protein that your body is able to digest after each meal. This is done by consuming digestive supports such as enzymes and hydrochloric acid tablets with each meal. These digestive supports can't add more than 5 to 10 percent to the amount of protein digested, but they *may* add enough to be of value to you.

There are a number of digestive-enzyme preparations available at health food stores. The most commonly used is papain, the digestive enzyme found in papaya. Usually multivitamin packs include these digestive aids with the other concentrated nutrients; read the label to make sure.

For most women bodybuilders the diet outlined in this section is appropriate for use during an off-season cycle. The exception to this rule is a woman who consistently experiences great difficulty in achieving contest-level muscularity. She should follow a low-calorie diet during both off-season and precontest cycles, unless she prefers to gauge her fat level by increasing her activity levels with low-intensity aerobics.

FAT–LOSS DIET

The only sure way to lose body fat is to eat fewer total calories than your body burns each day. One pound of body fat represents 3,500 stored calories; therefore you must create a caloric deficit of 3,500 to lose one pound of fat, whether you intend to lose this body fat to regain your youthful and sensuous body or to gain greater muscular definition for an upcoming bodybuilding competition.

There are two basic ways in which to create a caloric deficit: (1) Eat less calories each day; and (2) use up more calories in daily physical activity. In practice it's best to use a combination of these two techniques to create a caloric deficit sufficient enough to burn off between one and two pounds of body fat each week. While it is possible to lose fat at a faster pace than this, you could harm you body if you do so, and it's not very much fun.

As hinted at earlier, it's easiest to cut your caloric intake by reducing the amount of fat you consume each day. Merely replacing beef and/or pork in your diet with poultry (remove the fatty skin before cooking it, however) and/or fish will result in a substantial reduction in the number of calories you consume each day. You should also avoid salad and cooking oils, ice cream, egg yolks, full-fat milk and milk products, and all other fatty foods when attempting to restrict your caloric intake.

Here is a sample low-fat, low-calorie weight-reduction plan for one day:

Breakfast—egg whites (cooked without oil or butter), bran cereal with nonfat milk, coffee or tea with lemon, multipack of vitamins and minerals
Lunch—tuna salad made with water-packed tuna and a minimum of low-calorie mayonnaise, slice of melon, iced tea with lemon and/or sweetener substitute
Dinner—broiled chicken breast, steamed rice, salad with vinegar as a dressing, iced tea, multipack of vitamins and minerals
Snacks—cold chicken or turkey breast, fresh low-calorie fruit, nonfat yogurt, raw vegetables.

You should monitor your relative energy levels and adjust your caloric intake upward or downward according to how you feel. When you have developed a correct caloric deficit, you should feel *slightly* fatigued throughout the day. However, if you have gone too deeply into caloric debt, you will feel quite fatigued and experience hunger pangs. Those sensations should be avoided, since they will lead to binge eating and the ultimate defeat of any weight-loss diet. I know it's time-consuming to record your food intake on paper; however, you'll be glad you did months later when you're thinking back on how you can get into such fantastic shape again.

After two weeks of strict dieting, you can feel free to have a healthy serving of a high-fat food such as ice cream every five or six days. That will help you to keep your sanity without spoiling your weight-loss momentum. It is only by regularly overeating that you grow obese, and an occasional treat won't spoil your chances of reducing body-fat levels.

Remember that you should also try to burn calories through exercise to enhance the caloric deficit that you develop with a low-calorie diet. You should concentrate primarily on aerobic activity, since only aerobic work burns calories derived from body fat. Anaerobic exercise, such as hard bodybuilding training, burns only glycogen from the muscles, bloodstream, and liver. On the other hand, low-intensity aerobic exercise is an excellent method of melting off unwanted fat.

For most women bodybuilders the low-fat, low-calorie diet discussed in this section is suitable for use during a precontest cycle. In combination with plenty of aerobic training it will strip all vestiges of visible fat from your body.

Carbohydrate Loading

Many bodybuilders follow a plan of carbohydrate deprivation followed by carbohydrate loading during the last week before a competition. For three of four days they eat a minimal amount of carbohydrates and train nearly to exhaustion. Then, for twenty-four to thirty-six hours, they increase carbohydrate consumption. The carbohydrate-loading plan, when correctly used, will give you full-appearing muscles, prominent vascularity, and sharp muscularity.

There are a couple of tricks you should master when carbo loading. The first is that your physique will appear flat and lacking in mass during the carbohydrate-deprivation phase of this cycle, particularly on the last day before beginning to load up on carbos. Unless you expect this to happen, it will depress you so much that you will consider dropping out of the competition.

Second, you must experiment with the amounts of carbohydrate eaten while loading, as well as with the time you begin carbohydrate loading. You must avoid refined and simple carbohydrate foods; instead, eat only the complex carbohydrates in potatoes, vegetables, and some fruit. If you consume more than 1 to 1½ grams of carbohydrate per pound of body weight each twenty-four-hour period that you load, you will probably discover that your glycogen-depleted liver and muscles will fill up with sugar, after which excess carbodydrates will help to accumulate excess water beneath your skin. So the trick is to eat just enough carbohydrates to fill out your muscles, but not enough for water to spill over into other tissues.

It's also a good idea to restrict water intake to the point of feeling moderately thirsty all day for one or two days prior to competing. Combined with an influx of carbohydrates, water restriction actually diverts water from your skin and other interstitial tissues to your muscles, which results in much sharper muscularity.

Sodium Regulation

The mineral sodium has a great affinity for water; indeed, it can hold more than fifty times its weight in water. Therefore, when you have excess sodium in your body just prior to competition, you will retain too much water, spoiling your muscularity. It's essential that you learn to control your sodium intake while peaking. Even if you have no desire to peak for a competition, you may have a very important interview for a new job, or you may be planning to look your very best for a special date or to fit into a form-fitting outfit. Well, salt can mean the difference between what you want to look like and total disaster. Excess salt for the average person causes puffy eyes, feet, and fingers, and a general overall swollen look. Be very careful to fluctuate your sodium intake and, for the most part, keep it to a minimum.

There are several nutrition books that list the sodium content of a wide variety of foods, and you should study one regularly until you have a thorough knowledge of which high-sodium foods to avoid in your diet. Table salt is the biggest offender among sodium foods, but such seemingly innocent foods as celery are quite high in sodium.

You must reduce sodium intake to an absolute minimum for the final four days before a show, as well as during the day of your competition. Up to the four-day point, however, I personally maintain a normal intake of dietary sodium. I will even drink a margarita, complete with salt, from time to time. To most serious bodybuilders this revelation will be heresy, but there's a valid reason why I consume salt during a peaking cycle.

By taking detailed notes of each peaking attempt,

I have learned that my body becomes hypersensitive to sodium when I restrict it in my diet for more than a few weeks. Even a small slip in my sodium regulation can result in a high degree of water retention when I have been restricting sodium. In contrast, my body doesn't hold nearly as much water when sodium is a regular part of my diet. So, by restricting sodium intake for only four days, I can more or less trick my body into briefly holding less water than it would under normal conditions. Give this method a try and see if it works equally well for you.

Final Precontest Meals

It's advantageous to have a small waist when onstage competing, so you should consume only low-bulk, quickly digested foods during the day before and day of your contest. For example, chicken and fish are much more easily digested than fatty beef, and a piece of dried fruit (be certain that it contains no sulfur or sodium) is much smaller in bulk than its fresh counterpart. You might also consume high-fiber foods during the day before you compete in order to flush out your stomach and bowel system the next morning.

Many bodybuilders actively encourage a greater-than-normal bowel movement the morning of a competition to minimize waist size. This is most safely done by consuming naturally laxative fruit such as prunes the day before a show. Alternatively you can take a mild herbal laxative to encourage elimination. However, you should strictly avoid using harsh chemical laxatives.

VEGETARIAN DIET

I mentioned earlier in this chapter that there have been several sucessful lacto- and/or ovovegetarian bodybuilders. The *lacto-* prefix refers to the use of milk products in conjunction with a purely vegetarian diet, while *ovo-* refers to the use of eggs in a vegetarian diet. Of course, many vegetarians use both milk products and eggs in their diets.

The strictest form of vegetarian diet is called a vegan diet. Vegans consume only foods derived from vegetable sources, such as grains, seeds, nuts, fresh vegetables, fruit, and legumes. A vegan diet is so low in protein content that it would be difficult if not impossible for a serious bodybuilder to develop any high degree of muscle mass when following it. Indeed, I have never heard of a vegan bodybuilder who has won a title.

Several lactovegetarians have won bodybuilding titles, since the liberal addition of milk products to a vegan diet dramatically increases its protein content. The same holds true for an ovovegetarian diet. And the vegetarian diet highest in protein is a lacto-ovo-vegetarian regimen.

Since vegetarians eat primarily fresh, organically grown foods that have not been processed or refined, their diets help to promote health and increase personal energy levels. The diet is much lower in saturated fats than most other bodybuilding diets, so it particularly helps to prevent heart and vascular diseases. People who follow vegetarian diets also report increased aerobic endurance, reduced levels of aggression, less illness, more peace of mind, and less chronic joint soreness.

CYTOTOXIC DIET

One of the newest diets to gain wide popularity is the cytotoxic diet. The word *cytotoxic* is a hybrid of two words, *cyto-* (relating to the cell) and *-toxic* (capable of killing). Therefore cytotoxic foods are those that can kill cells in your body, and when they are eliminated from your diet you will experience fewer food-addiction problems, fewer illnesses and physical maladies, and fewer problems with excess body-water retention.

Cytotoxic foods are addictive, just as nicotine in tobacco is addictive. No one who smokes can tell you that their first cigarette was a pleasant experience. Because nicotine is a poison, it can cause nausea and a host of other unpleasant symptoms. But it can also cause the body's basic immune system to swing into action to eliminate the toxins brought into the body in tobacco smoke. The body literally goes into high gear to fight off the nicotine, which causes the person who just smoked the cigarette to experience a brief high. When this high abates, the person feels compelled to recreate it by smoking another cigarette. Soon the person is literally addicted to smoking, a major reason why it is so difficult to quit the habit.

Your body is also allergic to cytotoxic foods, although in a mild manner. You won't get hives right after you eat a cytotoxic food, but that food nonetheless subtly damages your body. When you eat a cytotoxic food, your body goes into high gear to eliminate the toxins in it, giving you a subtle high. You may not consciously notice this high, but your subconscious mind takes due note of it and induces you to eat frequently the food that results in the high. As a result, cytotoxic foods are just as addictive as nicotine.

A large number of physical and psychological maladies can be caused by chronic consumption of cytotoxic foods. Some of these maladies are body infections (leading to acne and other ills), inflammations (including arthritis), lack of energy, binge eating, nervousness, insomnia, irritability, excessive accumulations of mucus, slurring of words, diminished neuromotor coordination, itching ears, joint and muscle pains, body-water retention, frequent urges to urinate, and chronic depression.

To precisely identify your allergenic foods, you must have a sample of your blood analyzed. The white blood cells are removed from your whole blood, then placed on microscope slides with concentrates derived from more than one hundred fundamental foods. I say "fundamental" because, for example, you will be allergic to all milk products—hard cheese, cottage cheese, yogurt, ice cream, butter, and so forth—if you are allergic to whole milk. Therefore only whole milk must be tested.

After two hours a technician examines the white blood cells on each slide. If there is no allergy to the food being tested, the cells will retain their normal shapes. But if a moderate food allergy exists, the outline of the cell wall will be distorted. With a serious allergy the cell wall will actually rupture.

This test is widely available from physicians who practice internal medicine, as well as from many general practitioners. The cost of the test ranges in price from about $50 to more than $300 at some clinics.

If you lack the financial means to have a cytotoxic test done, or can't find a physician to give you the test, it is possible to determine allergenic foods by careful observation and note taking. For example, one prominent cytotoxic expert estimates that 90 percent of all men and women are allergic to milk products and/or grains, and merely eliminating those foods from your diet will lessen the cytotoxic impact on your body.

To discover your allergenic foods, you must restrict your food intake to only two or three basic foods per day, taking note of how you feel and how your body reacts the day after eating those foods. If you have a headache, are irritable, or experience any of the symptoms listed earlier in this section, you are probably allergic to one of the foods you consumed. If you experience more than two or three symptoms, you are certainly allergic to one or more of the foods. You can determine the cytotoxic culprit by eating the foods that caused a reaction in conjunction with other foods and noting new reactions.

You may need to spend one or two weeks manipulating food combinations to discover each cytotoxic food. Even then your determination won't be as precise as that revealed in a laboratory test, so I recommend taking the cytotoxic blood test if at all possible.

Once you have identified your cytotoxic foods, you should immediately eliminate them from your diet. You should also rotate your foods, attempting not to consume the same food two days in a row. Rotation is important because research and observation has revealed that people favor eating cytotoxic foods, and that eating a food too frequently can cause it to turn cytotoxic.

It normally takes four or five days to break a cytotoxic food addiction, and you won't feel very good those first few days. Chances are good that the withdrawal process will give you a persistent headache. You will also probably experience acute symptoms of cytotoxic poisoning, such as very sore joints. Stick it out, however, because around the fifth or sixth day on a cytotoxic diet you will experience a rejuvention of your body. You will look and feel markedly better than when you eat allergenic foods, and all of your cytotoxic symptoms will quickly abate. As a side effect, you will probably lose about five pounds of weight per week for the first two weeks you're on the cytotoxic diet, primarily from a reduction in bodywater retention.

The cytotoxic diet's ability to minimize water retention makes it ideal for use during a peaking cycle. Eliminating allergenic foods from your diet quickly and dramatically decreases water retention, so at a minimum you should eliminate milk products and grains from your diet the final week before you compete. You'll notice the difference if you do!

FASTING

Fasting has been highly touted as a means of losing excess body fat and cleansing the body. As a result, I tried fasting for three days prior to a competition, eating nothing and drinking only water in an attempt to drop a couple of stubborn pounds that were preventing me from looking my best. I *did* lose four pounds, but in the process I sacrificed more muscle tissue than fat, which resulted in a worse physical appearance than if I hadn't fasted at all!

It's little wonder that I don't recommend fasting for weight loss, particularly prior to a competition. For internal body cleansing, however, you can use a special type of juice fast for one or two days with very good results. However, you should only undertake a cleansing fast once a month at the most, and then only during an off-season cycle.

When following a juice fast, you simply drink diluted fruit and vegetable juices whenever you feel hungry during the day. It's best to avoid juices that are high in acid content, e.g., citrus juices and tomato juice, since they can result in a brief episode of gouty arthritis. But if you drink nonacid juices throughout the day, you will experience very little hunger and only a minimal decrease in energy.

Follow a juice fast no longer than three days, and be careful to break slowly back into eating a normal diet once you're off the fast. Break the fast for the first day by eating only soups, light breads, and one or two pieces of light fruit. Then by the second day you can resume normal eating, knowing that you have cleaned out your digestive system and made it much more efficient than it was prior to your fast.

WHEN TO EAT

There is a host of research that "proves" eating late in the day promotes storage of body fat. As a result, many women who are on a diet, as well as bodybuilders on a precontest diet, carefully avoid eating even a morsel of food after six in the evening. It would blow their minds to learn that I routinely eat dinner between nine and ten at night, and I have never had a problem with excess body-fat accumulation.

However, you must understand how active I am all

day, in order to appreciate why I can safely eat so late. My entire day is filled with workouts, business appointments, film and commercial work, and a myriad of other activities. I seldom have time—other than when peaking for a major bodybuilding competition—to do my aerobic workout during the day. I literally *can't* eat my dinner until nine or ten. I'm that busy.

The research I mentioned a moment ago revealed that there was an increase in body-fat stores because low levels of physical work and exercise during the evening hours failed to burn up the calories consumed. However, I normally do my daily aerobic workout—most frequently a half-hour session on the Lifecycle I have installed in my den—after eating each evening or first thing in the morning. This burns off any excess calories consumed at dinner, preventing them from making me fatter.

Unless you exercise after your evening meal, it would be best to follow the researchers' advice and consume your last food for the day no later than six or seven in the evening; this will prevent you from storing excess calories. But if you perform either your weight workout or an aerobic session late in the evening, you can eat later as long as you dine *before* you train.

With time you will instinctively discover that it's a poor practice to eat sooner than one hour after a workout or to train sooner than one hour after a meal. Research has proven that exercise dulls the appetite for up to one hour after a workout. And due to the digestive process, you will find yourself lacking in energy right after a meal. But the bottom line remains the same: Burn up more calories than you take in and you'll be okay, even if you eat at midnight every night.

FOOD SUPPLEMENTS

At the beginning of this chapter, I outlined the importance of supplementing your diet with one or two multipacks of vitamins, minerals, and trace elements each day during off-season training. Prior to a competition, however, your diet is fairly restricted, warranting inclusion of individual nutrient supplements.

Over a six-month to one-year period you can determine the relative effects of individual vitamins, minerals, and other nutrients on your bodybuilding progress. You must simply try each nutrient by itself for one or two weeks, taking careful note of its influence on your energy levels, rate of recuperation between workouts, speed of muscle hypertrophy, and so forth. But how do you know which supplements to test first?

In order of importance to a bodybuilder, here is a hierarchy of individual food supplements: vitamin C, vitamin B-complex, potassium, calcium, magnesium, dessicated liver, other individual minerals, and oil-soluble vitamins (A, D, E, K, and P). Generally speaking, it's most important to take those vitamins and minerals that are water-soluble. Oil-soluble vitamins are stored in body fat, then released into the system whenever too little of these nutrients is consumed.

It's worth noting that many health-conscious women, athletes, and bodybuilders use kelp and brewer's yeast supplements. The iodine in kelp is supposed to enhance the basal metabolic rate (BMR), but it actually has the opposite effect (physicians administer Lugol's solution, a liquid high in iodine content, to hyperthyroid patients to suppress the metabolic rate); however, kelp is a good source of minerals and trace elements.

People take brewer's yeast to add B-complex vitamins to their diet, but in reality brewer's yeast is a poor source of B vitamins. It is actually better to take synthetic B vitamins in tablet or capsule form, since synthetics have superior potencies of each B-complex vitamin.

During an off-season cycle—when you are attempting to balance your proportions and generally add mass to your physique—you can make good use of a protein supplement mixed according to the instructions presented earlier in this chapter. But you should discontinue use of protein supplements at least two weeks prior to a show, because protein drinks tend to bloat the body.

As you will recall, the best-quality protein comes from animal sources, so the optimal type of protein powder is derived from milk and eggs, usually with egg albumen making up the largest percentage of the powder. Proteins derived from yeast, soybeans, and other vegetable sources are definitely inferior to milk and egg proteins.

An even better source of protein supplementation, although a more expensive one, is a concoction of free-form amino acids that can be purchased in health food stores. These amino acids come in tablet, capsule, and powder form, and when consumed, they go almost directly into the bloodstream, where they can maintain a positive nitrogen balance in the body, resulting in a faster rate of hypertrophy.

I use massive amounts of amino acid capsules, particularly close to a competition, when I feel my protein requirements are higher than normal. It's quite easy to carry a handful of these capsules around with me during the day, taking them whenever I feel an energy lull or might miss a meal. They really work great! I'll probably supplement my diet with these free-form amino acids for the rest of my life.

RED VERSUS WHITE MEAT

While I occasionally enjoy having a serving of steak or some other type of red meat, I primarily eat the white meats from poultry and fish. White meat is considerably lower in calories than red meat, which makes it ideal for either maintaining or losing body fat. If you consume red meat frequently, you will discover that its high uric acid content will lead to chronically sore joints and cause you to be irritable. So it's best to consume primarily chicken, fish, and turkey as sources of animal protein.

TYPES OF CARBOHYDRATES

There are three general classifications of carbohydrate foods. The first of these is *refined* carbos, such as found in table sugar and white flour, as well as in any food made from these ingredients. Arnold Schwarzenegger rightly calls these foods "white death," and all serious bodybuilders should avoid eating them on any regular basis.

A second type of carbohydrate food is the *simple* carbs found primarily in fruit. This type of natural sugar is easily broken out of the foods you eat and transferred into the bloodstream. As a result, simple carbohydrates are an excellent source of "quick" energy fuel. When your energy reserves are being de-

Photo by Emmanuel Tanjala

pleted in a workout, you can often give them a quick refill by eating a piece of fruit in mid-workout.

You can gain a more sustained source of energy fuel by eating the *complex* carbohydrates found in grains and most vegetables. It takes your body longer to break these sugars loose from the food that you eat, which in turn yields a longer, more even energy release.

MY PERSONAL DIET

During the off-season I attempt to eat 1,600 to 1,700 calories per day and 75 to 100 grams of protein. The following is a sample menu illustrating how I personally eat in the off-season:

	Calories	Protein	Fat	Carbs
		(grams)	(grams)	(grams)
BREAKFAST				
• three scrambled eggs (only two yolks)	150	20	10	—
• dry whole wheat toast	120	1	—	28
• bran muffin	150	3	2	25
• coffee w/cocoa	50	—	3	9
SNACK				
• papaya (lots!) w/amino acids	150	8	—	35
LUNCH				
• tuna salad (*Flex Appeal* recipe)	170	30	2	6
• whole-wheat croissant	150	1	5	25
• iced tea (unsweetened)	0	—	—	—
SNACK				
• more tuna salad on a cracker	130	20	2	10
DINNER				
• half broiled chicken w/sauce (skin not removed prior to cooking [I forgot])	400	34	15	30
• half a chocolate bar [Darn it!]	150	2	8	17

TOTAL CALORIES = 1630
TOTAL GRAMS OF PROTEIN = 120

Prior to a competition, I drop the chocolate from my diet for approximately six weeks to reach a level of intake of 1,500 calories per day. Otherwise my diet is almost the same as it is during the off-season cycle.

FLEX APPEAL RECIPES

In this chapter I will give you four basic bodybuilding recipes with a number of variations, all of which add up to a great variety of dishes that you can either serve to yourself or the bodybuilder in your life.

The first recipe is for a delicious egg soufflé that you can have for breakfast. Depending on the ingredients, you can also use this soufflé as a delicious dessert or as the perfect between-meals snack. This is my favorite dish, and I've been experimenting with it for many years and exchanging ideas with my friend Jeanine back in Texas. We've come up with a number of "safe" bodybuilding soufflés that you can enjoy.

Basic Soufflé Recipe

Ingredient List

- 5–10 egg whites
- fruit (banana, papaya, pineapple, strawberries, etc.)
- powdered spices (cinnamon, cloves, allspice, etc.)
- powdered fructose or powdered sugar substitute (I prefer aspartame or Equal—this ingredient is optional, but I recommend it!)

Step One. Using a food processor or electric egg beater, whip up the egg whites until they are nice and fluffy (like meringue). Sprinkle in the sweetener as it's whipping up.

Step Two. In a nonstick Silverstone pan (spray it with Pam first for easier removal of the soufflé when it's done), cook diced fruit over a very low heat for 2 to 3 minutes, sprinkling it with spices as it cooks. Be sure to line the pan evenly with fruit so that it cooks evenly. If water accumulates as it usually does with strawberries or pineapple, pour it off and save it. Thickened with a pinch of cornstarch, you can use this liquid as a sauce for the soufflé.

Step Three. Spoon the whipped egg whites over the fruit and sprinkle it with a colored spice, such as cinnamon, for visual effect. Cover the dish and wait for the egg whites to become stiff.

Step Four. The soufflé is ready when the top is firm to your touch. Or you can tell it's done by stabbing it with a thin knife and seeing it separate and release steam. I love this soufflé so much that I often will stab it all over when it's about half done, just to speed up the cooking process, even though this is a very quick dish to fix in the first place. Another way to speed up the cooking—especially if you're using many egg whites—is to place the entire pan for a minute or so in an oven preheated to 400 degrees.

Note. Actual cooking time depends on how many egg whites you use in the dish. The number of egg whites used also dictates the size of the cookware that you use, since more egg whites require the use of a deeper pan. In any case a relatively deep pan is needed, because the egg whites briefly expand during cooking and will lift the lid off a shallow pan.

How to Serve. Simply invert the pan over a plate, upside-down-cake–style. The soufflé should be sliced like a pie unless you have made a smaller "individual serving." Serve the soufflé with fruit garnish and/or with the sauce you made from water thrown off during the initial fruit-cooking process.

This is probably the best recipe for fat loss you'll ever have!

Soufflé Variations

The following are variations of fruit ingredients that you can use in your soufflé with five to eight egg whites:

Variation #1—one ripe banana, two tablespoons of raisins and/or diced dates, and your pick of any or all of these spices: cinnamon, cloves, ginger.

Variation #2—one-half papaya, one-half ripe banana, one date (optional), and cloves (I usually only sprinkle a little powdered cloves on top of the soufflé).

Variation #3—one banana, half a pint of sliced strawberries, and no spices.

Other Variations—You can use just a half pint of sliced strawberries, just a banana, or a diced apple (with cinnamon, of course). Or you can use virtually any other fruit that you like. The beauty of this recipe is that you can experiment with any type of fruit that you want, creating your own personalized dishes.

A Nonfruit Ingredient—Along with the fruit, you might also sprinkle on some whole-grain granola to soak up the fruit juices. This ingredient can make your soufflé taste like a delicious dessert cobbler! Also, to give the egg-white meringue a little more body, you may wish to sprinkle on nonfat powdered milk or protein powder for extra flavor and extra grams of protein.

Comments. Since this soufflé recipe has virtually no fat (unless you add nuts—cashews, almonds, pecans, etc.—in the off-season), it's a great precontest taste treat. The soufflé is also a good source of unsaturated fat in your diet when you do add nuts, which provide essential fatty acids necessary for growth, healthy blood, healthy arteries, healthy nerves, and beautiful, supple skin.

This soufflé is filling and satisfying, in addition to being great-tasting. It's one of the most perfect bodybuilding foods one could ask for; it makes you feel like you're not depriving yourself of desserts and other goodies prior to a competition; it's easy to make, easy to eat, and easy to digest. You definitely should include a soufflé in your diet several times a week!

Good Old Tuna

Tuna fish is a staple of most bodybuilders' diets, and it's an excellent bodybuilding food when properly prepared. Unfortunately a lot of bodybuilders, particularly the men, just eat dry old tuna out of the can. Yuk! There are tons of delicious ways in which you can prepare a tuna salad. All you need is water-packed tuna (*never* use oil-packed tuna), a variety of vegetables, and a low-calorie dressing.

My basic tuna salad begins with one can of tuna that has been drained and then rinsed. For a dressing you can use either just enough low-fat, unflavored yogurt to moisten the tuna, or a little whipped low-fat cottage cheese (use the seasonings of your choice). If it isn't closer than two weeks to your show and you aren't behind schedule in losing body fat, you can use Henri's Lo-Fat yogurt dressing with your tuna. The Thousand Islands dressing makes a fabulous tuna salad.

Various Other Ingredients (Just mix them into the tuna salad.)

- minced onions and celery
- minced green olives (A couple won't hurt you!)
- grated carrots
- diced tomatoes
- diced cucumbers
- diced zucchini
- diced apple
- chopped walnuts
- chopped boiled eggs—extra whites

Note. Be creative. Just about any diced raw vegetable tastes great when added to the basic tuna salad recipe. It's up to you to determine how many calories you can get away with, although I've already eliminated as many calories as possible from my basic tuna salad recipe. Raw fruits and vegetables don't add many calories to the tuna salad, but use common sense when adding olives and nuts close to a competition!

Serving Suggestions. Stuff a tomato; use it in a whole-wheat–bread sandwich or on a bran cracker; eat the tuna salad by itself; or add tuna salad to a fresh vegetable salad. Take time to prepare this recipe by making two or three cans at a time. Keep it refrigerated and when you come home starving for anything to eat, you'll be really glad that good ol' Charlie is waiting for you!

Cooking Chicken

Chicken is high in protein and relatively low in fat content, particularly if the fatty skin is removed from the chicken prior to cooking it. Here is my basic chicken recipe, which will be followed by several tasty variations:

Ingredients

- 3 boned and skinned chicken breasts (The chicken breasts should be slightly frozen to make them easier to slice.)
- 1 tablespoon of lemon juice and ¼ teaspoon of corn, safflower, or soybean oil
- seasoning to taste (cayenne pepper, herbs, spices, etc.)
- your choice of vegetables (sprouts, celery, etc.)

Step One. Slice the chicken very thin. Spray Pam on a nonstick Silverstone pan. Add the chicken and lemon juice and cook for 2 to 4 minutes over a moderately high heat, stirring the chicken constantly until it is cooked.

Step Two. Remove the chicken. Coat the pan with ¼ teaspoon of oil (or spray with Pam) and stir fry the vegetables for 2 to 4 minutes. Add the chicken and seasonings, stir for a moment to mix all ingredients well, and serve.

Chicken Recipe Variations

German-Style Chicken—To the basic recipe, add the following ingredients:
- vegetables—shredded cabbage, minced scallions, minced onion
- seasoning—caraway seeds, apple cider vinegar, black pepper, a dash of fructose or sugar substitute.

Chinese-Style Chicken—To the basic recipe, add the following ingredients:
- vegetables—minced onion, cilantro or parsley, bean sprouts, celery, snow peas
- seasonings—ginger, dried mustard, 1 teaspoon of soy sauce (Remember that soy sauce contains salt!).

Italian-Style Chicken—To the basic recipe, add the following ingredients:
- vegetables—minced onion, green and/or red bell peppers, zucchini, mushrooms, cherry tomatoes
- seasonings—basil leaf, oregano, garlic and onion powder, pepper, sage.

Mexican-Style Chicken—To the basic recipe, add the following ingredients:
- vegetables—onions, green bell peppers, zucchini and one jalapeño pepper (if you're brave!)
- seasonings—ground cumin, garlic powder, onion powder, chili powder.

How to Serve Chicken. Serve on a bed of brown or wild rice or by itself with a baked potato, a salad, or a vegetable.

My Protein Cake Recipe

A slice of this cake makes a great dessert, or you can have it for breakfast or at snack time.

Ingredients

- 4 apples *or* 2 apples and 1½ pints strawberries, chopped finely or food-processed
- 1 cup of milk and/or egg protein powder
- 7 eggs (If you're worried about calories, throw out 2 or 3 yolks, but no more, or else the cake will come out mushy.)
- ¼ cup nonfat dry milk powder
- ⅛ teaspoon ground cloves
- ½ teaspoon nutmeg
- 1½ teaspoons baking soda
- 1 cup bran
- 1 teaspoon vanilla extract
- 1 tablespoon Sweet 'n Low *or* 1½ –2 tablespoons Equal *or* 3–5 tablespoons fructose

Step One. Mix together apples (or apples and strawberries), protein powder, and eggs.

Step Two. Mix together nonfat dry milk powder, cloves, nutmeg, baking soda, bran, vanilla extract (or other flavoring), and Sweet 'n Low, Equal, or fructose.

Step Three. Blend everything together and bake in a nine-by-twelve-inch pan (spray first with vegetable oil) for 30 minutes at 375 degrees.

The Perfect Breakfast

Ingredients

- ⅔ cup whole-grain raw rolled oats
- 1½ cups purified water
- 2 tablespoons milk and/or egg protein powder
- aspartame sweetener
- 1 heaping teaspoon psyllium husk

Boil the purified water and cook the oatmeal in it for about 5 minutes, the way you normally would. Add cinnamon if you like.

Meanwhile, in a blender, combine 1 cup water with the protein powder, aspartame sweetener, and psyllium husk. Blend slowly, then mix in with oatmeal when it's almost finished cooking and continue cooking until it's all mixed.

Caution: Make sure the saucepan is large enough because this magic recipe grows right before your eyes!

Variations: Add raisins, diced apple, diced dates, nuts, etc. (Here, again, use common sense with regard to the additional calories.)

Serves 2–3. The Perfect Breakfast is very filling, very low in calories, very satisfying, very delicious, and a great source of complex carbohydrates and additional protein. It's also fantastic for your digestion—another one of my favorites.

Oatmeal has always been one of my favorite foods. Every time I eat it, I feel so good inside. It's definitely a comforting food. I guess I associate my beloved mom's love and warmth and security with oatmeal whenever I eat it. It was a regular part of my diet when I was growing up. Now, as a grown-up body-builder, I can feel good on the inside and look great on the outside because of my revised recipe (sorry, Mom).

EAT LIKE A CHAMPION!

If you haven't paid much attention to your diet in the past, you've been shortchanging yourself and holding back your bodybuilding progress. Diet is at least 50 percent of the battle in bodybuilding, and as much as 90 percent of the fight prior to a competition. Eat correctly and you're on the way to championship status!

LOOKING AHEAD

In Chapter 9, I will discuss many competition-level training techniques that will allow you to prepare yourself perfectly for an upcoming physique contest. Some of the topics discussed include the cycle training and dietary philosophy; contest grooming, tanning, and suit choice; pumping up; secrets of posing for all three rounds of judging and the posedown; onstage conduct; the winning look and attitude in a body-builder; the role of aerobic training in peaking; secrets of my success as a competitor; my personal precontest routines; isotension contraction training; and a method of sharpening your physical condition when you come up a bit short of top shape the day before a show.

CHAPTER 9

competition-level training

*P*reparing every fiber of one's being to win a major bodybuilding competition is probably one of the greatest and most soulful challenges an athlete can undertake. And it takes a rare breed of woman to win a high-level bodybuilding title. Of the hundreds of thousands of women around the world who call themselves bodybuilders, only an elite few win state, provincial, regional, national, or international titles.

In my approach to bodybuilding competition, I have a two-month countdown (i.e., a concentrated preparation period) for each major contest that I enter, but I am actually preparing for competition 24 hours a day, 365 days a year. I *live* a bodybuilding life-style continually. I suppose I'm blessed with a fitness awareness that is very conducive to making me a top contender in every major bodybuilding competition I enter. How else could I have won two Miss Olympia titles?

We've all seen women who train like crazy and go on terribly restricted diets for six to eight weeks prior to a bodybuilding competition in an effort to look their best onstage. The combination of severe training and

an even more severe diet does get them fairly ripped up, but they usually end up burning off several pounds of muscle mass while trying to reach competition condition! As they sacrifice muscle in their effort to lose body fat, they also sacrifice any chance of appearing healthy, fresh, and at their best onstage. Then after the competition, because their entire preparation was such an ordeal for them, they stop training and start eating like gluttons. They quickly puff up like balloons and you'd hardly recognize them as bodybuilders anymore. A few months later another competition rolls around and the burden is taken up all over again. Up and down, up and down: Sooner rather than later, women who follow this misguided approach burn out on bodybuilding and leave the sport altogether.

Bodybuilding contest preparation doesn't have to be a period of mental and physical suffering. If you make consistent training and good diet a regular part of your daily life-style, you will be in relatively good shape—perhaps 85 to 90 percent of your best contest condition—all year round. Then it's a relatively easy and painless process to put the finishing touches on your physique, personal appearance, onstage presentation, and psychological preparation so that when you appear onstage, you'll be in spectacular condition.

However, I can't honestly tell you that every woman can become a champion bodybuilder, nor do I think every woman would *want* to! Gaining an ultimate peak demands several key qualities: self-discipline, consistency, a positive mental approach, pride, a never-ceasing energy focus, visual imagery, and an aggressive, positive anticipation toward contest preparation. All champion bodybuilders possess these character traits. Most unsuccessful bodybuilders don't. Those who don't must undertake the difficult task of developing these traits if they hope to be successful in competition. It may not be easy, but it *can* be done. As I said earlier, it takes a rare breed to become a champion bodybuilder. And if you really want it, well . . .

CYCLE TRAINING

No bodybuilder can train at precontest intensity—particularly if she is also dieting strictly—for more than a few weeks at a time. It doesn't take long for the mind and body simply to rebel at the rigors of such a regimen, and soon it's impossible to face the idea of going into the gym for another long, hard workout; regardless of how hard you train, your body will simply refuse to respond.

It's also impossible to add muscle mass to your physique before a contest when you're training very hard yet consuming so few calories that you don't have the energy to handle weights heavy enough to induce muscle growth or even to repair and maintain existing tissue. Precontest training and diet do only one thing, and they do it well: They get you into contest shape by reducing fat deposits throughout your body, shaping and separating your muscles, and generally improving muscular details. It's impossible to add even an ounce of muscle tissue the last two or three weeks prior to a competition.

In order to build muscle mass, you must train with heavy weights in all of your exercises. To have large muscles, you must have *strong* muscles. Of course, this degree of strength is relative, because favorable muscle attachments, bone lengths, etc., can allow you to lift heavier weights in an exercise than a woman

with larger muscles and less favorable leverage factors can. But the fact remains that the stronger you become, the larger your muscles will be.

Since you probably won't be using heavy poundages during a precontest cycle, you must seek to add muscle mass to your body during the off-season. Champion bodybuilders train with heavier weights and consume slightly more calories during the off-season, plus reduce aerobic activity, in order to build muscle. Then they switch to slightly lighter weights, longer aerobic sessions, and a more restricted diet during a precontest cycle in order to reduce body fat and enhance muscular detail.

Later in this chapter I'll discuss in great detail how I prepare myself for a competition and you can compare this program with the typical off-season workouts already presented. For the moment, as a sort of preview, let me give you the key elements of my training and diet during these two cycles:

Off-Season Training

(1) Use maximum weights and strict exercise form.

(2) Extend a set past failure through cheating reps, forced reps, descending sets, and/or burns, but only after you do at least 5 or 6 reps on your own.

(3) Use primarily basic exercises for each muscle group.

(4) Perform relatively low repetitions (in the range of 5 to 8 for upper body exercises and 8 to 12 for lower body movements).

(5) Follow a four-day split routine in which you train each muscle group twice a week.

(6) Rest sixty to seventy seconds between sets.

(7) Perform no more than 8 to 10 total sets for large muscle groups (back, chest, thighs, and deltoids) and no more than 5 or 6 total sets for smaller muscle groups.

(8) Do aerobic workouts (each session lasting 30 to 60 minutes) three to five days per week, the frequency depending on the relative severity of your diet.

Precontest Training

(1) Use moderately heavy weights (80 to 90 percent of what you used during the off-season) and do the exercise in *very* strict biomechanical form. Move the weights relatively slowly on each repetition.

(2) Either extend a set of strict reps past failure through cheating, forced reps, and burns, or superset your exercises (pre-exhaustion supersets are particularly valuable).

(3) Include more isolation exercises for muscle shape and separation, but still use at least one basic movement per muscle group to retain overall muscle mass.

(4) Do higher repetitions. (I prefer 10 to 15 reps on upper body movements and 15 to 25 reps for leg exercises, but you must instinctively determine the correct rep ranges for your body.)

(5) Follow a six-day split routine in which you train each major muscle group either two or three days a week.

(6) Rest as little as thirty to forty seconds between sets.

(7) Slightly increase the total number of sets you do for each muscle group (10 to 20 percent more sets will be adequate).

(8) Do one or two hours of aerobic work *every day,* depending on the intensity of aerobic activity and relative severity of your diet. (I've done up to three or four hours of aerobics per day at times when the fat wasn't coming off quickly enough.)

(9) Work on your tan if you're fair-skinned.

(10) Practice posing as much as possible (frequent, hard tensing of your muscles will greatly improve overall muscularity).

Off-Season Diet

This topic is thoroughly discussed in Chapter 8, but I will give you a few brief tips here nonetheless.

(1) I firmly believe in keeping my body fat relatively low (around 10 to 12 percent), and I strongly suggest that you do the same. Never allow yourself to go more than five to seven pounds above your competition weight. This means, of course, that you'll have to make healthy eating a regular part of your life-style.

(2) Due to their high fat content, red meats should be avoided; eat them no more often than once each week or two. Consume 1/2 to 1 gram of protein

per pound of body weight each day. You can never go wrong when you eat fresh fruits and vegetables as well as whole grains. Avoid drinking your calories (in other words, don't drink high-calorie liquids).

(3) Use a moderate amount of food supplementation, e.g., a multipack of vitamins, minerals, and trace elements with breakfast or lunch each day.

Precontest Diet

(1) Your precontest diet doesn't have to be too radical if you've kept your body fat low during the off-season, or if you start dieting well in advance of your competition to reduce overly large fat stores. Simply lower your caloric consumption to a level approximately 10 to 15 percent below your caloric maintenance needs by limiting fat intake even more than normally. (There are more than twice as many calories in a gram of fat as there are in a gram of protein or carbohydrate.)

(2) If you've kept your body-fat percentage low, diet gently for no more than six to eight weeks prior to a competition; allow your increased aerobic activity to help you burn off body fat.

(3) Avoid dietary sodium intake for the final week prior to your competition.

(4) Increase your consumption of vitamin and mineral supplements to compensate for nutrients lost while on a restricted diet. You will particularly need to consume water-soluble vitamins and minerals, which are lost through perspiration.

AN INSEPARABLE DUO

Even though I've made a clean division between diet and exercise in the foregoing section, it's absolutely impossible to isolate training from diet. In competitive bodybuilding, training and diet are inseparable. You simply *must* pay careful attention to both if you hope to achieve maximum results.

True, I've seen some excellent women bodybuilders pay almost no attention to diet during the off-season while they trained as hard as they possibly could. But as a competition approaches they have to go to the other extreme. Then they're forced to adhere to an

800-calorie diet, which leaves them with so little energy that they can hardly train, let alone work out with heavy weights. They end up looking ripped if they've dieted extremely enough, but they also end up so unhealthy that they look like death warmed over onstage—unappealing, to say the least!

However, as I said before, no woman bodybuilder ever needs to suffer like this if she intelligently combines diet and year-round training in her bodybuilding philosophy. This makes common sense to me, and it should to you as well; not only will you find it easier to reach peak shape during your competition countdown, but you'll also look a lot better—much more like a real bodybuilder—in the off-season. Isn't that a pretty fair exchange for missing out on a few desserts here and there when everyone else is pigging out?

CONTEST PERSONAL APPEARANCE

Your grooming, your suit choice, your tan, and the amount of oil you apply can have a great deal to do with whether or not you place high in a bodybuilding competition, so we should discuss each of these topics in detail.

Posing-Suit Choice

During the first couple of years that I competed in bodybuilding, there wasn't that much choice in either style or color of posing suits. There *still* isn't, for that matter; I mean, how many ways can you make a little bitty bikini look? Bathing suits purchased at beach shops or boutiques were the rule of the day, although sometimes you'd see a custom-designed suit. Kamali-designed bathing suits displayed the most muscle in the best styles, so they gained early popularity.

Today we have a wide variety of costumes designed specifically for women's bodybuilding. These are advertised in bodybuilding magazines. I'm a bit biased, but I feel that the Flex Appeal Competition Bikini that I sell through my mail-order business is one of the best posing suits available, since it allows obvious places where you can alter the suit to make it appear custom-made. Of course, you *can* sew your own suit

to fit the exact contours of your body, but unless you are a very experienced seamstress, a homemade suit looks, well, homemade.

The main requirement of a posing bikini is that it be cut in a stylish manner to reveal all of your hard-earned muscularity without revealing too much or riding up your body as you pose. Incidently, you can prevent the common problem of bra slippage in the middle of a free-posing program by placing two small pieces of two-sided tape between your body and the bra. Theatrical supply stores sell this type of tape.

Never wear a bikini made of patterned cloth; not only is this against the rules of bodybuilding competition, but the pattern also draws attention away from your physique. Similarly you must avoid garish colors. Once you find a bikini with a flattering cut to it, purchase at least two of them (perhaps in different colors) for use in competition. After the bikini you wore in the prejudging is marked with body oil or otherwise soiled, it's good to have a fresh one available for the evening show.

Color choice is important. At a Miss Olympia competition you'll see a rainbow of colors. While I've worn other colors in the past, I feel I look best in white and have won most of my contests while wearing a white bikini. Pick a color in which you can feel comfortable, one that harmonizes well with your own coloring. And please don't go overboard trying to design a unique suit that may run the risk of being disqualified.

Such was the problem I had during the competition filmed for the movie *Pumping Iron II—The Women.* My original custom-made posing suit was disqualified, and I was not allowed to compete in it. The reason? It had clear plastic sequins (not garish, gaudy, or the least bit distracting) interspersed on the posing suit. The affect I wanted to achieve onstage was a wet-look white posing bikini. It was absolutely beautiful (not to mention expensive), but I was not allowed to wear it onstage.

Well, I had brought *another* suit, just in case. It was disqualified as well: It had metallic-looking threads that were sewn in with the fabric. I said to Oscar State, the director of judges, in my not-so-usual tone of voice that the judges' decisions were not exactly fair, since only a month and a half before, a handful

A posing bikini should be cut in a stylish manner to reveal all your hard-earned muscularity.

of Miss Olympia and American Championships contenders had competed in *metallic suits with metallic sequins.* All he said in his British accent was that it was against the IFBB rules.

This conversation took place close to midnight the night before the competition. I went back to my room at Caesars Palace and immediately called Christian, my ever-present supporter, mentor, and training partner, to please come to my room to help me figure out what to do. He immediately sensed something was wrong when his telephone rang that late at night, especially since it was by me: I was supposed to be in bed with sweet dreams of victory the following day!

At 2:30 A.M., the morning of the competition, I finally got in touch with Heidi, my seamstress, and tearfully told her the situation. She said the only thing she could do was to send the sample from which the original was made. We both knew that the top would be too big, since it was made when my body-fat percentage was a bit higher, especially in the breasts. (The bottoms would be okay; I would just pull them up higher on my hips.) Heidi said she'd take care of the top by sewing in foam-lined interfacing along the top to smooth out the wrinkles in it and so it wouldn't look so baggy, and also so that it would add a little shape and contour. Big deal!

This had to be taken care of, done, flown in from L.A., and on my body within hours. Luckily my attorney, Scott, was flying out later that same morning; he would pick it up from my seamstress at five-thirty A.M. in order to make his flight, and bring it to me in time for the prejudging. Saved! Or was I?

Listen to this: *After* the prejudging, minutes before the evening presentation, I was called away from the dressing area by some of the "officials." There had been complaints made to the judges and officials by fellow competitors about the "padding" in my bra (which, throughout the entire ordeal, I had openly admitted to having), and they demanded that I be disqualified, for the third time, again because of my suit. Maria Shriver and I were doing a segment for *PM Magazine* and *World News Tonight* and she was appalled at all this nonsense.

"Where's some scissors! A knife! Anything!" was all I could say (scream). "I'll cut out every bit of the lining this very second!" Maria frantically looked in her purse for some manicure scissors, which she found, and we immediately started tearing away. Of course, the camera crew of *Pumping Iron II* was hovering over me so as not to miss any juicy con-

troversial detail for the film. When every bit of lining was hacked out of my suit, I sarcastically asked if it made a radical distinction to go onstage with a less-than-perfect-fitting top.

Did it really matter? How did it change the way my body looked in reference to how it was being judged? It didn't! So my top was somewhat ill-fitting and loose; when I did particular poses, I just had to be extra careful not to give the spectators a peek in my suit if and when it flapped open. I suppose I should have left the suit exactly as it was or, better yet, posed in my beautiful white-sequined suit, because points were deducted anyway. I admit, I felt a little picked on, but I guess that's show biz!

Grooming

Every facet of your appearance, especially your grooming, must be presented at its best onstage at both the prejudging and the evening show of a women's bodybuilding contest. How can you spend literally hundreds of hours preparing your body and then totally ignore your head? Grooming includes your hairstyle, makeup, and skin tone.

No doubt you already have a hairstyle that conforms to the competition rule requiring your hair to be put up and off your shoulders where it won't obscure upper back and shoulder development. Many women have had their hair cut short enough for everyday wear to conform to this requirement. Others, myself included, have longer hair that must be specifically styled for a competition, such as over to the side of the head.

Experiment with a variety of hairstyles to discover one that flatters your facial features. If you can't discover one on your own, it's worth the moderate investment to consult a professional hairstylist.

The only guidelines I can give you about makeup are: (1) Be certain it enhances your features; and (2) it must be somewhat heavier than normal. Bright stage lighting washes out normal makeup, which means you'll have to wear heavier makeup onstage. If you can't get backstage to see how much makeup the contestants are wearing prior to entering a show yourself, experiment with differing amounts from show to show and have a friend in the audience evaluate how it looks.

Tanning

Good skin tone is essential onstage. The darker your skin, the harder your physique will appear, so fair-skinned individuals must have either a natural or artificial tan. It's best to lie out in the sun, gradually increasing exposure time to avoid sunburn. A sunburn draws water into the skin, making you body appear devoid of some of its actual muscularity.

If the sun isn't out consistently, you may have to use a solarium. I personally prefer using one simply because it's safe and it takes up less time. I've used solaria extensively, and the resulting tan has been acceptable, with minimal risk of burning or otherwise harming my skin.

There is also a wide variety of "quick-tan" products available for use in the winter if you don't have access to a solarium. It's best to try several tanning preparations before your competition to decide which cream is best for your unique body. Whatever you do, try your absolute best to have something of a base tan before you start to put on this "barbecue sauce." The last thing you want is to look jaundiced onstage with yellow- or orange-appearing skin. And be sure to apply the cream with rubber gloves to avoid staining your hands, or wash them *many* times afterward.

Skin Oiling

The final touch is applying the body oil that will highlight your muscularity onstage. Use a light, even coating of vegetable oil (almond and apricot kernel oils are popular) that soaks into your skin and then gradually emerges from your pores as you lightly perspire onstage. Nothing looks as unsightly as a heavy coating of mineral oil lying on your skin like a neglected oil slick.

I mix metallic eye-shadow powder with my oil for an interesting effect. A *maximum* of 1/8 teaspoon of powder per 1 1/2 cups of oil greatly enhances muscle highlights. Pick a light peachy color. Never use dark colors of eye-shadow powder, thinking that it'll improve your tan color; you'll end up with a filthy suit and streaky-looking tan. Even if you do use a lighter shade, just for the glow effect, be careful not to stain your suit with it.

Experiment with different amounts and varieties of oils on your body well before your competition. To help ensure consistency of application, try to have the same person who helped you in the days prior to the competition also help you apply your oil backstage. Remember, a light and even coating is best, and be sure to tell the person applying the oil not to get any on your suit!

PUMPING UP

Technically speaking, as soon as you have finished a set of any exercise, blood flows quickly and profusely into the muscle that has just been worked in order to flush away local fatigue by-products and carry new glycogen (muscle sugar) and oxygen into the muscle. This profusion of blood in a trained muscle group makes that muscle temporarily larger than normal.

At a competition experienced bodybuilders take advantage of this temporary "muscle pump" by exercising less impressive muscle groups backstage just before going out onstage in an effort to make those body parts more in correct proportion to the rest of their physiques.

It's best first to warm up your entire body with light, high-rep movements, then pump only two or three of your weakest muscle groups with several light sets each. It's impossible to pump up more than two or three muscle groups adequately, since you only have a certain amount of blood volume to engorge your muscles, so it would be senseless to try pumping your entire body. You should also be careful to avoid overpumping a muscle group with too many sets, as this may cause your muscularity in that body part to smooth and tire out.

Normally there is a variety of barbells, dumbbells, and benches provided backstage for the entrants to use in pumping up. If you don't have weights available, however, you can do high-rep sets of various calisthenic exercises (push-ups, freehand calf raises, etc.) for good effect. Or you can use a partner to provide resistance by pushing or pulling against your hands or some other body part. I prefer to pump the shoulders, arms, and calves before going onstage.

Backstage at the 1980 Miss Olympia—getting pumped up to pose.

Photo by R. Ruoti

SECRETS OF POSING

In this section I will simply try to help you prepare your first posing routine. Once you have a basic program of poses mastered, you can gradually refine the routine and add more sophisticated poses.

The first thing you should try to understand is that you will have three distinctly different rounds of posing. Round one of the AFWB/IFBB judging system consists of five standardized compulsory poses. Round two consists of displaying your physique from the front, back, and both sides in a semirelaxed state with your arms down at your sides. Round three is the stylized free-posing to music. If you are in the top five after three rounds of judging, you will enter a fourth round, called a *posedown,* in which you'll vie with the other four finalists for a few final, crucial points.

The five compulsory poses in round one are front double biceps, left side chest, back double biceps, right side triceps, and front abdominals-and-thigh poses. These standardized poses can be improved on to a great degree merely by slightly shifting your foot, leg, hand, arm, head, and body positions, although there is a fine line between slightly shifting and altogether changing a compulsory pose, running the risk of being "called" on it, and perhaps even having points deducted from your score for persistently performing the pose incorrectly.

By the way, you will find out that you will keep practicing the poses of all three rounds throughout your bodybuilding career, always improving them. As your physique grows better and better you'll want to subtly alter round one and round two poses to reveal this improvement. Also, as your physique matures, you will discover more and more optional poses in which you'll look great. For example, I had been competing at the international level for nearly three years before I could hit a good three-quarters back shot. Prior to that I simply didn't have the degree of development to pull it off successfully. Never, and I mean *never,* strike a pose that serves no useful purpose, that is, one that doesn't show your physique at its best.

Although most women avoid it, you *must* practice the semirelaxed stances of round two. If you watch enough prejudgings, you'll notice that there are subtle shifts in body position that make your physique look more impressive. These can only be discovered though consistent practice. If you've ever seen a prima ballerina in action, you know that there is a difference between standing and *standing*!

As a general rule, prior to a competition I spend 20 to 25 percent of my posing time on round one, 20 to 25 percent on round two, and the remainder of my time on my free-posing program. Unfortunately many bodybuilders break their percentages down something like this: zero percent, zero percent, 100 percent. Round one and round two make up two-thirds of your score, so *practice* the poses in those two rounds of judging.

It takes plenty of time to develop a free-posing program, so start working on round three at least two to three months before your competition. You will need at least two months to develop optional poses, choose appropriate music, choreograph your program, and totally make the routine uniquely your own.

It's natural that as your physique begins to improve, you will want to spend more time trying out and practicing new poses in front of a mirror. These first efforts will more than likely form the basis of your free-posing routine. You can initially mimic poses you like from photos in *Muscle & Fitness* and other bodybuilding magazines. Usually the pose won't look great the first time you try it, but work on subtle body shifts to develop it gradually and personalize it to suit your own unique body. Once you have it down to the point where you know exactly how each muscle should feel in the stance, practice it without the mirror. This is important for all poses, as well as your round-three routine: There aren't any giant mirrors set up in the audience to help you.

I know it's tough, but try to practice without any mirrors from time to time. Here's a little trick that really helped me improve my posing. I'd practice various poses for a couple of days *without* a mirror until I felt I had the right "feel" for each pose. Then, to test out my perception of a pose, I'd step in front of the mirror and strike the pose with my eyes closed, open my eyes, and... well, that told me I needed to spend a little more time practicing each pose both with and without the mirror.

For your first free-posing routine you'll need ten to twelve *good* poses. While you're choosing them, keep in mind that ten good poses are much better than twenty to thirty mediocre ones. I also feel that you should avoid repeating more than one or two of the earlier compulsory poses in your free-posing routine. The judges and audience will have already seen these compulsory poses, so why bore them by running

through all of the round-one poses another time?

While working on your optional poses, you should also be searching for a piece of music that suits your personality or, better yet, a selection that really inspires you and makes you really want to move with it from the inside. This selection shouldn't last for more than two or three minutes, and it's permissible to fade out the music on your recorded cassette partway through it if you don't have enough great poses to fill the complete recording. It's a safe practice to bring *two* cassettes of your musical selection because you just never know what might happen to your tape. Some sound systems have been known to destroy a tape or two.

Your next step is to assemble your poses with smooth and dramatic transitions between each stance, and you must then choreograph all of this to your musical selection. Even though I'd never seen a women's competition before entering the United States Championships in early 1980, my dance background enabled me to choreograph a smooth and effective routine. The way I did some of my individual poses was really amusing, especially by today's standards, but the video cassette I have of the routine does show good, solid choreography and smooth, graceful transitions.

If you don't have a dance background or a good coach to help you develop a routine, I suggest that you seek the help of a dance choreographer to assist you. Simply call several dance studios (they're listed in the Yellow Pages) to see who would be interested in helping you and compare prices for this type of assistance. To get the most out of a choreographer or dance instructor, make sure you've already settled on your individual poses. You'll probably have to spend three or four hours with a choreographer to develop effective transitions. Finally, you'll have to practice for several weeks to lock the routine into your mind and body.

Ultimately you will learn to incorporate a relatively high degree of theatricality into your free-posing routine. Certain facial and body gestures convey specific emotions to your audience. Once you have developed such good communication with an audience that you can actually move and emotionally inspire them, you are a *master poser*! But whatever you do—and I can't stress this too much—*don't try too hard.* The facial expressions and gestures must come from within your very soul, because this free-style posing moment (it seems like you've been out there for only a moment when you're posing well) is a pure act of communication between you and your audience.

Charisma

Charisma is the final competitive quality of a superstar bodybuilder, and it's a quality that exudes from within. Charisma is an inner quality that is expressed in body language to make you stand out as a superhealthy, superalive *winner onstage*!

Two basic factors lead to the development of charisma: experience and mental programming. By observing and competing in a large number of women's championships, you will learn the little tricks of playing to your audience that were mentioned in the earlier discussion of contest posing. These subtle techniques develop a communication link between you and the audience. With communication comes audience support and a degree of emotional rapport. All of these factors combine to build your personal onstage charisma.

You can also enhance your charisma through visualization, the mental programming technique discussed in Chapter 11. Essentially, if you realistically visualize yourself as a winner onstage at your next competition, you *will* have the body language, attitude, and charisma of a winner. This allows you to project your positive personality to the audience, which in turn results in even greater personal charisma onstage.

I've been told that I had a high level of charisma right from the start in competitive bodybuilding. If this is true, it no doubt came about because, as a former dancer and cheerleader, I was used to being in front of an audience. When you're comfortable and at ease with your audience, you'll project your charisma much more easily. And *that* will move you from champion to superstar!

Charisma can also be described as inner joy, happiness, or pulchritude that comes from *knowing* that you've done your homework, that you've prepared yourself fully, and sacrificed lesser pleasures in order to win, and that the moment you step onstage you are

During the prejudging round at the 1981 Miss Olympia.

so ready that you *love* it. Enjoy yourself and let the contest be an extension of your labors of love in the gym. At that point you will have the aura of a winner, and *winning* is what we're all after.

ONSTAGE CONDUCT

Being onstage at a prejudging for a bodybuilding competition is a learning experience. Therefore, above all else, you must be alert for every change in tempo that you will encounter at a prejudging. Even though you will have attended several competitions prior to actually entering one, things will happen to you onstage that are totally unexpected. And nothing looks worse than a bodybuilder standing in line with several others and turning to the right when everyone else in line is turning to the left on a judge's command.

You have to be a sponge up there, absorbing as much useful information as possible during the first few competitions. What does it feel like to be competing when you have butterflies in your stomach? How can you learn to control your knees when you're bouncing up and down from fright? How do the other competitors react to you onstage? How do *you* react to *them* onstage? How does the audience accept you? How do you keep a pleasant look on your face when your back is cramping up from standing in the lineup for an hour at prejudging? Do you feel confident and in command, or are you a little afraid and lacking in self-confidence? What do you find that you most need to work on before entering another competition?

These are questions that can only be answered in a test of fire. Once you have answered them to your own satisfaction, you'll be better able to project your personality and charisma as well as your highly trained physique.

AEROBICS

Lately aerobics have had a great deal of media attention, and everyone seems to be doing aerobic training of some sort. Aerobics have been sloppily labeled and abused for the sake of the good old buck. *Aerobic* means simply ''with oxygen,'' and aerobic training is work carried out at a low enough intensity that your body is able to supply oxygen to your working muscles at least as quickly as it is being used up.

Aerobic workouts are an essential part of my training, particularly during a peaking cycle. Unfortunately, I had to experience a second-place finish at the 1981 Miss Olympia show to discover the value of aerobic training. Prior to my first competition (the United States Championships), I had been teaching several half-hour, hour, and two-hour aerobic classes per day, and I was tight-looking and fat-free as a result.

Aerobic workouts like cycling and running are an essential part of my training.

Photo by Luke Wynn

Photo by Luke Wynn

I then moved from Texas to California to train, and I began meeting all of the champion bodybuilders I'd read about in various bodybuilding magazines. The many new techniques I learned from them led to a series of experiments. During that time I neglected my aerobics. That in turn led to a regression in my muscular detail. As hard as I tried—or thought I tried!—I just couldn't get ripped up for the '81 Olympia. And it's not a good practice to experiment with new techniques just prior to such an important competition.

After that loss you'd better believe that I went back to working hard at my aerobic training, and I've never had a problem peaking completely since then. During a defining phase I increase my aerobic activity, doing at least a solid two hours of aerobics each day. Sometimes I spend three to four hours a day on aerobic training. I tend to stick to playing racquetball, taking aerobics classes, cycling, and running. To keep this training from becoming boring, I rotate my aerobic activities from day to day.

The amount of aerobic activity I perform keeps me from having to crash diet just before a competition as so many bodybuilders do. I never have to go under 1,500 calories per day, even when the competition is only one or two weeks away. And with the higher number of calories I consume, I can maintain a greater degree of muscle mass when in a fully defined state of physical condition.

To have both mass and muscle quality, *you must eat.* I've tried going down to 600 to 700 calories a day—and have even fasted for a day or two—just before a competition in an effort to achieve peak muscularity. I did reduce my body fat to a low point of 6.3 percent, but I lost several pounds of hard-earned muscle mass in the process!

Aerobic training allows you to eat more food and retain muscle mass as you gradually burn off body fat through the added physical activity. Rather than starve yourself, diet less strictly for a longer period of time, train with heavy weights, and place greater emphasis on your aerobic workouts. Then you will have both mass and cuts, as well as a superfit cardiorespiratory system.

ISOTENSION CONTRACTION

During the weeks leading up to the 1980 United States Women's Championships, where I scored my first bodybuilding victory, I noticed that the more I practiced my posing and the harder I held the muscle contractions in each pose, the more muscular I seemed to become. It was as if tight muscle flexing made my muscles harder.

Later I learned about the isotension contraction technique that most top male bodybuilders use to harden and add detail to their muscles. This bodybuilding technique—which is actually nothing more than a good, hard form of isometric contraction—was very similar to the hard posing practice I was putting in each day prior to my competition.

When practiced regularly in the weeks leading up to a competition, isotension contraction definitely hardens the muscles and brings out the most muscular detail. It also gives you two added benefits. One of these is the ability to flex your muscles more completely in each pose (anaerobic conditioning), which makes the pose more impressive. The other is an ability to hold compulsory poses at a competition prejudging for up to twenty to thirty seconds, as is often required, without becoming exhausted and shaking like a leaf.

Isotension contractions consist of "rep" flexes of a muscle group. Simply flex a muscle as hard as you can for eight to ten seconds, then relax it for ten to fifteen seconds. Keep performing these isotension contractions of a muscle group until you have done 8 to 10 reps. Gradually, over a six-to-eight-week peaking cycle, you can work up to thirty to fifty isotension contractions of each muscle group nearly every day. And believe me, that is a workout in itself!

Experience has shown me that you should flex each muscle group in a variety of positions when practicing isotension contractions. For example, you can flex your quadriceps muscles with your leg held totally straight, slightly bent, or markedly bent. Do fifteen isotension reps in each position during every isotension workout, and you'll add greatly to your frontal thigh muscularity.

Many bodybuilders practice isotension between sets or normal weight work for the muscle group they're training. I prefer to practice isotension on its own, either as a workout in itself or at odd times during the day. It's easiest to do it at odd times—while driving my car, air traveling, talking on the phone, watching a film, and so forth. Do you think I'm nuts? I think it's great, and it feels good too!

The keys to isotension are using the technique regularly and flexing your muscles as hard as possible. Performed in this manner, isotension contractions are imperative for competitive bodybuilders.

MY SECRET OF SUCCESS

I love to have variety in my precontest training, so I'm constantly changing my training methods. There's nothing new about injecting maximum variety into bodybuilding workouts. The human body adapts very quickly to any external stimulus—high reps, low reps, heavy weights, moderate weights, high-fat foods, low-fat foods, varying sleep patterns, and different types of aerobic workouts.

Muscles grow larger and more detailed when they are stressed with a heavier weight than they are accustomed to handling, but they very quickly adapt to this new weight and cease growing. They will also rapidly adapt to a particular workout. By constantly changing my training programs, however, I'm able to keep my muscles off balance, so to speak. I shock them so they can't adapt to a consistent stress, and they're therefore forced to grow larger and more detailed. I *never* allow my muscles to adapt to a set type of work load. Essentially, I follow a sort of "nonroutine routine," and it works wonders for me!

I also add considerable variety to my workouts by changing the way I actually perform an exercise from one training session to the next. The reason for this can be boiled down to three words: *muscle contraction specificity.* You must do a movement in a particular way if you want to achieve a predetermined appearance in the muscle affected by the exercise. I discovered this many years ago back in Texas, long before I began serious competitive training.

If you place your feet wide apart as you do squats, for example, it stresses the inner thigh muscles, particularly higher up. A narrow stance hits the central section and the outer sweep of the quadriceps. Doing squats with your toes angled outward places greater stress on the vastus medialis quadriceps muscle on the inside of your thigh, just above the knee. Done with your toes pointed slightly outward, squats stress the lower and outer sections of your thighs.

A better example would be when doing buttock "lifting" exercises. I truly believe that the contraction you impose on your buttocks will render the shape of lift that you are striving for. Sure, you can do general movements to affect your whole butt area, such as squats, but I'm sure we've all heard horrifying reports of the broadening effect squats can have on a person's butt. Well, that's not what I'm after. I don't want muscles just for the sake of having muscles; I want them to be beautiful and shaped the way *I* want them.

Such performance variations exist for virtually every exercise, and I do every possible variation, especially just before a competition. At that time I want to hit a muscle group from every possible angle to promote complete development. At other times I generally use the performance variation of any exercise that stresses the part of a muscle that needs additional shape or contour.

I've learned these performance variations over more than seven years of steady training and experimentation. I used to spend up to fifteen hours a day working at the Sport Palace in Harlingen, Texas. I didn't want to become bored, so I filled my unoccupied time with every possible exercise variation on each available piece of equipment.

All of the years you put into your training can yield so much more when you consciously use your brain to get the most out of each exercise. *Think* about how you can better a movement to achieve a unique muscle contraction or to stress an area that hasn't been stressed before. You'll be light-years ahead of the bodybuilders who don't think of such fine points!

MY PRECONTEST PROGRAM

Below is a sample precontest training program to show you how I peak for a competition. Remember that the program is only a *sample* and that my training is constantly changing.

MONDAY AND THURSDAY

Note: Brackets enclose exercises that are supersetted.

Morning—Chest and Arm Workout

Exercise	Sets	Reps
(1) Cable flyes	4	10–15
(2) Incline dumbbell presses	4	10–15
(3) Cable crossovers (various angles; last set to total failure)	3–4	15–20
(4) Pulley push-downs	3	10–15
(5) Reverse-grip push-downs	3	10–15
(6) Lying triceps extensions	2	10–15
(7) Two-arm dumbbell triceps extensions	2	10–15
(8) Standing barbell curls	2	10–15
(9) One-arm pulley curls	2	10–15
(10) Incline dumbbell curls	2	10–15

Afternoon—Aerobics and Posing

(1) Run three to five miles (moderate pace).
(2) Pose for one hour.

Evening—Abdominal Workout

Exercise	Sets	Reps
(1) Nautilus crunches	3	30
(2) Lying leg raises	3	50
(3) Roman chair sit-ups	3	50
(4) Seated twisting*	2–3	3–4 minutes

*With a strong contraction on each rep of the first two minutes of each set.

TUESDAY AND FRIDAY

Morning—Thigh and Calf Workout

Note: The workout begins with ten to fifteen minutes of cycling on a stationary bike, followed by at least five minutes of stretching as a warm-up.

Exercise	Sets	Reps
(1) Leg curls	5	15–25
(2) Hack squats	5	15–25
(3) Leg extensions	4	15–25
(4) Vertical leg presses	4	15–25
(5) Lunges	3	30
(6) Standing calf raises	4	15–20

Note: At this point I stretch my calves for five minutes.

Exercise	Sets	Reps
(7) Seated calf raises	4	15–20
(8) One-legged calf raises	2	to failure

Note: After each set of exercise (8), I stretch my calves for approximately two minutes.

Afternoon—Aerobics and Posing

(1) One hour of aerobics class (my own; see Chapter 10)

(2) One hour of easy cycling

(3) One hour of posing practice

Note: I do either (1), (2) *or* (1) *and* (2) with (3), according to my energy levels and body-fat percentage.

Evening—Buttocks Workout

Exercise	Sets	Reps
(1) Pulley leg-hip movements (three ways)	3	15–20
(2) Hip hyperextensions (with buttock contractions at the top of each repetition)	3	15–20
(3) Floor-exercise buttock lifts (see Chapter 10)	3	to failure
(4) Floor-exercise buttock tighteners (see Chapter 10)	3	20–30

WEDNESDAY AND SATURDAY

Morning—Shoulder and Back Workout

Exercise	Sets	Reps
(1) Shoulder presses (warm-up)	2–3	20–30
(2) Side laterals	4	10–15
(3) Military presses	4	10–15
(4) Dumbbell front raises	2	10–15
(5) Barbell shrugs	2	10–15
(6) Bent laterals	4	10–15

Note: At this point I do an additional back warm-up that includes stretching exercises. The main stretching movement consists of grasping a sturdy upright bar, with feet close to the bar and hips as far away from the bar as possible, then stretching the lats with straight arms. It feels great, but Joe Gold, owner of the World Gym in Santa Monica, California, accuses me of bending up all of his equipment when I do this!

Exercise	Sets	Reps
(7) Stiff-arm lat pull-downs	4	10–15
(8) Wide-grip front pull-downs	4	10–15
(9) Seated pulley rowing	3	10–15
(10) T-bar rowing	3	10–15
(11) One-arm dumbbell bent rowing	3	10–15

Afternoon—Aerobics and Posing

(1) One or two hours of cycling (easy pace)

(2) One hour of posing

Note: When practicing posing, the first half hour is devoted to holding the mandatory poses until I almost faint while still holding the pose and still smiling. The second half hour is devoted to practicing my free-posing program.

Evening

Same abdominal program as on Mondays and Thursdays.

SUNDAY

Sundays are devoted to rest and perhaps some light aerobic training and posing.

IF YOU COME UP SHORT

Despite your best efforts, you may mistime your peak and come up a bit short of optimal condition the day before a competition. In that case you can improve your muscularity somewhat by taking a mild herbal diuretic the evening before competing.

You should avoid using the harsh chemical diuretics favored by many bodybuilders. They disrupt the electrolyte balance in your body and actually make your muscles look smaller. (Muscles are more than 75 percent water, so using a harsh diuretic can reduce their mass.) Chemical diuretics indiscriminately remove water from every area of your body—fat cells, the dermis, blood, muscles, viscera, and so on. Stay away from them, because they are both dangerous and counterproductive to bodybuilding.

being an orchestra conductor, who has to blend the sounds of a wide variety of musical instruments to yield the sweet sound of a Tchaikovsky symphony.

Each time you attempt to peak, it's essential that you take detailed notes on how each variable affects your physique. This will help you to develop an idea of how you should look at one-week intervals for the last six to eight weeks before a competition and how you should look at daily intervals the last week. Plus it will give you a good indication of what it will take to bring your body to the condition required at each checkpoint.

When you get this down pat, you'll know exactly how much less you must eat or how much more aerobic exercise you must do to reach your checkpoint if you're a bit overweight. You'll also know how much to back off if you're peaking too quickly. Then you can peak precisely on the date of your competition, and *that's* the art required to *win*!

THE ORCHESTRA CONDUCTOR

Peaking completely and precisely on the day of a competition makes you a master of your craft. There are scores of variables that you must correctly control to reach the exact peak you want. Among these variables are all of the permutations of bodybuilding training, aerobic workouts, and diet. It's almost like

LOOKING AHEAD

In the next chapter I will discuss valuable home exercises. Topics discussed will include how to work out at home with weights, home calisthenics exercises, a home stretching program, a program of home training with improvised resistance exercises, and a personalized home aerobics program.

CHAPTER 10

home training

I have found that the absolute best way to get the most out of bodybuilding is to combine it with aerobics. Heavy bodybuilding workouts build muscle mass, but they are anaerobic exercises that rely on muscle glycogen to meet their energy requirements.

Weight workouts burn off minimal body-fat stores. Only sustained, low-intensity aerobic training sessions meet their energy requirements by burning stored fats. This is the key reason why I am a strong believer in near daily aerobic exercise.

Aerobic workouts are an essential facet of my training philosophy, although it took me a while to realize their importance. Prior to my first competition, the 1980 United States Championships, I had been teaching aerobic exercise classes, and I was very tight-looking as a result. After I really got into bodybuilding, however, I did less and less aerobic training due to my hectic schedule.

When I began meeting bodybuilding champions in person, I learned many new training techniques from them. This led to a series of experiments, during which I neglected my aerobics, which in turn made it more difficult to get cut up for a competition. That type of oversight is allowed only once in a professional bodybuilder's career!

During a defining phase I increase my aerobic activity, doing at least a solid two hours of aerobics, and often up to three hours. I tend to rotate between playing racquetball, taking or giving aerobic classes, cycling, and running. For best results from aerobic training, I have to change my aerobics sessions in order to keep my body from adapting to the fat-burning effects. I've pointed out the fact that the human body remarkably adapts to the uniform stress imposed upon it on a regular basis. That's why I rotate my aerobic activities from day to day—to keep my body off balance, so to speak. The last thing I need is for my body to adapt itself to a five-mile run every morning!

The closer a competition, the more crucial diet becomes to me, but I'm no fanatic. I do enough aerobic training so that I never have to go under 1,500 calories a day, even just prior to a competition. It took me years to understand that I have to *eat* to have both mass and quality onstage, and that I have to *do aerobics* to burn off excess stores of body fat.

It is especially important for a woman to be more activity-oriented instead of starving herself in order to get ripped, for the simple reason that she is less muscular than a man and cannot afford to sacrifice hard-earned muscle because of some silly diet.

To give you an idea of how various types of aerobic activity stack up against each other, here is a chart of how many calories you can expect to burn off with sixty continuous minutes of brisk exercise in each mode:

Aerobic Activity	Calories Burned
Running (10 mph)	900
Bicycling (15 mph)	700
Swimming (1 mph)	650
Racquetball	500
Tennis	400

I like running and I love the results even more, which is probably why running is America's most popular form of aerobic activity. More than thirty million men and women run on a regular basis. However, I don't believe in running daily because of the high risk of injury when running more often than two or three days a week. Since all of your body weight is coming down on one foot, ankle, shin, knee, thigh, and hip countless times a session, there is a great potential for injury in this activity, especially if you don't have proper running shoes or proper running form.

A bicycle seat supports much of your body weight and reduces the risk of leg injuries to a minimum, so cycling and stationary cycling present less risk of injury. But that alone isn't reason enough to cycle. I cycle because it's a superefficient fat burner that doesn't sacrifice one bit of lean body mass in the process. It's also fun! And swimming is an even less risky form of aerobic exercise—as long as you *can* swim, of course—since all of your body weight is buoyed by the water when you swim.

Ultimately the choice of aerobic activities that you make will be highly individual. You may even wish to concentrate solely on one type of aerobic training, but I'm sure that in the long run you will find it easier to stick to an aerobic exercise program if you frequently switch from one mode of aerobics to another.

The collection of exercises I present here are some of the best ones that I have always counted on over the years. This is a near perfect combination of movements to use in conjunction with your bodybuilding program. I have also maintained my level of fitness with this program during extended periods of time (up to one month) when I was unable to go to a well-equipped gym. These exercises have been invaluable to me, and I hope you get the same satisfaction out of them.

WARM–UP EXERCISES

JUMPING JACKS

(A) Emphasis. This is a vigorous full-body movement that particularly stresses the calves and the torso muscles that articulate your arms.

(B) Starting Position. Stand erect with your feet close together and your arms at your sides.

(C) Movement Performance. Bend your legs and sharply straighten them to spring from the floor. Simultaneously swing your arms directly out to the sides and upward until your hands touch overhead, and spread your legs a bit wider than shoulder width. Land with your legs slightly bent to absorb the shock of landing, then immediately spring up and return to the starting point. Repeat the movement.

RUNNING IN PLACE

(A) Emphasis. This is another vigorous full-body movement, but it particularly stresses the leg and arm muscles.

(B) Starting Position. Stand erect with your feet about shoulder width apart and your arms at your sides.

(C) Movement Performance. You can perform this exercise either with your arms down at your sides throughout the movement or rhythmically moving your arms forward and backward in coordination with your leg movements. Start jogging in place, lifting your feet only a few inches off the floor, then steadily build up the height of your knee lift until you are lifting your knees at least up to waist level each step. Continue running in place for one or two minutes.

BEND AND REACH

(A) Emphasis. This is a good warm-up exercise for stretching out the muscles of your hamstrings, pelvic girdle, lower back, and upper back.

(B) Starting Position. Stand with your feet set 6 to 8 inches wider than your shoulders on each side. Place your hands on your hips and stand erect.

(C) Movement Performance. Keeping your legs straight, bend forward at the waist and touch your hands on the floor about eighteen inches in front of your feet. Come partially erect and stretch back down to touch the floor directly between your feet. Bounce partway up one more time and go back down to touch about a foot in back of your feet, then come erect. Repeat the entire movement 5 to 10 times.

SIDE–TO–SIDE LUNGING STRETCH

(A) Emphasis. This vigorous warm-up movement stresses all of the muscles of the lower body, particularly those of the thighs, hips, and buttocks.

(B) Starting Position. Stand with your feet set about three feet apart, your toes pointed directly outward. Bend your legs until your thighs are in a position parallel with the floor. Lean forward and grasp your ankles. (Alternatively you can extend your arms directly forward from your shoulders to aid body balance.)

(C) Movement Performance. Shift your weight toward your left leg, simultaneously straightening your right leg. Then immediately shift your weight toward your right leg while straightening your left leg. Continue lunging from side to side in this manner for 10 to 15 repetitions to each side.

STRETCHING EXERCISES

STANDING QUADRICEPS STRETCH

(A) Emphasis. You can use this movement to stretch all of the muscles of your quadriceps and hip flexors.

(B) Starting Position. Stand near a high, sturdy surface, or a solid upright in the gym, and grasp it with your right hand to steady your body in position during the exercise. Or if you've been doing the exercise as long as I have and are confident in your ability to balance on one leg, you can do the movement freehand. Reach down with your left hand and grasp the ankle of your left leg with that leg bent at about a 90-degree angle.

(C) Stretched Position. Pull upward on your ankle to as high a position as possible, or until you reach the pain zone.

STANDING HAMSTRINGS STRETCH

(A) Emphasis. This exercise stretches the muscles at the backs of your thighs and your lower back.

(B) Starting Position. Stand with your feet close together, your toes pointed directly forward. Keeping your legs straight and your spine as straight as possible, slowly bend forward at the waist.

(C) Stretched Position. Grasp your ankles and pull your torso toward your thighs until you reach the pain zone. If you find it easy to place your torso on your thighs, you can make the exercise more intense by placing one foot in front of another and crossing your legs; in this case you should alternate the foot that you place forward each time you perform the stretch.

HURDLER'S STRETCH

(A) Emphasis. This exercise stretches virtually all of the muscles of your thighs, hip girdle, and lower back.

(B) Starting Position. Sit on the floor with your right leg extended forward and held straight during the movement. Your left leg should be fully bent and placed on the floor at the side of your hip.

(C) Stretched Position Number One. Lean forward over your straight leg until you either enter the pain zone or have placed your torso flat against your thigh.

You can grasp your ankle to help pull your torso down to your leg.

(D) Stretched Position Number Two. Supporting your body weight on your elbows, lean backward until you either enter the pain zone or your back is flat on the floor.

(E) Stretched Position Number Three. Sitting erect, twist your torso as far away from your extended leg as possible.

Note: Be sure to do an equal amount of stretching for each side of your body.

WAIST AND INNER THIGH STRETCH

(A) Emphasis. This movement stretches the muscles of your inner thighs as well as the muscles at the sides of your waist and upper torso.

(B) Starting Position. Sit on the gym floor with your right leg extended directly out to the side and held straight during the exercise and your toes pointed.

Bend your left leg and place the sole of your left foot against your upper right thigh as illustrated. You can do the stretching movement either with your hands held behind your head or with the arm held straight toward your extended leg.

(C) Stretched Position. Lean directly to the right until you enter the pain zone or until the side of your torso is resting on your thigh. Be sure to do an equal amount of stretching to each side.

TURTLE STRETCH

(A) Emphasis. This unique exercise stretches the inner thighs, lower back, hamstrings, and buttocks.

(B) Starting Position. Sit on the floor, bend your legs, place your feet together, and grasp your feet with your hands as illustrated. Sit erect.

(C) Stretched Positions. With your back rounded and your chin against your chest, bend your torso forward as far as comfortably possible. In this bottom position, and without moving any other part of your body, slowly raise your head up as high as possible, then arch your back and slowly come erect. Repeat the entire movement up to 10 times.

SEATED SPLIT STRETCH

(A) Emphasis. This exercise stretches the inner thigh, hamstring, hip girdle, and lower back muscles.

(B) Starting Position. Sit on the floor and spread your legs out in a V position (the wider apart you can position your legs, the better). Keep your legs straight during the entire movement.

(C) Stretched Positions. Rotate your torso so you are facing your right foot, reach toward your foot, and pull your torso down on your leg in that direction. Return to the middle position and this time bend directly forward and lower your torso as close to the floor as possible. Finally, rotate your torso so you are facing your left foot, and do the forward bending movement in that direction. Repeat the sequence back in the same direction and continue it until you have stretched 10 times to each side.

SEATED HAMSTRINGS/LOWER BACK STRETCH

(A) Emphasis. This exercise stretches the muscles at the backs of your thighs, lower back, and upper back.

(B) Starting Position. Sit on the floor with your legs held straight out in front of you, your toes pointed.

(C) Stretched Positions. This movement is very much like the turtle stretch. Starting with your torso erect, incline your head forward until your chin is on your chest, round your spine forward, and bend forward until your torso rests on your thighs. After a moment in this bottom position, slowly lift your head, then arch your back and slowly return to the upright seated position. Repeat the entire movement up to 10 times.

MIDSECTION EXERCISES

BENT–KNEE SIT–UPS

(A) Emphasis. Sit-ups stress all of the abdominal muscles, particularly the upper section of the rectus abdominis.

(B) Starting Position. Lie on your back with your legs slightly spread. Bend your legs at about a 30-degree angle and keep them bent throughout the movement. Cross your arms over your chest as you do the exercise.

(C) Movement Performance. Sit slowly up by first lifting your head from the floor, then curling your shoulders, upper back, and lower back off the floor. Reverse the procedure to return to the starting point and repeat the movement, working up to 50 consecutive repetitions.

BENT–KNEE LEG RAISES

(A) Emphasis. Leg raises stress all of the abdominal muscles, particularly the lower section of the rectus abdominis.

(B) Starting Position. Lie on your back on the floor with your hands placed beneath your hips. Straighten your legs.

(C) Movement Performance. Simultaneously raise your feet from the floor and bend your legs to a 90-degree angle, continuing the movement until your knees are near your chest. Slowly straighten your legs until they point straight upward from your hips. Keeping your legs straight, slowly lower them back to the starting point and repeat the movement. Work up to 25 consecutive repetitions.

KNEE TUCKS

(A) Emphasis. This excellent movement works the entire frontal abdominal wall.

(B) Starting Position. Lie on your back on the floor with your hands tucked beneath your hips and your chin on your chest. Raise your heels just clear of the floor with your legs straight.

(C) Movement Performance. Simultaneously bend your legs fully and pull your knees up as close to your face as possible. Hold this fully contracted position for a moment, return slowly to the starting position (don't let your heels touch the floor, however), and repeat the movement. Work up to 25 reps.

BODY CURLS

(A) Emphasis. Body curls work the entire rectus abdominis muscle wall on the front of your midsection.

(B) Starting Position. Lie on your back on the floor with your arms crossed on your chest, your legs slightly bent, your heels on the floor, and your chin on your chest. Keep your legs pressed together throughout the exercise.

(C) Movement Performance. Simultaneously curl your torso from the floor and lift your legs upward (bending them to about a 90-degree angle) until your elbows touch your forearms. Slowly return to the starting position and repeat the movement for up to 25 repetitions.

(D) Exercise Variation. You can involve the intercostal muscles on the sides of your waist more intensely by doing body curls with a twist to alternating sides at the top of each repetition.

JET SIT–UPS

(A) Emphasis. This unique movement stresses virtually all of the abdominal muscles, including the rectus abdominis and intercostals.

(B) Starting Position. Lie on your back on the floor with your arms at your sides but held just off the floor. Bend your right leg to about a 45-degree angle and place your right foot firmly on the floor. Keeping your left leg straight, raise your left heel slightly off the floor.

(C) Movement Performance. Use upper abdominal strength to raise your torso off the floor, simultaneously using lower abdominal strength to raise your left leg upward, until both your torso and leg are at approximately 45-degree angles with the floor. If you have some difficulty in raising your torso from the floor, you can grasp the backs of your upper thighs with your hands to assist your abdominal muscles. Slowly lower your torso back to the floor, chin on your chest, simultaneously bending your left leg fully until your left foot is just above the floor, then straightening your left leg while pushing your foot parallel to the floor back to the original starting position. Do 10 to 15 repetitions in this position, then switch leg positions for another 10 to 15 reps.

BENT–KNEE LEG LIFTS

(A) Emphasis. This unique leg raise movement stresses all of the frontal abdominal muscles, particularly the lower section of the rectus abdominis.

(B) Starting Position. Lie on your back on the floor, supporting your torso on your elbows as illustrated. Bend your right leg fully and hold your knee over your abdomen throughout the movement. Raise your left heel just clear of the floor and keep your left leg straight as you do the exercise.

(C) Movement Performance. Moving only your left leg, raise your leg upward until it is perpendicular to the floor. Lower your left leg back downward until your heel almost touches the floor, then repeat the movement. Do 15 to 20 reps with this leg position, switch legs, and do 15 to 20 more reps raising your right leg from the floor.

SIDE LEG LIFTS

(A) Emphasis. Side leg lifts place relatively intense stress on your rectus abdominis, intercostal, and external oblique muscles.

(B) Starting Position. Lie on your left side on the floor, supporting your torso on your left elbow as illustrated. Orient your pelvis so that it is at a 45-degree angle with the floor throughout this exercise. Straighten your legs, press them together, and start the exercise with your legs just off the floor. Place your right hand behind your head.

(C) Movement Performance. Raise your legs upward until they are perpendicular to the floor, pulling your right elbow toward your knees at the top of the movement and contracting your upper abdominal muscles. Slowly lower your legs back to the starting point and repeat the movement for 15 to 20 repetitions. Switch sides and do 15 to 20 more reps in that position.

HIP AND THIGH EXERCISES

(A) Emphasis. Hip hyperextensions stress the muscles of the buttocks, hips, and lower back.

(B) Starting Position. Kneel on your hands and knees on an exercise mat. Shift your weight to your right knee, lift your left knee from the mat, simultaneously bend your left leg fully and tuck your left knee in to your chest, and round your back.

(C) Movement Performance. Extend your left leg to the rear while arching your back. From this position, use butt power to lift your left foot as high as possible. Return to the starting point and repeat the movement. Be sure to do an equal number of reps for each leg.

(D) Exercise Variations. I like to do peak contraction movements at the top point of the exercise, holding my working leg straight and doing just short, quick, partial reps at the top of the movement. I also frequently do hip hyperextensions while supporting my torso on my elbows rather than on my hands. A final variation begins with my leg bent and my knee toward the floor, from which point I straighten and extend my leg directly upward as high as I can.

COMBINATION HIP HYPEREXTENSIONS

(A) Emphasis. This combination movement stresses the muscles of the buttocks, hips, and lower back.

(B) Starting Position. Assume the same starting position as for hip hyperextensions.

(C) Movement Performance. Extend your leg to the rear on the first rep as you would for normal hip hyperextensions, but on the next repetition, extend your leg directly out to the side. Alternate extending your leg to the rear and then to the side for up to 25 total reps.

(D) Exercise Variations. At the end of your set, you can do about 15 repetitions of one of three movements directly out to the side. The first of these is leg kicks, in which you begin with your leg bent and then extend it directly out to the side. In the second variation you keep your leg straight and raise it upward from a position with your heel near the floor to the highest point comfortably possible. The third variation consists of a leg rotation, in which you move your foot in large circles with your leg held straight.

BODY WHIPS

(A) Emphasis. This is a fantastically dynamic leg, hip, and midsection exercise when performed correctly.

(B) Starting Position. Kneel on your left knee with your hands placed on the floor about two feet apart to support your torso parallel to the floor throughout the movement. Keeping your right leg straight and your right foot no more than two inches from the floor, whip your foot forward as far as you can, moving your torso toward your leg.

(C) Movement Performance. Whip your right leg backward, still with your foot just above the floor and as far across the midline of your body behind yourself as possible. As your leg passes the midline of your body, your hip must roll toward the floor to keep your foot near the floor. And as your foot reaches its full range of motion across the midline of your body, your torso is whipped forcefully toward it. Immediately your leg is whipped back to the starting point and the movement is repeated for up to 25 reps with each leg.

Training Tip: Momentum is very important in this exercise: You should make the most of leg momentum to increase the range of motion of your leg.

SIDE LEG RAISES WITH KICK

(A) Emphasis. This compound movement stresses the muscles of your thighs, hips, buttocks, and abdomen (the external obliques and intercostals).

(B) Starting Position. Lie on your left side on an exercise mat and support your torso on your left elbow as illustrated. Your left leg will remain straight and on the mat throughout the movement. Your right leg will also be held straight as you do the exercise, starting in a position resting against your left leg.

(C) Movement Performance. Raise your right leg straight upward until it is at least at a 90-degree angle with the floor. Lower your leg back to the starting position. At the bottom of the movement, rotate your pelvis and torso about 45 degrees toward the floor. In this position, use buttock strength to raise your leg up as high as possible. Lower your leg back to the starting point, rotate back to the initial position, and repeat the movement, alternating torso/hip positions for 25 repetitions.

Training Tip: At the end of 25 reps of the full movement, you can do partial peak contractions with your working leg bent and your torso rotated toward the floor. Be sure to do an equal number of sets and reps for each leg.

BUTTOCK TIGHTENERS

(A) Emphasis. This is a very intense movement stressing the buttocks and erector spinae muscles of the lower back.

(B) Starting Position. Lie on your back with the soles of your feet flat on the floor and your feet pulled up close to your pelvis. Place your hands on the sides of your waist.

(C) Movement Performance. Tense your buttocks and lower back muscles to raise your butt well off the floor. Hold this top position for a moment, return to the starting point, and repeat the movement. Often I'll place my hands against my sides and lower back to monitor my erector spinae contractions.

Caution: If you have any lower back problems, this exercise should be avoided.

(D) Exercise Variations. There are several variations of the foot and knee positions that you can use in this exercise. You should do the movement not only with your feet set shoulder width apart (as you will most frequently see the exercise performed) but also with

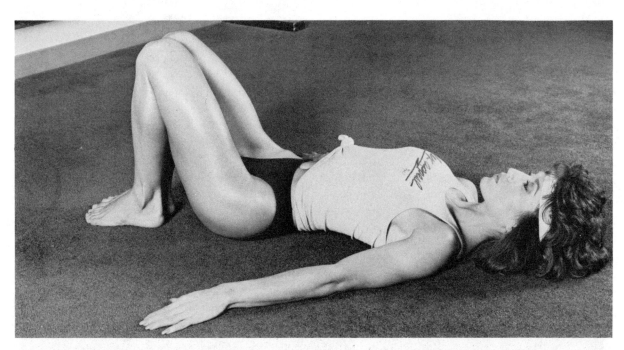

your feet together. You can also have your knees together, apart, or actually moving apart and together
during the movement. Finally you can do buttock
tighteners with one leg extended, which effectively
doubles the amount of resistance you feel in your
working buttock muscles.

HIP TONERS

(A) Emphasis. This is a good full-body movement that
especially stresses all of the muscles of the legs, lower
back, and midsection.

(B) Starting Position. Kneel on the mat with one
knee about two feet behind the other. Bend over and
place your hands shoulder width apart on the floor
directly beneath your shoulders. Lift your knees from
the floor so that your weight is supported on your
hands and feet.

(C) Movement Performance. Spring your feet from
the floor and quickly switch position with them before
they again land on the floor. Immediately spring back
in the air and again switch position. Continue switching leg positions until comfortably fatigued.

INNER THIGH LIFTS

(A) Emphasis. This excellent floor-exercise movement tones the adductor muscles of your inner thighs.

(B) Starting Position. Lie on your left side on the floor, supporting your torso on your elbow as illustrated. Straighten your left leg along the floor. If you have good quadriceps development, this will push your ankle and foot clear of the floor; otherwise your foot will rest lightly on the floor in this position. Bend your right leg past a 90-degree angle and place your toes and the ball of your foot on the floor with your foot extended, placing your toes even with your left knee. In the correct starting position, your right foot will rest on the floor behind your left leg.

(C) Movement Performance. Keeping your left leg straight, use inner thigh strength to raise it off the floor and upward to as high a position as you comfortably can without altering your upper body position (this will be a position in which your left foot is twelve to eighteen inches from the floor). Slowly lower your leg back down to the starting point and repeat the movement for 20 to 30 reps. Be sure to do an equal amount of work with your right leg.

INNER THIGH TOUCHES

(A) Emphasis. As with inner thigh lifts, inner thigh touches stress and tone the muscles of your inner thighs. But inner thigh touches also place significant stress on the abductor muscles of your hips and outer upper thighs.

(B) Starting Position. Assume the same starting position as for inner thigh lifts except keep both legs straight and initially raise your right leg upward until it is at about a 45-degree angle with the floor. Hold your right leg in this position throughout the movement.

(C) Movement Performance. Use inner thigh strength to lift your straight left leg slowly upward to touch against your right leg. Lower your left leg back to the starting point and repeat the movement for 20 to 30 reps.

(D) Variations. There are two commonly performed variations of inner thigh touches. In the first you hold your legs parallel to the floor and scissor them back and forth over each other, alternating 1 rep with your left leg on top and the next with your right leg on top. In the second variation you hold your right leg approximately perpendicular to the floor and raise your left leg from the floor up to your right leg over a much longer range of motion than in the basic performance method for this movement.

SQUAT THRUSTS

(A) Emphasis. This is an excellent movement that stresses all of the muscle groups of your body, but particularly your legs, hips, abdomen, lower back, and chest muscles.

(B) Starting Position. Stand erect with your feet close together and your hands on your hips.

(C) Movement Performance. Bend your legs and lean forward so you can place your hands shoulder width apart on the floor a bit in front of your feet. From this position, keep your arms straight and spring your feet from the floor so you can extend your body and land in a push-up position. Spring off the floor with your feet again, landing with your body flexed and your feet close to your hands. Return to the initial starting position and repeat the movement for 15 to 20 reps.

Note: You should do squat thrusts throughout your workout, whenever you feel your heart rate returning to normal. This might be as many as three or four times during a floor exercise session. I also prefer to finish off a floor exercise workout with a set of squat thrusts, followed by at least six to ten minutes more of stretching.

ISOMETRIC AND UPPER BODY EXERCISES

HAND–ON–KNEE ISOMETRIC PEC CONTRACTIONS

(A) Emphasis. All isometric pec contractions place intense stress on your pectoral muscles, shaping and defining the entire complex of chest muscles.

(B) Starting Position. Sit cross-legged on a mat on the gym floor. Reach across your body with your right hand and place your hand against the inside of your knee, your right arm held straight throughout the movement. I like to monitor the contraction in my right pectoral by placing the fingertips of my left hand against the muscle group.

(C) Movement Performance. Using my knee as an immovable object, I strongly contract my right pec muscle for four to six seconds, relaxing for a moment and repeating the contraction eight to ten times. By shrugging my shoulder upward a little, I find that I can more strongly contract the upper part of my pectoral muscles; sagging my shoulder downward allows me to place more intense stress on the lower part of my pectoral complex.

(D) Variations. In a crossed-arms pec contraction I cross my forearms and clasp my hands with my fingers interlaced as illustrated. This movement can be done with your arms angled downward from your shoulders or with your arms elevated at any angle up to one that places your arms parallel to the floor. In a clasped-hands pec contraction I clasp my hands at face level and force my elbows together to contract both pec muscles. Usually I'll start this exercise with my hands set at about hip level, then at mid-chest level and finally at face or forehead level. I'll do several reps at each hand level to stimulate my chest muscles thoroughly.

UPPER ARM SELF-RESISTED CONTRACTION

(A) Emphasis. Depending on your mental focus, you can use this movement to stress either your biceps or triceps with a good degree of intensity.

(B) Starting Position. Sit cross-legged on a mat on the gym floor. With your right palm facing upward and your right arm relatively straight, place your left hand palm down on your right wrist.

(C) Movement Performance. Push down with your left hand to provide resistance against your right wrist as you slowly bend your arm completely. Concentrate your mental energy on your right biceps as it slowly contracts and extends under resistance for 8 to 10 repetitions. Rest a moment and repeat the movement, this time concentrating on your left triceps muscle group as it pushes against your right wrist to straighten and then rebend your right arm. Be sure to perform an equal amount of work with both arms by switching hand positions frequently.

WAIST–OBLIQUE CONTRACTIONS

(A) Emphasis. Competitive bodybuilders practice this exercise a lot to gain good control over their oblique and intercostal muscles during a posing routine. You can do the same exercise to firm and tone the muscles at the sides of your waist.

(B) Starting Position. Place your feet together and stand erect. Place your hands behind your neck or head.

(C) Movement Performance. To get the correct contraction in this movement, you must do four tasks simultaneously: (1) Bend your right leg a few degrees and go up on the toes of your right foot; (2) consciously contract the muscles on the right side of your waist; (3) pull downward on your right arm and elbow with the muscles at the sides of your waist; and (4) forcefully blow out all of your air. When you do these four things at once, you will experience a very intense contraction in your oblique and intercostal muscles. Hold this contraction for four to six seconds, relax for a moment, and repeat the contraction eight to ten times. Be sure to do an equal number of contractions for the other side of your torso.

Training Tip: Once you have mastered the ability to contract intensely the muscles at the sides of your waist, you should "grind" the contracted position, moving your torso up and down, as well as from one side to the other, to feel out alternative areas in which you should work on your contractions.

PUSH–UPS

(A) Emphasis. Push-ups stress the pectorals, deltoids, and triceps.

(B) Starting Position. Assume a supported position on your toes and hands with your torso straight and your arms perpendicular to the floor. Your hands should be set about shoulder width apart on the floor, your fingers facing forward.

(C) Movement Performance. Bend your arms fully and lower your torso down until your chest touches the floor. Without resting your weight on the floor, push yourself back to the starting point and repeat the movement. Do 10 to 20 reps.

Training Tip: If you lack sufficient upper body strength to manage at least ten push-ups, you should do push-ups with your knees rather than your feet resting on the floor until you have developed enough chest, shoulder, and arm strength for the movement. However, don't do this easier variation of the exercise unless you simply can't do the more advanced form of exercise.

LOOKING AHEAD

In the final chapter I will discuss various ways in which you can use your mental powers to improve your bodybuilding goals. The primary subjects discussed include mental concentration, positive thinking, five-sense visualization, goal setting, and goal achievement.

CHAPTER 11

the mind and bodybuilding

T he human mind is one of the most awesome and powerful forces on earth. Properly utilized, your mind can help you to build one of the greatest bodies in the world.

In order for your mind to assist you to become a champion bodybuilder, however, you must *allow* it to help you. If you're like most people, you are your own worst enemy because you stand in your own way to progress. The standard cop-out is "That's too difficult for me to ever succeed at, so I won't even try." It's a cop-out because you refuse to take the risk of failing in order to have a chance at succeeding.

Everyone can improve. Indeed, you can improve your body to such an extent in only a year of dedicated bodybuilding training that you probably wouldn't recognize the new you. Every woman has the ability to improve her entire life dramatically if she will only *try* to improve. But first you must have the desire and then must go about it the right way with the proper mental attitude.

You have the power of God locked up in your mind. Let it pour forth and guide you to physical develop-ment that you won't believe possible at this point in time. Go for it as hard as you can rather than standing in your own way. Success is yours for the taking, so what are you waiting for? Here's how....

POSITIVE THINKING

Regardless of your walk in life, all successful people have one mental factor in common: They always think positively.

A person is basically what he or she thinks. Your personality is made up of the accumulation of your thoughts. You are today what your thoughts, beliefs, and convictions have made you. Many times you are defeated not by your circumstances and problems but by your attitude toward them. What you *think* about your problems is of utmost importance in overcoming them, and more times than not, it's a positive attitude that spells the difference between victory and defeat.

"For as a man thinketh in his heart, so is he."
—*PROVERBS 23:7*

I believe that the Holy Bible is the inerrant Word of God. I don't feel that it's out of place to express what I truly believe in this chapter concerning the subject of mind. Mind is not always "mental," so to speak, like a formal educational process. Nor is it stuffing your memory with facts. The development of mind is a nurturing growth process that takes place throughout your life. I am grateful that I have been gifted with faith in God to hunger for the way in which He wants me to live. It has taken scientists thousands of years to learn what God already revealed to us in the Bible: that we actually precondition our lives for sickness or health, prosperity or poverty, by what we think and say. Medical authorities tell us that most physical illness is psychosomatic, that is, it results from negative thinking, worry, or emotional stress. Have you ever met people who give you a rundown on their pains and afflictions when you greet them with a friendly "How are you today?"

So, apart from how we think, the next and equally important factor we need to deal with is our mouths.

"Thou art snared with the words of thy mouth."
—*PROVERBS 6:2*

I wish I could elaborate on the fundamental truths that have been the basis of my success; however, I feel I would get so carried away that this chapter would be a Christian book within a bodybuilding book.

CONCENTRATION

One of the first mental techniques that you can use to improve the results you receive from your training is *concentration*. Concentration is a consciously developed link between your mind and your working muscles during a set of any exercise. The stronger this mind-muscle link, the more you'll get out of each set.

You take your first steps toward supreme concentration by identifying which muscles are being stressed by each exercise you perform in a workout. Then you should focus your mind on these muscles during each set you perform of the movement chosen, attempting to be conscious of your muscles working against the weight. It won't take long to enable yourself to feel a working muscle, but at first it'll be difficult to focus your mind unwaveringly on that sensation.

When you are in a state of optimal concentration, your mind stays on the working muscles; it doesn't skip back and forth between that focal point and anything else that distracts you. And everything will seem to distract you when you are first learning to concentrate. The trick is to force your mind back immediately to the task at hand the moment you discover that it has wandered.

I'd be surprised if you can initially hold your attention on your working muscles for more than ten to fifteen seconds. Later, when you are more adept at workout concentration, you will be able to maintain your mental focus for more than a minute. You will actually be able to concentrate so completely that you will become oblivious to your surroundings.

There is a simple concentration-improvement exercise that you can do at odd times of the day. This involves focusing your attention on any object for as long as possible, forcing your mind back on it every time your concentration weakens. Since you are always breathing, I suggest that you focus your concentration completely on your inhalations and exhalations. Slow down the tempo of your breathing and concentrate on each breath for ten to fifteen minutes.

If you practice this little exercise consistently for several weeks, you can dramatically improve your workout concentration. If you also count individual breaths in groups of ten, you will be performing a rudimentary form of mantra meditation.

Once you have mastered the art of concentration in a bodybuilding setting, you will find that this rare ability also helps in every other aspect of your life. When you are able to concentrate fully on a task you have set for yourself, you will be able to complete it more quickly and in much better form than if you don't concentrate well.

Concentrating mentally on pec contractions using finger monitoring.

VISUALIZATION

If you've read about psychology or taken a college psych course, you may have heard about a psychological term called *self-fulfilling prophecy*. In a self-fulfilling prophecy, believing that something will happen sets the subconscious mind to making choices that will help bring that thought into reality.

You've no doubt seen examples of self-fulfilling prophecies over the years. Perhaps you knew a young girl who wanted to become a dancer, fantasized about it frequently, and—lo and behold!—became a professional dancer. Perhaps your sister wished to become a nurse or physician so badly that she became one, or a friend convinced herself she could become a cheerleader and did.

In everyday situations the subconscious mind is *unconsciously* programmed to seek a certain objective. It then becomes a tremendously powerful ally in helping you achieve that objective. Wouldn't it be great if you could *consciously* program your subconscious mind to help you to reach your bodybuilding goals more quickly and easily? Well, you can!

Through a mental technique called *visualization* you can consciously program your subconscious mind to make it easier for you to get good workouts, to avoid foods detrimental to your progress, and to discipline yourself in every way a champion woman bodybuilder must to succeed at her sport. And all visualization amounts to is a regularly applied program of "creative daydreaming."

After you have relaxed, begin to work on building a detailed three-dimensional image of your perfect physique. Imagine every ripple of muscle, each separation between the muscles, all of the veins, the tightness of your skin over your muscles. Make it *real*, as if your mind is a movie projector focusing this image against the insides of your eyelids. Once you have this image in sharp focus, savor it.

At first your mind will frequently drift away from your image. Force it back on target. Also, your image won't be in sharp focus initially. Work on bringing it into focus. Soon you'll be able to summon up a very sharp and realistic image of the way you want your physique to appear.

This is as far as all but an informed handful of male and female bodybuilders take the practice of visualization, and they get plenty out of it! But—and this is a *big* but—you can take the visualization technique far beyond where most people take it. Doing so can separate you from the pack and make you successful much more quickly!

Psychologists who are experts in visualization have concluded that to receive optimal benefit from the practice, you should involve all five of your senses: sight (or visual imagination), taste, hearing, olfactory ability, and touch. The type of visualization procedure described up till now usually involves only sight. Infrequently it will involve fleeting images of sound or touch. Therefore, to improve the results of your visualization, you must endeavor to include other senses in your imagined physical image.

One of the easiest senses to incorporate into your visualization is touch. The sense of touch includes the "feel" of being inside your superior new body, flexing, touching, experiencing your firm, tight muscles. So, after you have developed your visual image, the next logical step is to project yourself into it and realistically experience the feel of that fantastic body you'll soon have.

You can add sound to your image by projecting yourself into a training or competition situation. In the gym you can hear the clang of the weights or the voice of your training partner urging you on as you exercise your imagined body. Onstage you can hear the roar of the crowd and your music as you glide from one incredible pose to another.

It's difficult to *taste* what it's like to be inside your world-beater physique, but why not visualize yourself inside that body during one of your last meals before competing? At that point your diet will be pretty bland and boring, but merely adding the taste of the food or your lip gloss or anything else with a taste to the appearance and feel of your physique moves your visualization process forward.

The smell of being in your ultimate physique is easily symbolized by the scent of body oil onstage at a prejudging, or perhaps the subtle perfume of honest sweat in a gym. Just be certain to combine this olfactory sense with as many other senses as possible in your visualization practice.

The key here is to combine as many of the five senses as you can in your visualized self-image. Expert psychologists feel that including three of these five senses in visualization is all an athlete can expect to achieve. Obviously these scholars haven't had much experience with bodybuilders, because I've consistently managed to include all five senses in my visualized images of my ultimate physique!

A lot of bodybuilders, even a few of the superstars, feel that visualization is just so much window dressing. If someone tells you this, don't listen and immediately erase the experience from your memory bank. Visualization *does* work wonders for a bodybuilder, as long as the images are kept within the bounds of reality.

I wish I could give you a timetable for how long it will take you to master and benefit from each level of visualization, but individual aptitudes for mastering visualization vary considerably. Just *work* on it, master it, and use it to improve your physique and life in general!

I truly believe that each of our five senses is a God-blessed gift, perfect in every way. Depend on the senses and draw on the potential that they hold in store for you. Praise Him and be thankful; you are His greatest creation!

GOAL SETTING

One of the best methods of achieving success in bodybuilding—as well as in every other facet of your life—is *goal setting*. In life situations you probably won't achieve something if it appears to be too mind-boggling a project. This is where proper use of long- and short-range goals comes into play.

There are really three types of goals that you should set for yourself: final goals, long-term goals, and short-term goals. Final goals are usually set only once, because they should be so lofty in nature that it's unlikely that you would achieve one early enough in your life to warrant setting another. An example of a final goal may be to win the Miss Olympia title one day. It isn't a goal that is easy to attain, but rather something toward which you might strive for many years.

Long-range goals are set on a yearly basis, and reset when each has been attained. These long-term goals are way stations on your journey to the top. So if your ultimate goal is to win a Miss Olympia title, you might set yearly long-term goals of first winning a local championship, then state, regional, national, and international events, before aiming for the Olympia.

The value of long-range goals lies in breaking an incomprehensible ultimate goal into more manageable portions. But even long-term goals can be mind-boggling, so they should in turn be broken down into one-month or six-week short-range goals that are easily comprehended and relatively easily attained. Each time you reach a short-term goal and set a new and higher one, you have taken a step toward the top.

Lao-tzu, the noted Chinese philosopher reputed to have founded the Taoist religion, wrote: "The journey of a thousand miles is started with a single step." This aphorism is frequently quoted when people write or speak about the goal-setting process because goal setting is very much like taking a long cross-country walk. One step may not seem like such a big deal when compared to a walk of a thousand miles, but inevitably enough single steps add up to a thousand-mile journey.

You should never lose sight of your ultimate goal and your long-term goals, but most of your mental focus should be on setting and achieving short-term goals. This keeps you from overloading your mind and shorting out its enormous power. You end up taking one step at a time, and in the end you achieve each intermediate long-term goal as well as the cherished ultimate goal.

Let's look at an example of how you can use goal setting to help you achieve bodybuilding success. Assume that your final goal is to win the Miss Olympia title, and you realize that you can greatly improve the mass and quality of your legs and buttocks by increasing your leg press poundage by 180 pounds over the next year. Therefore you set as your long-range goal using 180 pounds more for a set number of reps within a year's time.

Adding 180 pounds to your leg press in a year is a realistic goal, given the relative mass and power of your thigh and butt muscles. It's important that all of your goals be realistically attainable, because they are useless if you can't reach each goal in the time you have allotted. If you aren't already an experienced weight trainer, you will soon gain a clear understanding or what is realistically attainable in bodybuilding training.

Returning to your long-term goal of adding 180 pounds to your training weight for the leg press: You should break that figure down into twelve monthly short-term goals. You divide 180 by 12 and get 15, so you must add 15 pounds to your leg press each month in order to reach your long-range goal of using 180 additional pounds.

Adding 15 pounds to a movement sounds a lot

more manageable than using 180 more pounds, doesn't it? In the answer to that question lies the beauty of using short-range goals to help you achieve your long-term goals, and of using long-term goals to achieve final goals: It's easier to eat a loaf of bread one bite at a time than all at once.

Goal Achievement

Obviously there is a lot to be said for being goal-oriented, but the concept goes over a lot of people's heads. I believe that this is due to the common inability to decide what is important in life. Do you know what you want in life? Some people don't.

One easy way to identify goals is to think in ultimate terms. One common general goal is security, and to achieve security, you need enough of an assured income to guarantee you freedom from want. What ways are open to you to attain that amount of earning power? The answer depends on how well you analyze and evaluate your native talents. I have a talent for bodybuilding; you may have a talent for music or medicine.

Once you have thought in more general terms, it's relatively easy to narrow your focus and begin to discover what you want out of bodybuilding and the rest of your life. But don't get the idea that these goals are carved in stone, because you will change them from time to time as your perception of basic needs changes.

You must also learn to analyze the sequential steps that you need to take in order to achieve a goal, because these steps eventually become your short-term goals. The route to attaining every long-range goal is not as easy to determine as it was in our example of adding 180 pounds to the exercise weight you use in a leg press movement. Sometimes the steps are hidden from view and you have to do some serious digging to uncover them.

As soon as you have determined what your long- and short-range goals should be, you can begin to go after them in a deliberate, step-by-step manner, which ultimately leads to success. You can use this approach equally well in any part of your life: It works in life's every facet.

TURNING THE DIAL

Like any success venture, bodybuilding competition contains an element of risk: You must accept the risk of losing in order to win. As a result, you will occasionally face negative situations. When you do, it's best to turn these to your advantage by changing your mental focus.

For example, I used to become discouraged from time to time because I was gaining muscle mass so slowly, which is the case with most women bodybuilders. Now I prefer to train for quality development rather than for pure mass because the mass will ultimately come if I follow this approach. And because I follow this approach, I'm no longer discouraged by slow gains.

The worst thing that can happen to a champion bodybuilder is to lose a major competition, but when I have lost in the past I've been able to use that loss to spur myself to train even harder than before. Losing the '81 Olympia was, in retrospect, one of the best things that could have happened to me, because reliving the experience has given me so much drive, enthusiasm, and training energy that it's pushed me to new heights of development. Also, an occasional loss keeps a bodybuilder from getting too cocky.

Rex Dante, my memory dynamics teacher, calls this process "turning the dial." You turn a negative experience into something positive. I'm a firm believer that everything happens to me for a purpose. I need only discover what that greater purpose is and use it to my advantage.

MOTIVATION

On the way to the gym I think about a variety of things to give me training drive. Often I listen to good rock music, and at other times I get psyched up by listening to classical music and inspirational cassette tapes, or by thinking about my competitors and how good they are. I sometimes think about my parents, all they've done for me over the years, and how it's now my turn to give something back.

All these methods work in rotation, and the variety is important. The mind can quickly adapt to a certain psyching stimulus and become inured to it, so you should never stick to any one psyching method. In the same manner, your body quickly grows used to a certain type of training program and stops increasing hypertrophically. That's why I frequently change routines.

SELF–CONFIDENCE

As you continue to make good gains from regular training, you will find that your self-confidence increases almost as quickly as your body improves. This is largely because you notice how much control you now have over the appearance of your body. With proper bodybuilding training and diet you can literally form your body to whatever specifications you desire, and that is a very heady experience.

Self-confidence is a valuable asset to anyone's life because it opens many doors. When you have self-confidence you are able to take chances that other people can't accept. If you have built up a pattern of success, it's difficult to believe that you will fail at any new undertaking. Of course, you *will* fail from time to time, but such infrequent failure is a small price to pay for the good things that will come your way as a result of your growing self-confidence.

Self-confidence can become your enemy, however, when it breeds the type of arrogant behavior I've seen in some women bodybuilders. It's certainly easy to believe that you have become a superior person as a result of your bodybuilding, but don't let that attitude color your interactions with other people. It's much better to maintain an air of humility and willingness to learn from others. Then you will be a credit both to yourself and to your chosen sport.

ALL IN PERSPECTIVE

In the event that you become a serious competitive bodybuilder, the best advice I can give you is to keep your sports participation in perspective: It should be a valuable adjunct to your life rather than the dominant factor. Don't sacrifice your family, friends, job, education, or morals in pursuit of a false god. Instead, treat your bodybuilding as an enjoyable, healthful hobby.

Living in southern California, the center of competitive bodybuilding in the United States, I've seen many male and female bodybuilders make their training and other preparations 100 percent of their lives. When that is the case, and they don't end up winning the big title and reaping its attendant riches, they have nothing to fall back on.

Bodybuilding is my occupation, but it doesn't rule my life. I train only two or three hours a day, and the rest of my day is spent in business pursuits, communing with my friends, and enjoying the varied kaleidoscope of life. I firmly believe that this balanced approach to bodybuilding is one reason why I have been successful in the sport. I get more out of bodybuilding when I don't let it rule me, and you will too.

Photo by Luke Wynn

Glossary
of Common Terms

Aerobic exercise. Sustained, low-intensity exercise (e.g., running, cycling, swimming, dancing) that builds endurance and helps burn fat. For an aerobic effect you must maintain your pulse rate at 80 percent of maximum (calculated by subtracting your age from 220) for at least twenty minutes. Aerobic excercise uses abundant supplies of oxygen to burn energy extracted from fat cells; therefore it is an excellent form of exercise for burning body fat.

AFWB. The American Federation of Women Bodybuilders, which governs women's amateur bodybuilding in the United States. The AFWB is affiliated internationally with the IFBB.

AMDR. Adult minimum daily requirement, or the level of a particular nutrient suggested for ingestion by adults each day by the US Food and Drug Administration (FDA).

Anaerobic exercise. Short-term, high-intensity exercise that burns more oxygen than the body can supply, thus creating an oxygen debt. This type of exercise burns primarily glycogen for energy. Since *weight training* is normally anaerobic work, you should also perform regular *aerobic workouts* to burn off body fat more efficiently.

Balance. One of the most desirable physical qualities that a competitive bodybuilder can possess, balance is an even proportional relationship between all of the muscle groups of a physique.

Bar. The metal rod four to six feet in length that forms the base of a BARBELL. (The bar of a DUMBBELL is usually ten to fourteen inches in length.)

Barbell. The most basic piece of equipment used in BODY-BUILDING training, consisting of a BAR, SLEEVE, COLLARS and PLATES. Barbells can be either adjustable or fixed in weight.

BMR. The basal metabolic rate, or the speed at which the body burns calories to meet its basic survival needs.

Bodybuilding. One of several subdivisions of WEIGHT TRAINING in which a person uses weight workouts and sound dietary practices to reshape his or her body. Most people use bodybuilding to solve problems of physical balance merely for their own satisfaction. For a smaller number of men and women, bodybuilding is an international sport on both amateur and professional levels.

Body sculpting. Usually used in a feminine context, this is another term for BODYBUILDING.

Burn. The pain caused by a buildup of fatigue by-products in a muscle that has been pushed very hard during a SET.

CAFB. The Canadian Amateur Federation of Bodybuilders, which administers amateur bodybuilding for men and women in Canada. Like the AFWB, the CAFB is affiliated internationally with the IFBB.

Cheating. A training method in which extraneous body motion is used to boost a weight past the point at which it normally would fail to move. Cheating is used to push a muscle to keep working past the point of normal failure (see TRAINING TO FAILURE).

Circuit Training. A special form of WEIGHT TRAINING that specifically increases cardiorespiratory (aerobic) fitness while toning and developing the body. With circuit training, a bodybuilder sets up approximately fifteen exercise stations around a gym, then moves with little rest between exercises from station to station until the entire circuit is completed.

Clean. The act of pulling a BARBELL or two DUMBBELLS directly from the floor to shoulder height. For example, a barbell must first be cleaned to the shoulders before a set of standing military presses can be performed.

Collar. The metal clamp used to secure plates in place on a BARBELL bar. Collars are either removable or permanently bolted or welded in place. Inside collars keep plates from sliding in toward the hands, and outside collars keep plates from slipping off the ends of the bar.

Contraction. The shortening and tightening of a muscle or muscle group during a REPETITION of an exercise. There are two types of muscular contraction: *isotonic contraction,* or exerting muscle force against a moving object (e.g., a BARBELL or exercise machine); and *isometric contraction,* or exerting muscle force against an immovable object (e.g., statically flexing the muscles while posing).

Couples competition. Often called mixed-pairs competition, this is a type of bodybuilding competition in which man-woman teams compete against each other. The newest form of bodybuilding competition, couples shows have become quite popular worldwide in both amateur and professional categories.

Cut up. A term referring to a fat-free, highly muscular degree of physical condition.

Definition. The state of being CUT UP, or having a high degree of muscular development and a low level of body fat.

Density. The hardness of a muscle. Muscle density is a prized quality in any contest-ready bodybuilder's physique.

Dumbbell. A short-handled version of the BARBELL, intended for use in one hand. While barbells are best for use in training large muscle groups, such as the thighs, back, and chest, dumbbells are best used to exercise the smaller muscle groups, such as the arms and shoulders.

Exercise. The actual movement that you are doing in a WORKOUT. In a calisthenics program a push-up or a sit-up would be an exercise; in bodybuilding an incline press is an example of an exercise. An exercise is often referred to as a *movement.*

FDA. The US Food and Drug Administration, which has researched and published findings on nutritional practices.

Flexibility. A limberness of joints and muscles that permits an exaggerated degree of joint movement. Flexibility is promoted by regular use of stretching exercises.

Forced reps. A training technique in which a training partner pulls up on the middle of a BARBELL to allow a bodybuilder to complete two or three repetitions past the normal point of failure. Like CHEATING reps, forced reps stress a muscle more intensely than in normal bodybuilding training, and thus promote a greater degree of HYPERTROPHY.

Hypertrophy. The increase in mass and strength in a muscle resulting from high-intensity WEIGHT TRAINING. This is sometimes referred to as growth, although no actual increase in the number of muscle cells occurs. There is only an increase in the cross-sectional area of each muscle fiber.

IFBB. The International Federation of Bodybuilders. Founded in 1946, this large sports federation has more than 115 national organizations affiliated with it internationally, making it the seventh largest international sports federation.

Intensity. Literally the quality of effort that you put forth during the performance of an exercise or an entire training ROUTINE.

Isolation. One of the most important concepts in BODYBUILDING training, this involves limiting effort in an exercise to a specific muscle group or often to only a part of that muscle. By carefully choosing exercises to isolate a particular part of a muscle or muscle group, you can actually alter the shape of the muscle(s).

Judging rounds. In the IFBB/AFWB system of judging, there are three main rounds of posing, followed by a posedown involving the top five competitors after three rounds of judging. In round one, five compulsory poses are evaluated; in round two the body is viewed in a semirelaxed attitude (with arms down at the sides) from the front, back, and both sides; and in round three an athlete's free-posing routine is evaluated.

Lifting belt. A wide leather belt that is worn tightly cinched around the waist to add stability to the middle of the body during heavy leg, back, and overhead pressing exercises.

Mass. The relative size or fullness of muscles. Mass is less prized among women bodybuilders than SYMMETRY, proportion, and MUSCULARITY.

Muscularity. The absence of body fat and fullness of muscle tissue that results in a highly defined physique. Muscularity is also called being defined, cut, or ripped.

Nutrition. The science of consuming various foods to assist in changing the form of a person's physique in a BODYBUILDING context. Primarily nutrition is used either to add MASS to the body or to strip away body fat for a contest.

Olympian. A woman who has competed in the Miss Olympia competition.

Olympic barbell. A specially machined BARBELL used in WEIGHT-LIFTING and POWER-LIFTING competition as well as for heavy leg, back, and chest exercises. An Olympic barbell is approximately seven feet in length and takes much larger PLATES than a normal exercise barbell.

Olympic lifting. A form of WEIGHT-LIFTING competition engaged in by some women that features competition in two lifts: the snatch, and clean and jerk. Men's Olympic weight lifting is the type included in the Olympic Games every four years.

Overload. The amount of RESISTANCE placed on a muscle group over and above what it is normally used to handling.

Peak. A peak is reached over a six-to-eight-week period of time when a bodybuilder achieves optimal competition condition. It takes an experienced bodybuilder to peak optimally and exactly on the day of a major championship.

PHA. A special type of CIRCUIT TRAINING featuring short four-to-six-EXERCISE circuits. Exercises are included for virtually all muscle groups within each short circuit of movements.

Plates. The flat metal or vinyl covered disks added to a BARBELL BAR to adjust the weight of the apparatus to the desired level.

Posing. The art of physical display onstage at a competition. A good free-posing ROUTINE includes a wide variety of symmetrical, artistic, and muscular poses, all connected together with transitions featuring gymnastics and dance movements.

Poundage. The actual weight of a BARBELL used in any BODYBUILDING exercise.

Power lifting. A popular form of competitive WEIGHT LIFTING engaged in by many women worldwide. Power lifting consists of three lifts: squat, bench press, and deadlift. In the United States and Canada, power lifting is much more popular among women than Olympic-style weight lifting, but both forms of competitive weight lifting lag far behind BODYBUILDING in popularity.

Program. The list of exercises, weights, SETS, and REPETITIONS performed in a single WORKOUT. A program is also referred to as a ROUTINE or TRAINING SCHEDULE.

Progression. The process of incrementally increasing the stress placed on a working muscle in any exercise. Progression can be accomplished in three ways: by doing more reps with a set weight, by using more weight in a movement, or by decreasing the amount of rest between sets in a training program.

Pump. The briefly larger size of a muscle after it has been exercised. Muscle pump is caused by a greater-than-normal influx of blood into the muscle; the blood removes fatigue by-products and replenishes the glycogen and oxygen that has been used up during a workout.

Quality training. A WORKOUT technique used during a precontest training cycle in which the amount of rest between SETS is systematically reduced. Quality training is quite hard work, but it greatly contributes to contest condition.

Repetition. Also referred to as a *rep,* this is each full and individual execution of an exercise. For example, when doing push-ups, a repetition would consist of the complete downward movement from a position with arms straight until the chest touches the floor, and then the return back up to the starting position.

Resistance. Like a POUNDAGE, this is the actual weight of a BARBELL being used in bodybuilding exercise.

Rest interval. The brief pause between SETS that allows the body to recuperate partially and regain its strength before the next set is initiated.

Ripped. A term often used to denote a high degree of MUSCULARITY, as in "She's really ripped for this show!"

Routine. The program of exercises, SETS, REPETITIONS, and POUNDAGES performed in a WORKOUT. Often a routine refers to the actual written schedule performed in each workout.

Set. A group of REPETITIONS (usually in the range of 8 to 15 for most exercises) done without a pause between reps. Several sets of each movement are ordinarily done with a rest interval between sets.

Sleeve. The hollow metal tube that fits over the BAR of a BARBELL or DUMBBELL. A sleeve is often scored with shallow grooves, called *knurlings,* that allow a bodybuilder a more secure grip when her hands are perspiring.

Spotter. A training partner who stands near you as you perform an exercise. One or two spotters are necessary for safe BODYBUILDING training.

Steroids. Anabolic steroids are artificial male hormones used by a minority of women to improve strength and muscle MASS. Intelligent women bodybuilders avoid using steroids because they tend to masculinize the body.

Sticking point. The point in time at which your muscles tend not to increase in HYPERTROPHY, regardless of how hard or regularly you train them. Sticking points are a normal occurrence, since the body tends to gain in mass and strength in spurts followed by short dormant periods.

Stretching. A type of exercise used to increase FLEXIBILITY of the joints and muscles.

Striations. Small grooves over the surface of a highly developed and fully defined muscle group.

Supplements. Concentrated vitamins, minerals, proteins, and other foods consumed by bodybuilders to supplement their normal diet.

Symmetry. The shape of the body, particularly when seen in silhouette. Good symmetry is a highly prized physical quality among women bodybuilders.

Training to failure. The process of continuing a set to the point where your working muscles are so fatigued that they can no longer complete a full REPETITION.

Vascularity. A prominence of surface veins over the muscles and beneath the skin. Vascularity is most evident in a woman's forearms, and it is only visible when a woman is carrying a low degree of body fat.

Weight. The amount of RESISTANCE being used in a BODYBUILDING exercise.

Weight class. To prevent larger bodybuilders from having an unfair advantage over smaller women, many competitions are conducted in weight classes. In many shows two classes are contested: a lightweight class (under 114 pounds) and a middleweight class (over 114 pounds). In the largest contests, such as the annual American Championships, three weight classes are used: lightweight class (under 104$\frac{1}{2}$ pounds), middleweight class (up to 114 pounds), and heavyweight class (over 114 pounds).

Weightlifting. A competitive form of WEIGHT TRAINING in which women compete in well-defined events to determine who can lift the most weight. The most popular form of competitive weight lifing is called POWER LIFTING, in which three lifts are contested: squat, bench press, and deadlift. A somewhat less popular form of competition is Olympic-style weight lifting (often called simply OLYMPIC LIFTING), in which two lifts are contested: snatch and clean, and jerk. Weight lifters also compete in WEIGHT CLASSES, but there are many more classes in weight lifting competition than in bodybuilding events.

Weight training. A general activity in which BARBELLS, DUMBBELLS, and other resistance apparatus are used to change the appearance, health, and physical condition of the human body. Within the general classification of weight training are a number of subclasses: BODYBUILDING, competitive WEIGHT LIFTING, injury rehabilitation, and so forth.

Workout. A specified, usually predetermined training session.

Sources

BOOKS

Darden, Ellington. *The Nautilus Bodybuilding Book*. Chicago: Contemporary Books, 1982.

Darden, Ellington. *The Nautilus Book*. Chicago: Contemporary Books, 1980.

Dobbins, Bill. *"High Tech" Training*. New York: Simon & Schuster, 1982.

Dobbins, Bill, and Sprague, Ken. *The Gold's Gym Weight Training Book*. New York: Berkley, 1981.

Douglass, Stephen B. *Managing Yourself*. San Bernardino, CA: Campus Crusade for Christ, International, 1978.

Freeman, Hobart E. *Positive Thinking and Confession*. Warsaw: Faith Publications, 1980.

Hatfield, Frederick C. *Aerobic Weight Training*. Chicago: Contemporary Books, 1983.

Kennedy, Robert. *Bodybuilding for Women*. Buchanan, NY: Emerson Books, 1979.

Mentzer, Mike, and Friedberg, Ardy. *Mike Mentzer's Complete Book of Weight Training*. New York: William Morrow, 1982.

Neal, Wes. *Athletic Perfection*. Milford, MI: Mott Media, 1981.

Olinekova, Gayle. *Go for It!* New York: Fireside, 1982.

Pirie, Dr. Lynne. *Getting Built*. New York: Warner Books, 1984.

Reynolds, Bill. *Bodybuilding for Beginners*. Chicago: Contemporary Books, 1983.

Reynolds, Bill. *Complete Weight Training Book*. Mountain View, CA: Anderson World, 1976.

Reynolds, Bill. *Weight Training for Beginners*. Chicago: Contemporary Books, 1982.

Schaeffer, Franky. *Addicted to Mediocrity*. Westchester, IL: Crossway Books, 1981.

Schwarzenegger, Arnold, with Hall, Douglas Kent. *Arnold's Bodyshaping for Women*. New York: Simon & Schuster, 1979.

Sprague, Ken, and Reynolds, Bill. *The Gold's Gym Book of Bodybuilding*. Chicago: Contemporary Books, 1983.

Weider, Betty, and Weider, Joe. *The Weider Book of Bodybuilding for Women*. Chicago: Contemporary Books, 1981.

Weider, Joe, ed. *Bodybuilding and Conditioning for Women*. Chicago: Contemporary Books, 1983.

Weider, Joe, ed. *Women's Weight Training and Bodybuilding Tips and Routines*. Chicago: Contemporary Books, 1982.

MAGAZINES

Bodybuilder, Charlton Publications, Charlton Building, Derby, CT 06418.

Flex, 21100 Erwin St., Woodland Hills, CA 91367.

Iron Man, Box 10, Alliance, NE 69301.

Muscle Digest, 10317 East Whittier Blvd., Whittier, CA 90606.

Muscle & Fitness, 21100 Erwin St., Woodland Hills, CA 91367.

Muscle Mag International, Unit Two, 52 Bramsteele Rd., Brampton, Ontario L6W 3M5, Canada.

Muscle Training Illustrated, 1665 Utica Ave., Brooklyn, NY 11234

Muscle Up, Charlton Publications, Charlton Building, Derby, CT 06418.

Muscle World, Charlton Publications, Charlton Building, Derby, CT 06418.

Muscular Development, Box 1707, York, PA 17405.

Strength & Health, Box 1707, York PA 17405.

AUTHORITATIVE BODYBUILDING COURSES

I sell seven authoritative women's weight training and bodybuilding courses by mail order. For information on these courses, write to Rachel McLish, Box 111, Santa Monica, CA 90406.

FEDERATION ADDRESSES

American Federation of Women Bodybuilders, Box 658, Niwot, CO 80544.

International Federation of Bodybuilders, 2875 Bates Rd., Montreal, P.Q. H3S 1B7, Canada.

© Harry Langdon

53